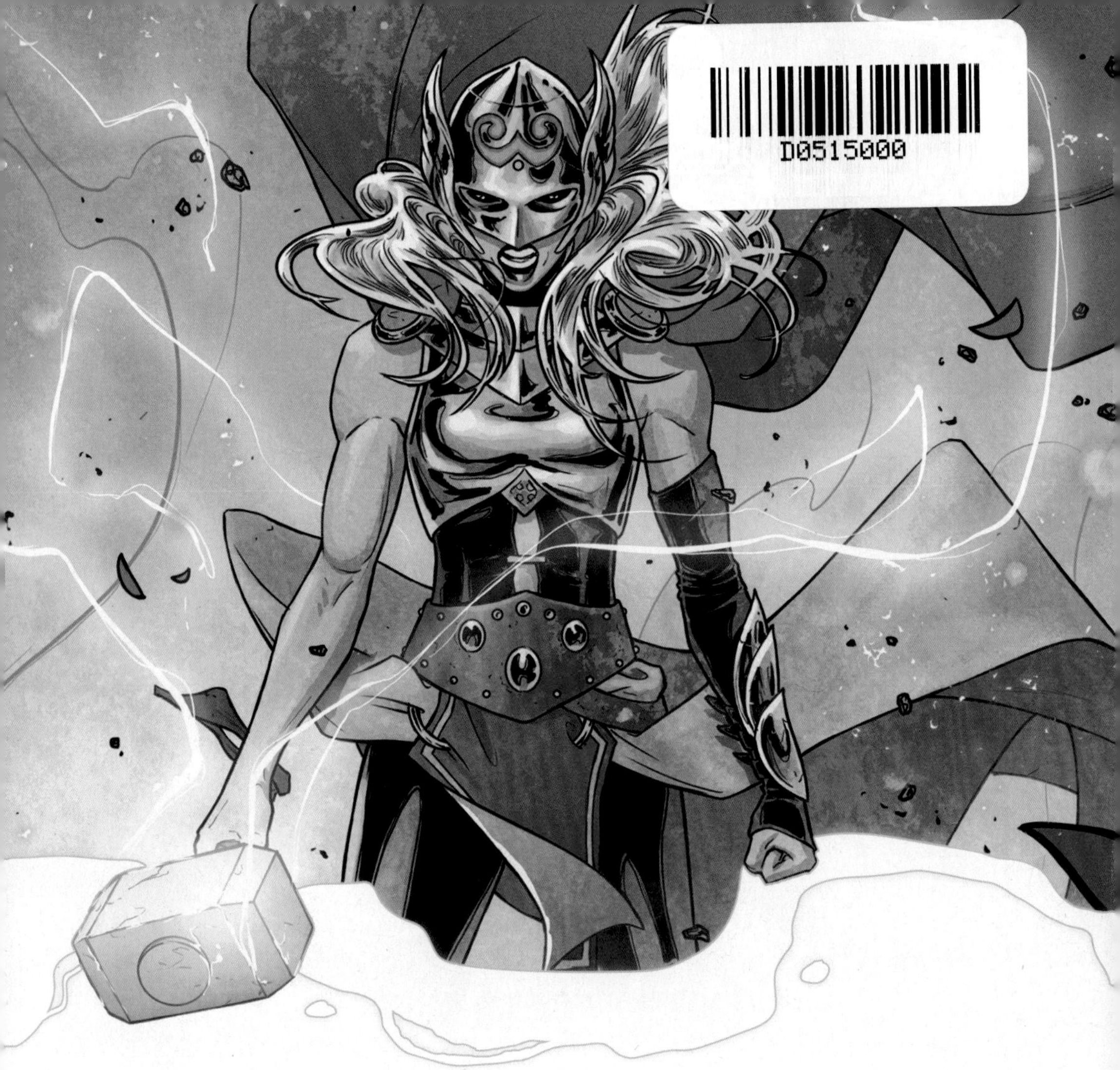

COLLECTION EDITOR: **JENNIFER GRÜNWALD**
ASSISTANT EDITOR: **DANIEL KIRCHHOFFER**
ASSISTANT MANAGING EDITOR: **MAIA LOY**
ASSISTANT MANAGING EDITOR: **LISA MONTALBANO**
VP PRODUCTION & SPECIAL PROJECTS: **JEFF YOUNGQUIST**
BOOK DESIGNER: **ADAM DEL RE**

SVP PRINT, SALES & MARKETING: **DAVID GABRIEL**
EDITOR IN CHIEF: **C.B. CEBULSKI**

THOR CREATED BY **STAN LEE, LARRY LIEBER** & **JACK KIRBY**

MIGHTY THOR VOL. 1: THUNDER IN HER VEINS. Contains material originally published in magazine form as MIGHTY THOR (2015) #1-5. Third printing 2021. ISBN 978-0-7851-9965-6. Published by MARVEL WORLD, INC., a subsidiary of MARVEL ENTERTAINMENT, LLC. OFFICE OF PUBLICATION: 1290 Avenue of the Americas, New York, NY 10104. © 2017 MARVEL No similarity between any of the names, characters, persons or institutions in this book with those of any living or dead person or institution is intended, and any such similarity which may exist is purely coincidental. **Printed in Canada.** KEVIN FEIGE, Chief Creative Officer; BUCKLEY, President, Marvel Entertainment; JOE QUESADA, EVP & Creative Director; DAVID BOGART, Associate Publisher & SVP of Talent Affairs; TOM BREVOORT, VP, Executive Editor; NICK LOWE, Executive Editor, Content, Digital Publishing; DAVID GABRIEL, VP of Print & Digital Publishing; JEFF YOUNGQUIST, VP of Production & Special Projects; ALEX MORALES, Director of Publishing Operations; DAN EDINGTON, Managing RICKEY PURDIN, Director of Talent Relations; JENNIFER GRÜNWALD, Senior Editor, Special Projects; SUSAN CRESPI, Production Manager; STAN LEE, Chairman Emeritus. For information regarding advertising in Comics or on Marvel.com, please contact Vit DeBellis, Custom Solutions & Integrated Advertising Manager, at vdebellis@marvel.com. For Marvel subscription inquiries, please call 888-511-5480. **Manufactured b** 11/19/2021 **and** 12/21/2021 **by** SOLISCO PRINTERS, SCOTT, QC, CANADA.

10 9 8 7 6 5 4 3

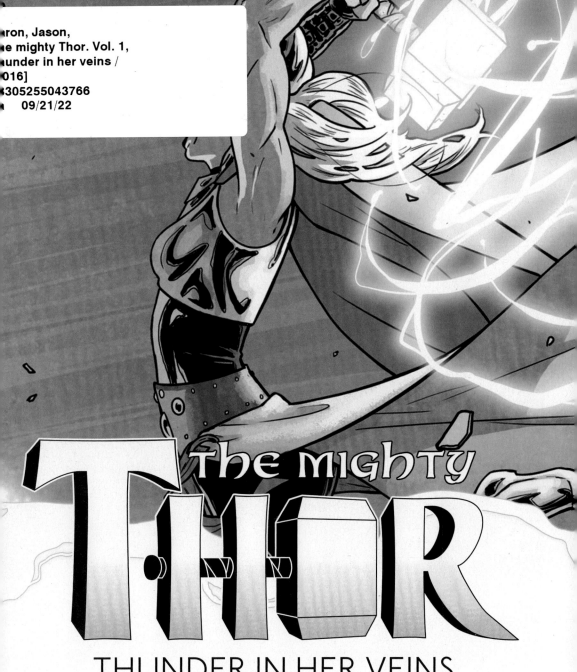

THE MIGHTY THOR

THUNDER IN HER VEINS

WHEN **DR. JANE FOSTER** LIFTS THE MYSTIC HAMMER MJOLNIR, SHE IS TRANSFORMED INTO
THE GODDESS OF THUNDER, THE MIGHTY THOR!
HER ENEMIES ARE MANY, AS ASGARD DESCENDS FURTHER INTO CHAOS AND WAR THREATENS
TO SPREAD THROUGHOUT THE TEN REALMS. YET HER GREATEST BATTLE WILL BE AGAINST
A FAR MORE PERSONAL FOE: THE CANCER THAT IS KILLING HER MORTAL FORM…

WRITER	ARTIST
JASON AARON	**RUSSELL DAUTERMAN**

COLOR ARTIST	LETTERER	COVER ART
MATTHEW WILSON	**VC'S JOE SABINO**	**RUSSELL DAUTERMAN & MATTHEW WILSON**

ASSISTANT EDITOR	EDITOR	EXECUTIVE EDITOR
CHRIS ROBINSON	**WIL MOSS**	**TOM BREVOORT**

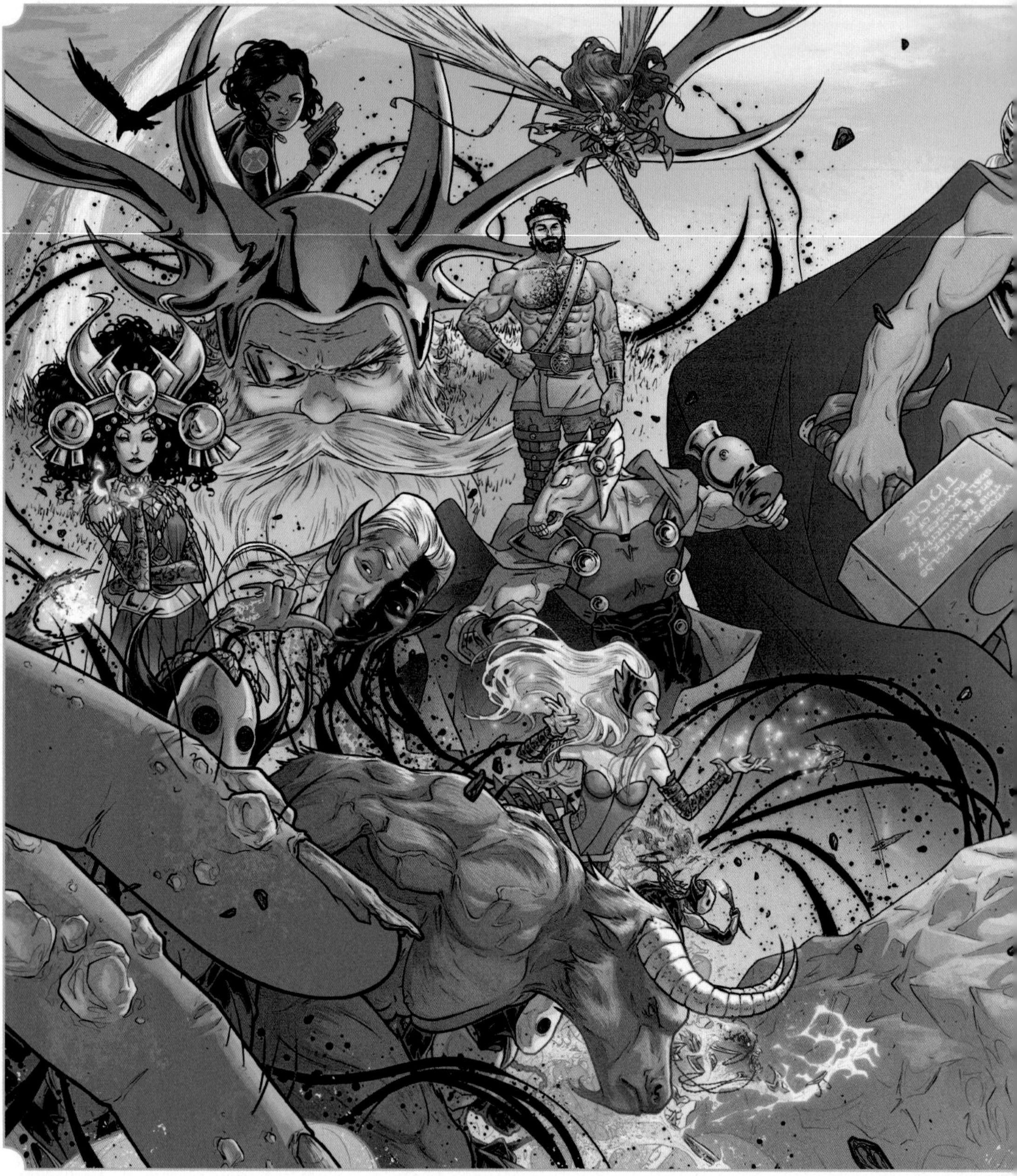

1

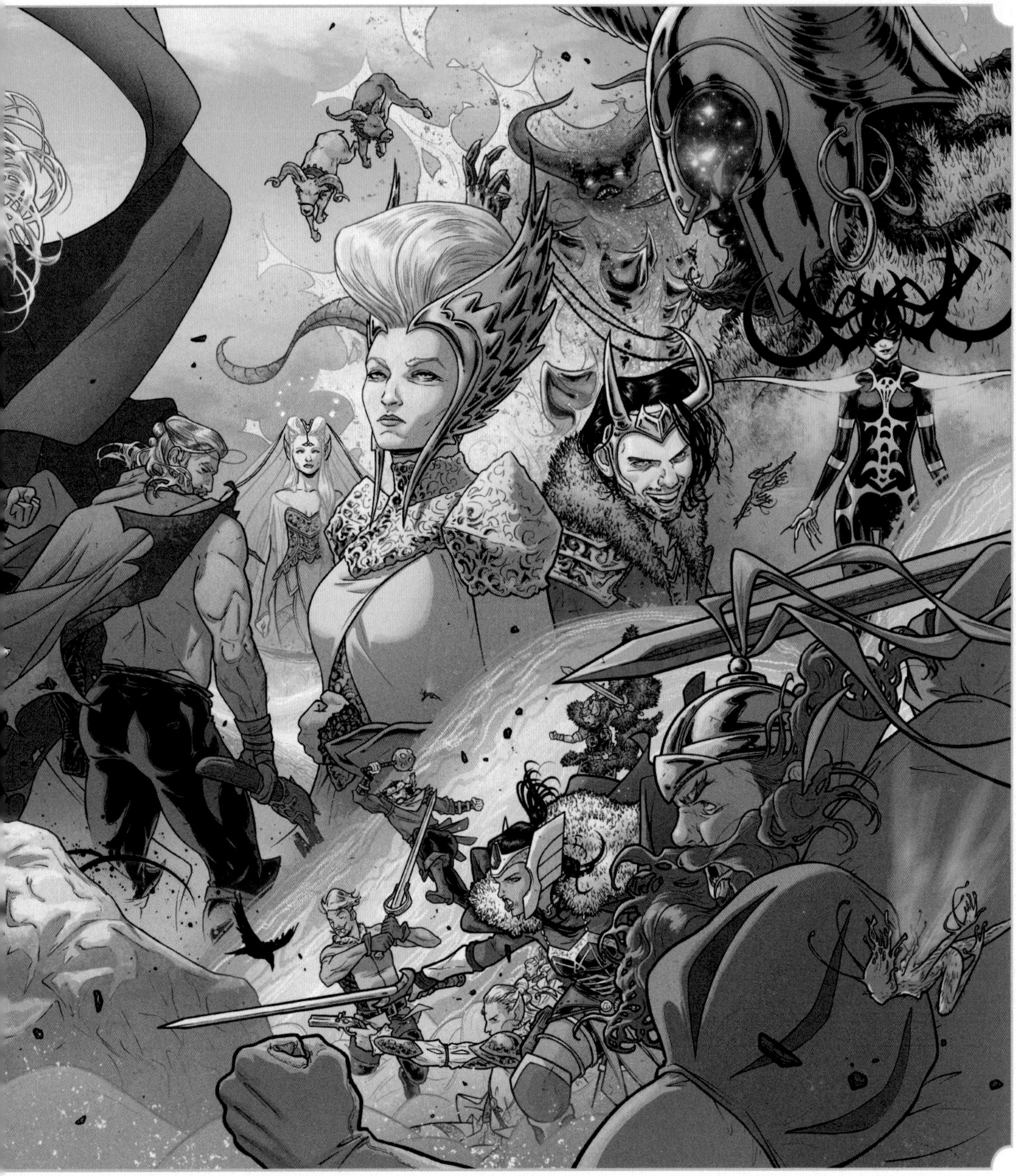

THUNDER IN HER VEINS

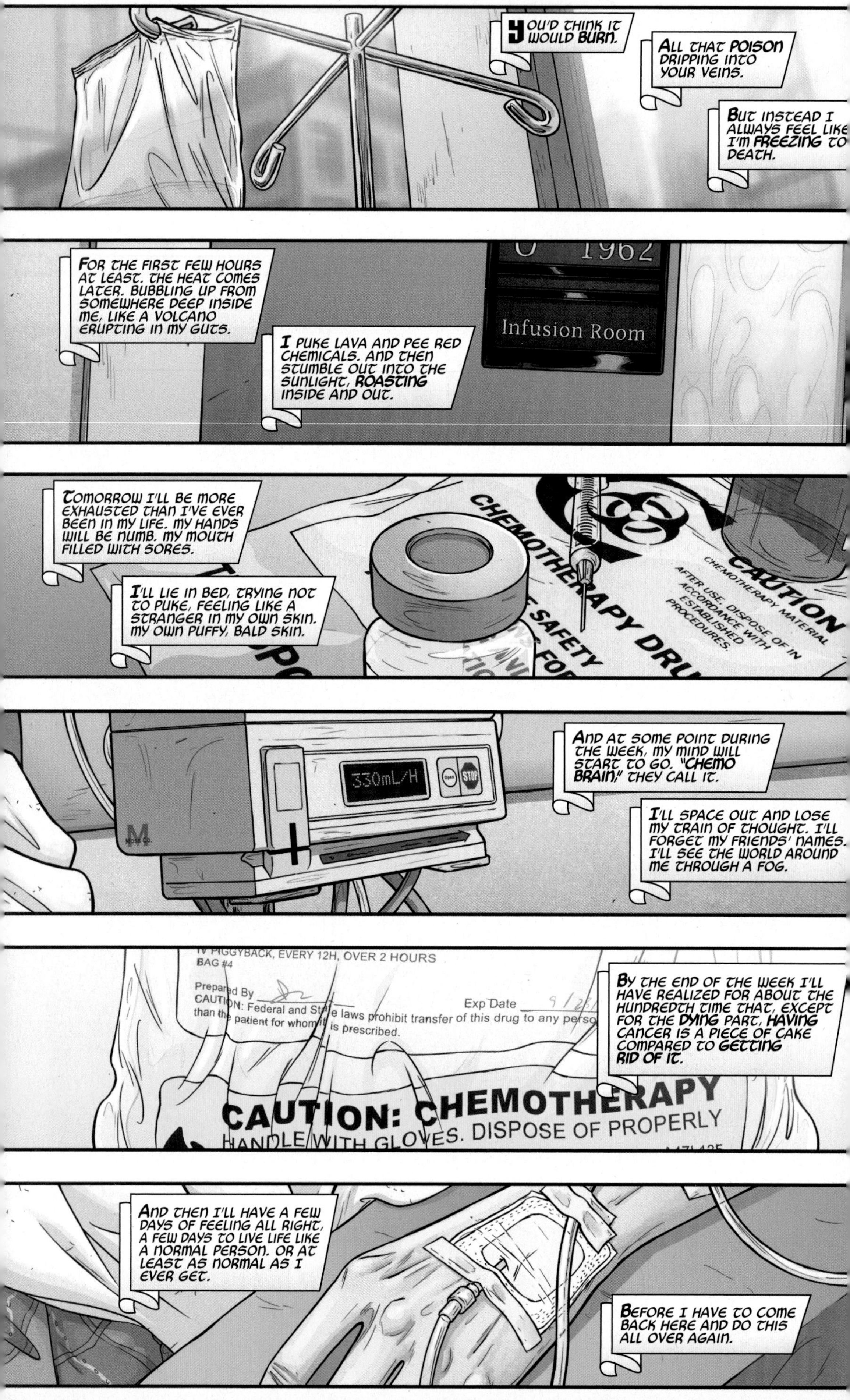
YOU'D THINK IT WOULD BURN.
ALL THAT POISON DRIPPING INTO YOUR VEINS.
BUT INSTEAD I ALWAYS FEEL LIKE I'M FREEZING TO DEATH.
FOR THE FIRST FEW HOURS AT LEAST. THE HEAT COMES LATER. BUBBLING UP FROM SOMEWHERE DEEP INSIDE ME, LIKE A VOLCANO ERUPTING IN MY GUTS.
I PUKE LAVA AND PEE RED CHEMICALS. AND THEN STUMBLE OUT INTO THE SUNLIGHT, ROASTING INSIDE AND OUT.
Infusion Room
TOMORROW I'LL BE MORE EXHAUSTED THAN I'VE EVER BEEN IN MY LIFE. MY HANDS WILL BE NUMB. MY MOUTH FILLED WITH SORES.
I'LL LIE IN BED, TRYING NOT TO PUKE, FEELING LIKE A STRANGER IN MY OWN SKIN. MY OWN PUFFY, BALD SKIN.
CAUTION
CHEMOTHERAPY MATERIAL
AFTER USE, DISPOSE OF IN ACCORDANCE WITH ESTABLISHED PROCEDURES.
330mL/H
STOP
AND AT SOME POINT DURING THE WEEK, MY MIND WILL START TO GO. "CHEMO BRAIN," THEY CALL IT.
I'LL SPACE OUT AND LOSE MY TRAIN OF THOUGHT. I'LL FORGET MY FRIENDS' NAMES. I'LL SEE THE WORLD AROUND ME THROUGH A FOG.
IV PIGGYBACK, EVERY 12H, OVER 2 HOURS
BAG #4
Prepared By
Exp Date
CAUTION: Federal and State laws prohibit transfer of this drug to any person other than the patient for whom it is prescribed.
BY THE END OF THE WEEK I'LL HAVE REALIZED FOR ABOUT THE HUNDREDTH TIME THAT, EXCEPT FOR THE DYING PART, HAVING CANCER IS A PIECE OF CAKE COMPARED TO GETTING RID OF IT.
CAUTION: CHEMOTHERAPY
HANDLE WITH GLOVES. DISPOSE OF PROPERLY
AND THEN I'LL HAVE A FEW DAYS OF FEELING ALL RIGHT, A FEW DAYS TO LIVE LIFE LIKE A NORMAL PERSON. OR AT LEAST AS NORMAL AS I EVER GET.
BEFORE I HAVE TO COME BACK HERE AND DO THIS ALL OVER AGAIN.

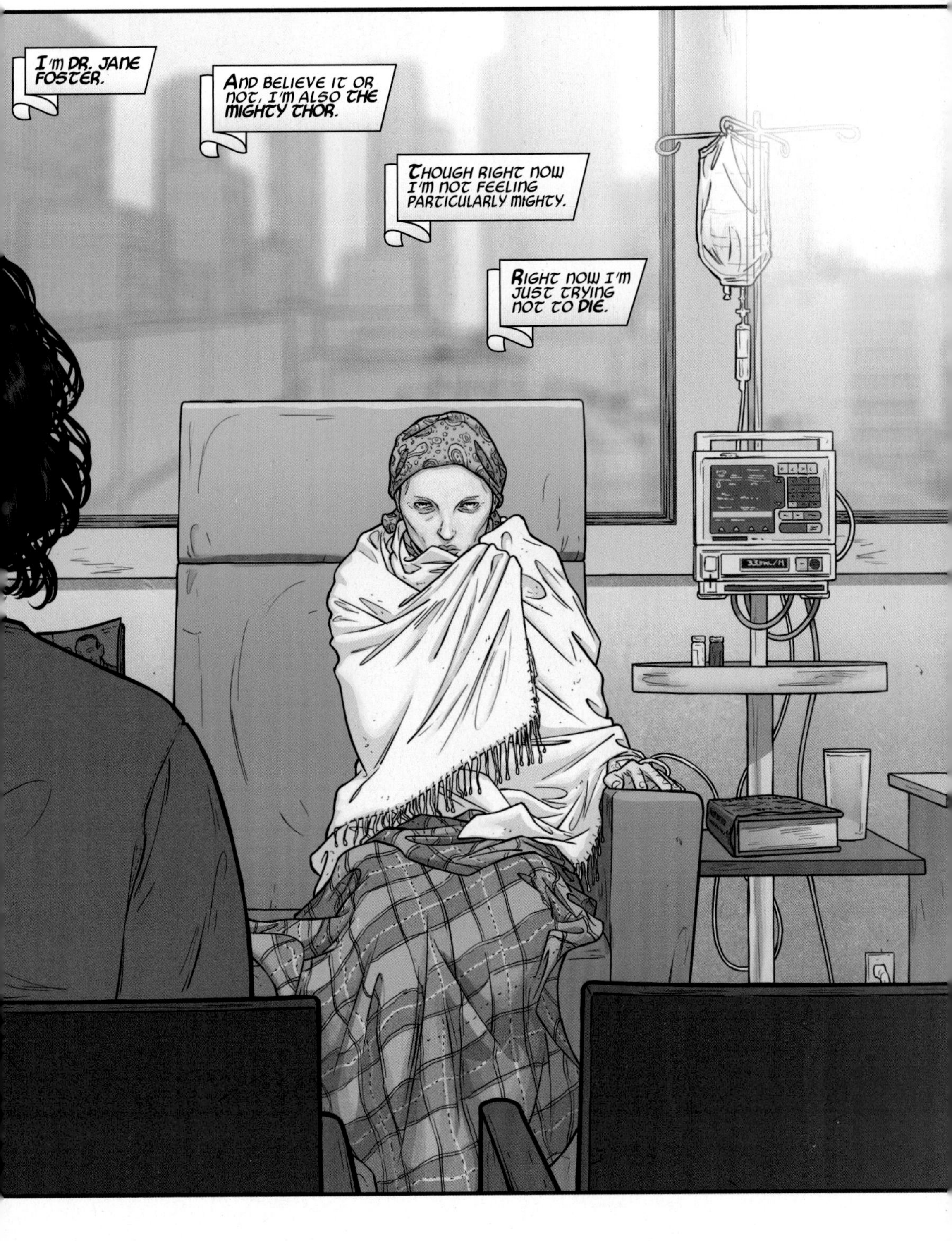
I'M DR. JANE FOSTER.
AND BELIEVE IT OR NOT, I'M ALSO THE MIGHTY THOR.
THOUGH RIGHT NOW I'M NOT FEELING PARTICULARLY MIGHTY.
RIGHT NOW I'M JUST TRYING NOT TO DIE.

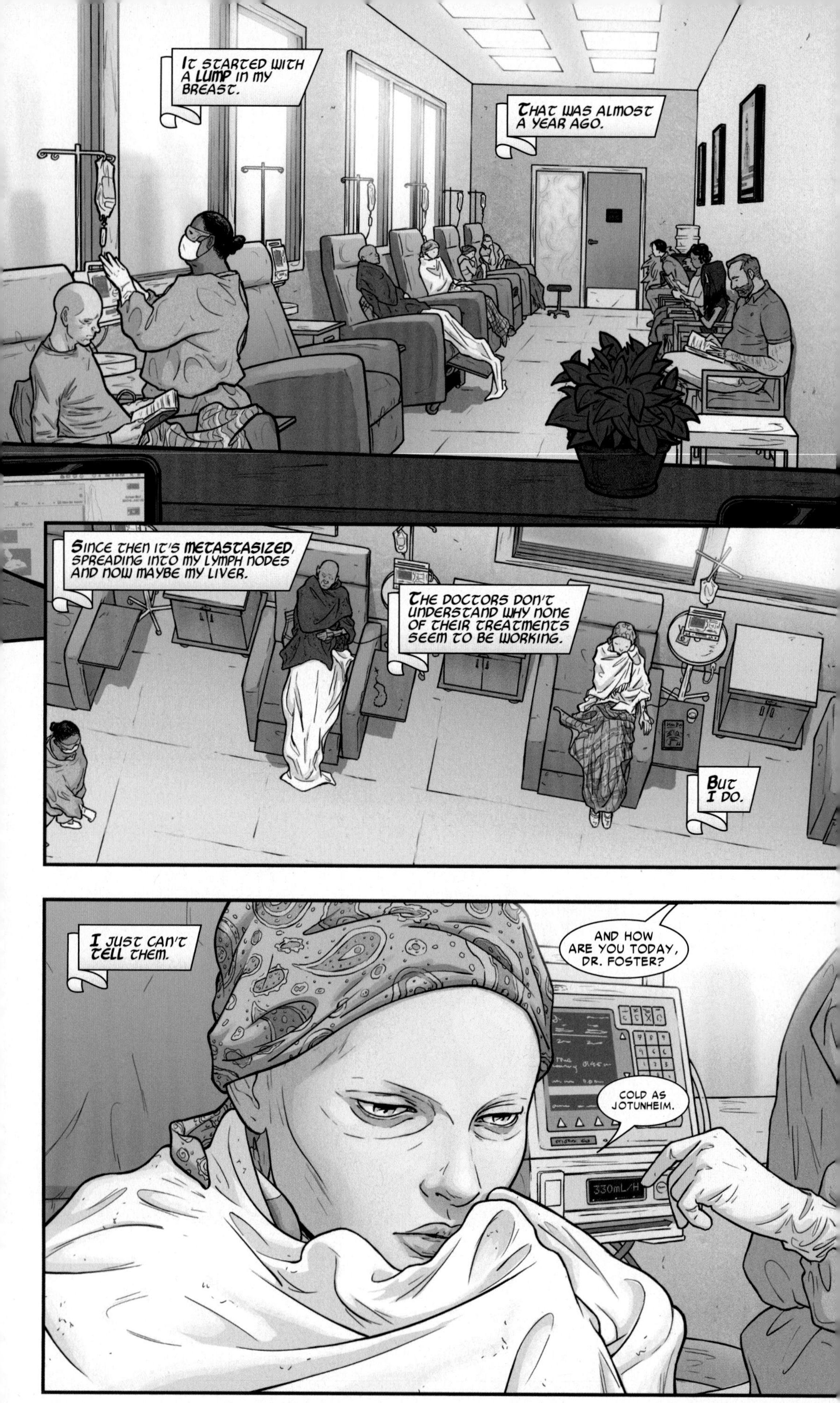
IT STARTED WITH A LUMP IN MY BREAST.
THAT WAS ALMOST A YEAR AGO.
SINCE THEN IT'S METASTASIZED, SPREADING INTO MY LYMPH NODES AND NOW MAYBE MY LIVER.
THE DOCTORS DON'T UNDERSTAND WHY NONE OF THEIR TREATMENTS SEEM TO BE WORKING.
BUT I DO.
I JUST CAN'T TELL THEM.
AND HOW ARE YOU TODAY, DR. FOSTER?
COLD AS JOTUNHEIM.
330mL/H

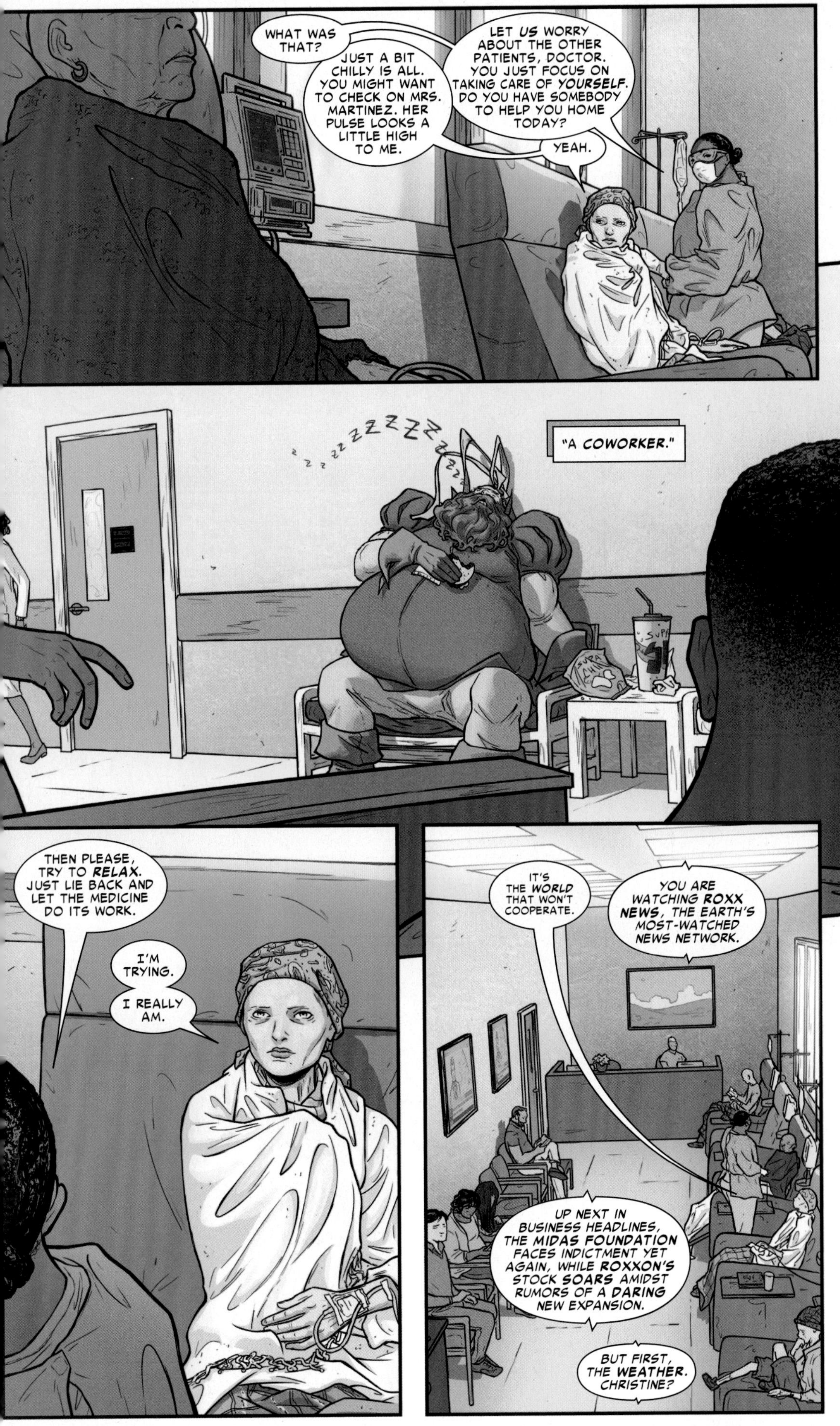

WHAT WAS THAT?
JUST A BIT CHILLY IS ALL. YOU MIGHT WANT TO CHECK ON MRS. MARTINEZ. HER PULSE LOOKS A LITTLE HIGH TO ME.
LET US WORRY ABOUT THE OTHER PATIENTS, DOCTOR. YOU JUST FOCUS ON TAKING CARE OF YOURSELF. DO YOU HAVE SOMEBODY TO HELP YOU HOME TODAY?
YEAH.
"A COWORKER."
zzzzzZZZZZ
THEN PLEASE, TRY TO RELAX. JUST LIE BACK AND LET THE MEDICINE DO ITS WORK.
I'M TRYING.
I REALLY AM.
IT'S THE WORLD THAT WON'T COOPERATE.
YOU ARE WATCHING ROXX NEWS, THE EARTH'S MOST-WATCHED NEWS NETWORK.
UP NEXT IN BUSINESS HEADLINES, THE MIDAS FOUNDATION FACES INDICTMENT YET AGAIN, WHILE ROXXON'S STOCK SOARS AMIDST RUMORS OF A DARING NEW EXPANSION.
BUT FIRST, THE WEATHER. CHRISTINE?

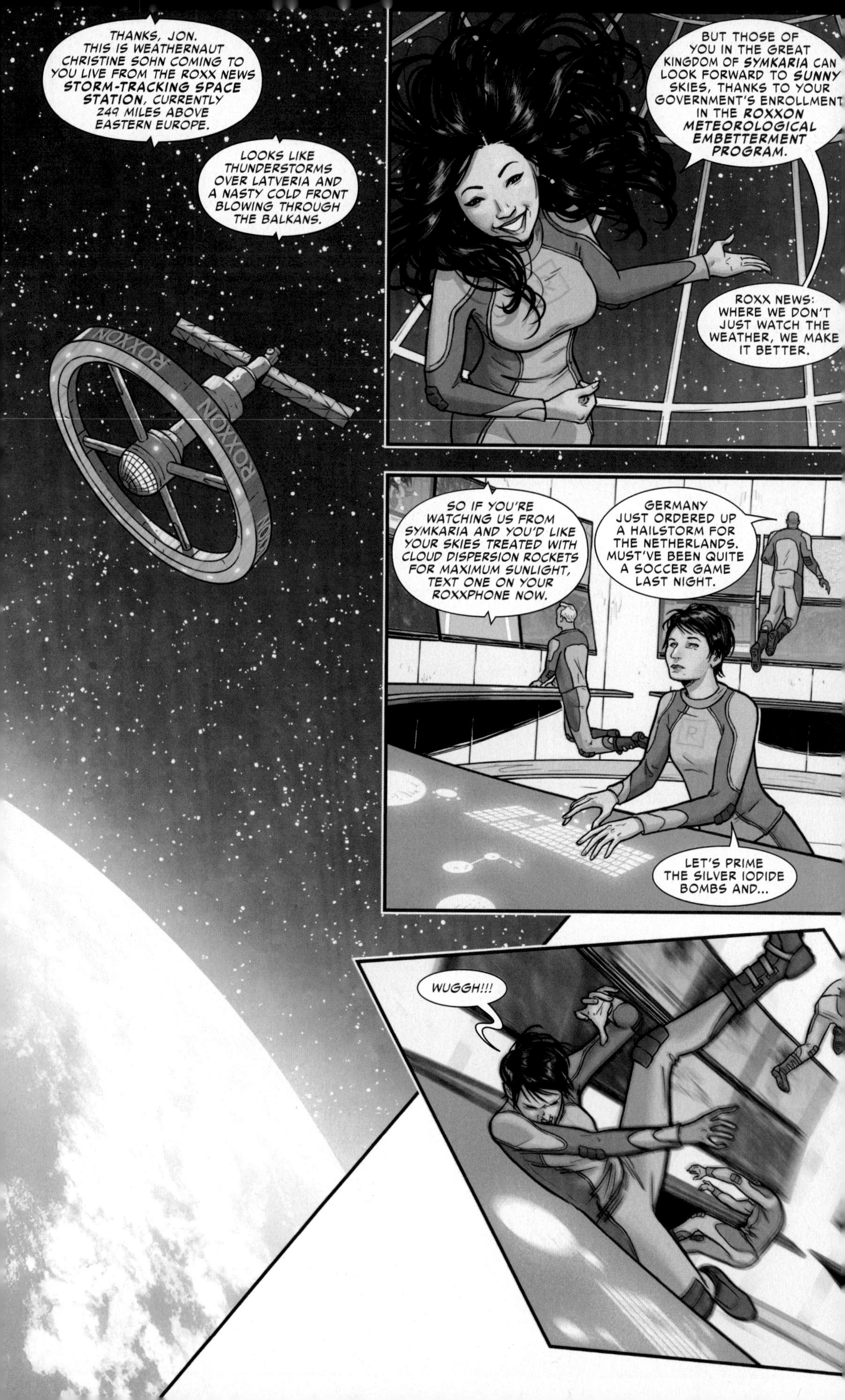

THANKS, JON. THIS IS WEATHERNAUT CHRISTINE SOHN COMING TO YOU LIVE FROM THE ROXX NEWS STORM-TRACKING SPACE STATION, CURRENTLY 249 MILES ABOVE EASTERN EUROPE.
LOOKS LIKE THUNDERSTORMS OVER LATVERIA AND A NASTY COLD FRONT BLOWING THROUGH THE BALKANS.
ROXXON
BUT THOSE OF YOU IN THE GREAT KINGDOM OF SYMKARIA CAN LOOK FORWARD TO SUNNY SKIES, THANKS TO YOUR GOVERNMENT'S ENROLLMENT IN THE ROXXON METEOROLOGICAL EMBETTERMENT PROGRAM.
ROXX NEWS: WHERE WE DON'T JUST WATCH THE WEATHER, WE MAKE IT BETTER.
SO IF YOU'RE WATCHING US FROM SYMKARIA AND YOU'D LIKE YOUR SKIES TREATED WITH CLOUD DISPERSION ROCKETS FOR MAXIMUM SUNLIGHT, TEXT ONE ON YOUR ROXXPHONE NOW.
GERMANY JUST ORDERED UP A HAILSTORM FOR THE NETHERLANDS. MUST'VE BEEN QUITE A SOCCER GAME LAST NIGHT.
LET'S PRIME THE SILVER IODIDE BOMBS AND...
WUGGH!!!

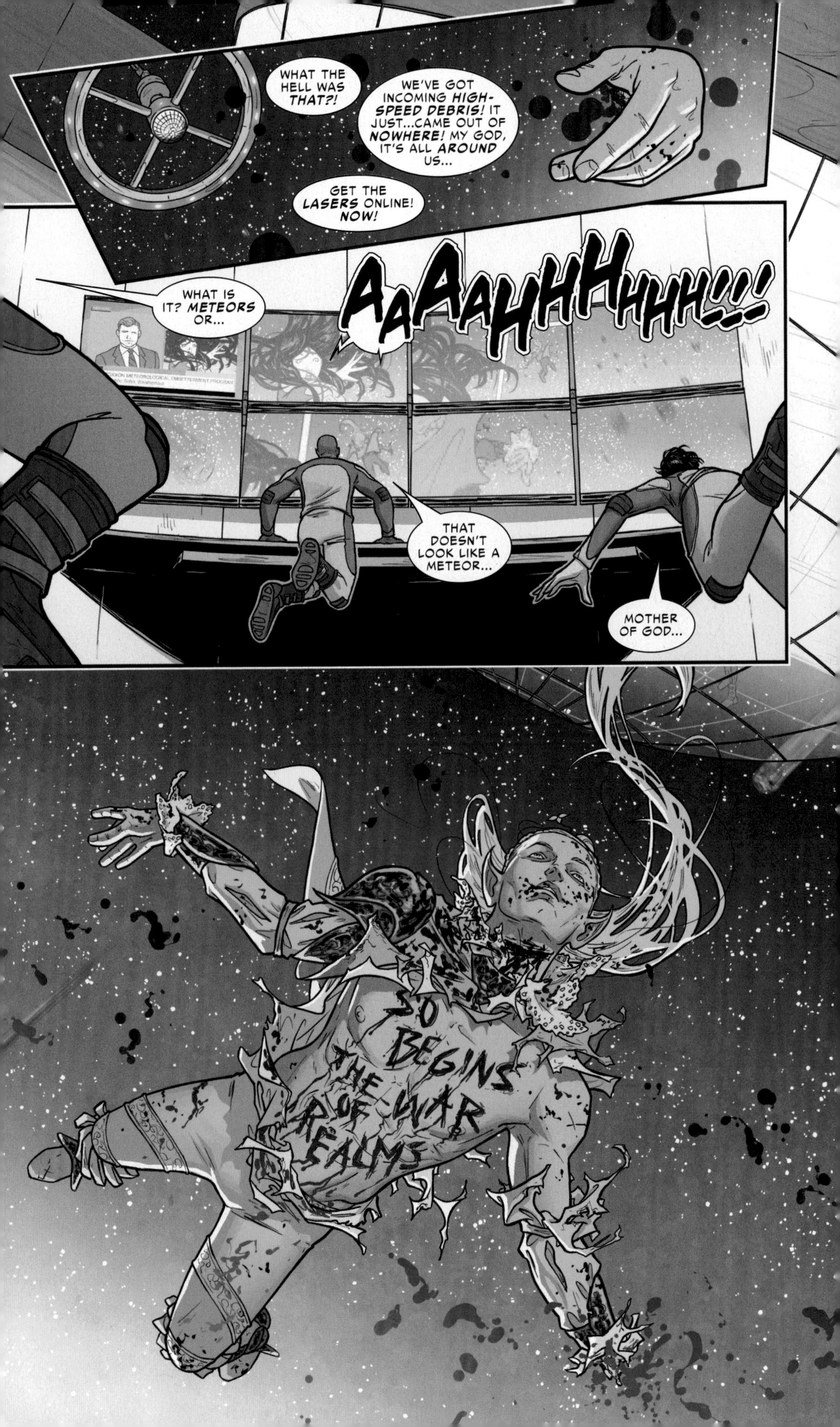

WHAT THE HELL WAS THAT?!
WE'VE GOT INCOMING HIGH-SPEED DEBRIS! IT JUST...CAME OUT OF NOWHERE! MY GOD, IT'S ALL AROUND US...
GET THE LASERS ONLINE! NOW!
WHAT IS IT? METEORS OR...
AAAHHHHHHH!!!
THAT DOESN'T LOOK LIKE A METEOR...
MOTHER OF GOD...
SO BEGINS THE WAR OF REALMS

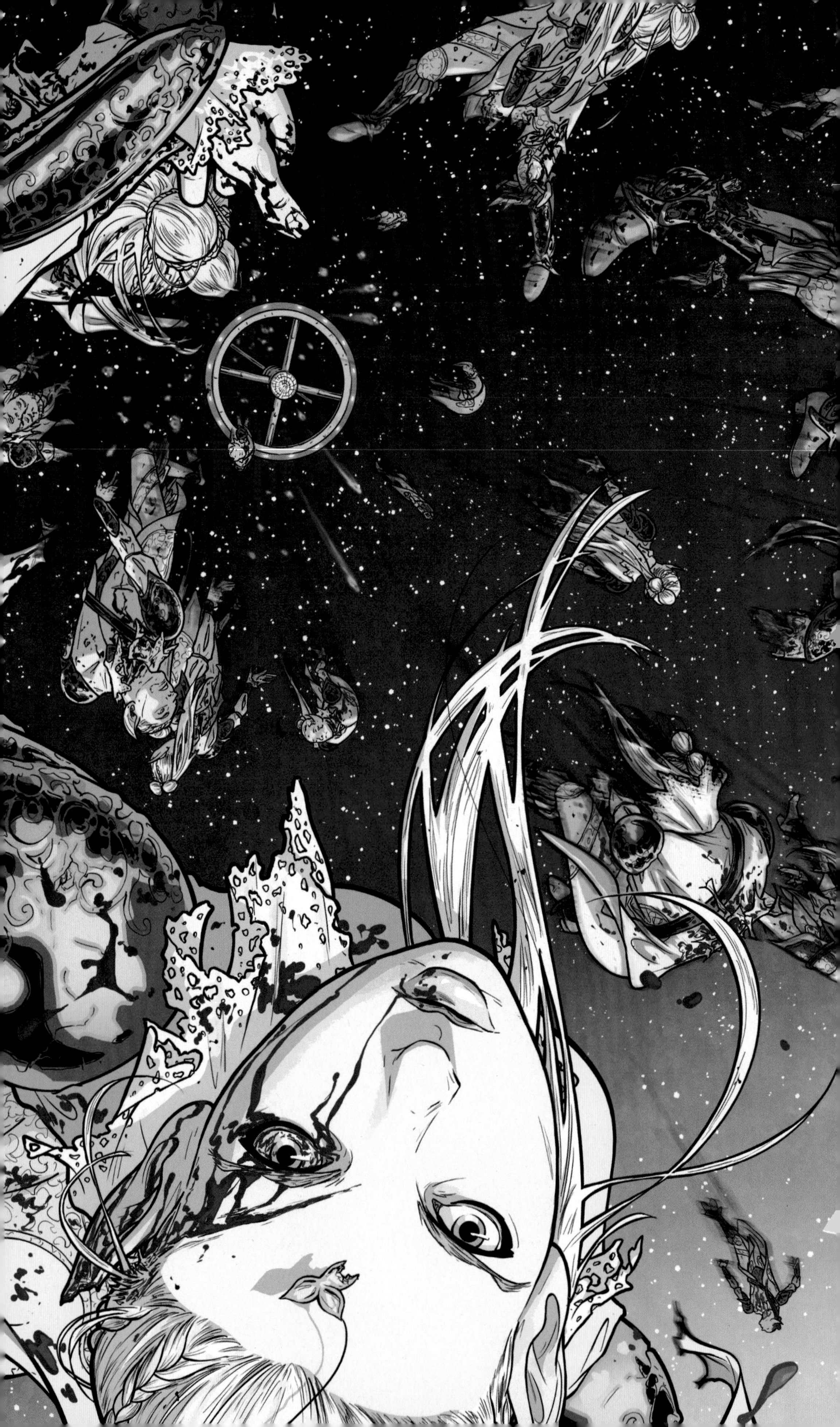

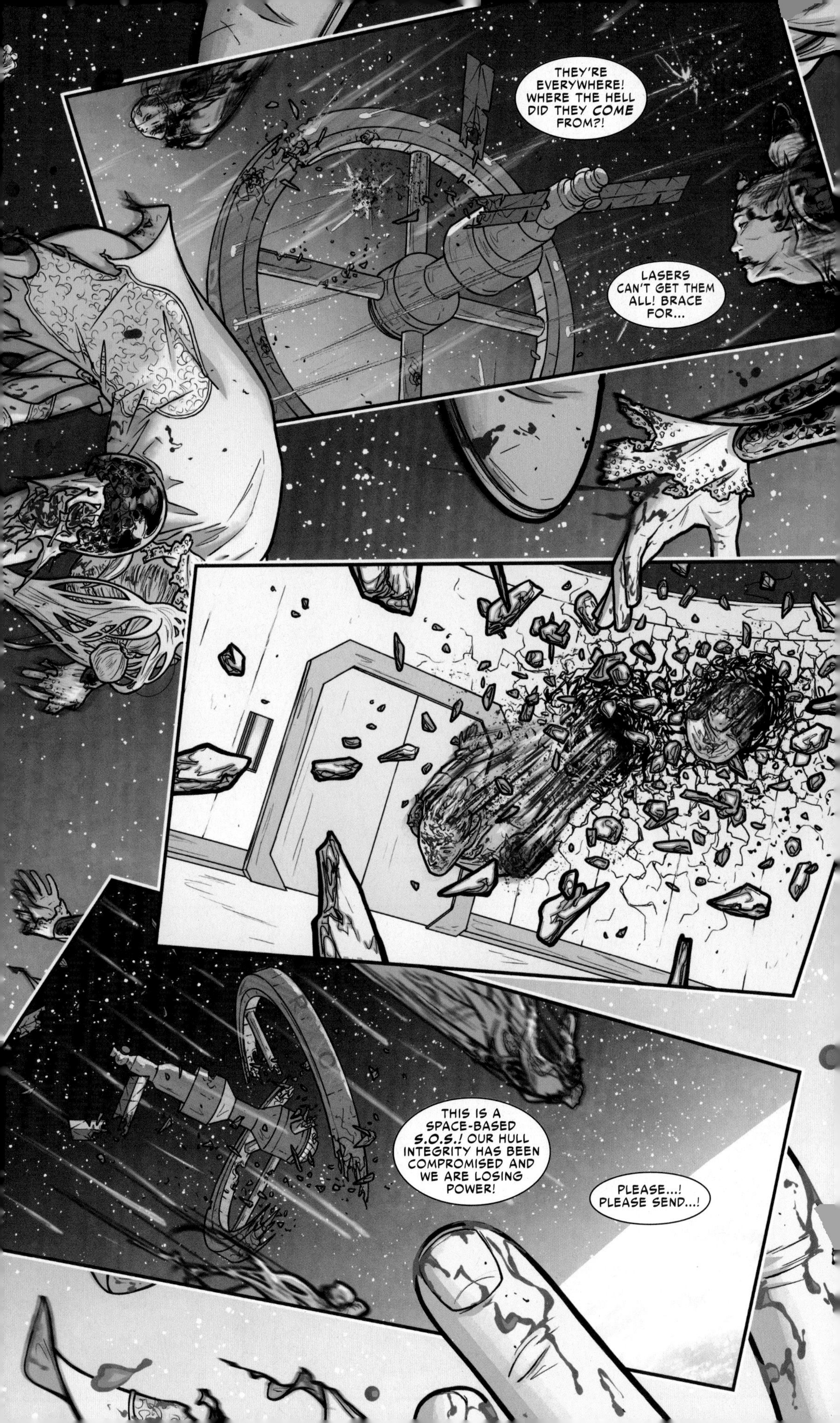
THEY'RE EVERYWHERE! WHERE THE HELL DID THEY COME FROM?!
LASERS CAN'T GET THEM ALL! BRACE FOR...
THIS IS A SPACE-BASED S.O.S.! OUR HULL INTEGRITY HAS BEEN COMPROMISED AND WE ARE LOSING POWER!
PLEASE...! PLEASE SEND...!

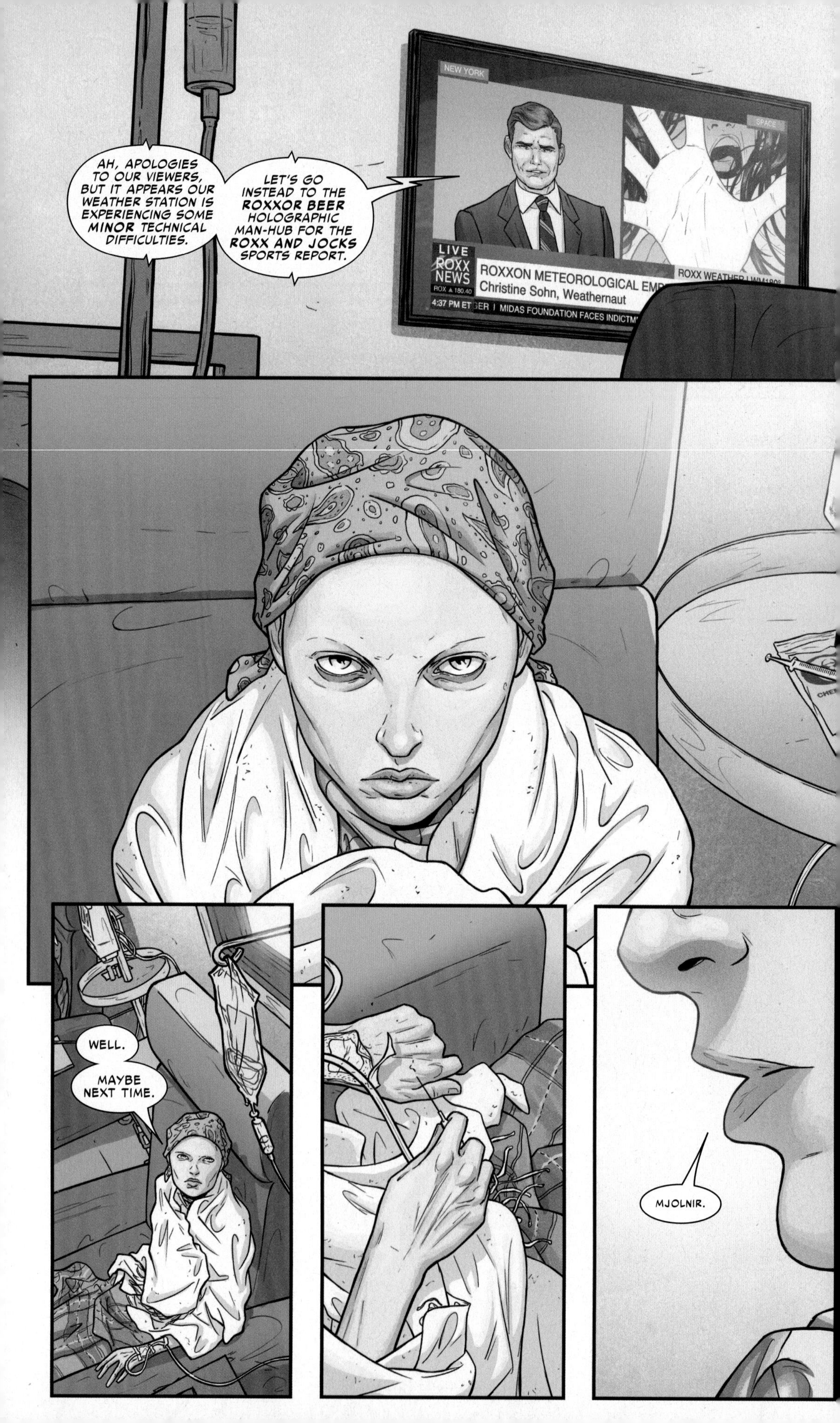
NEW YORK
SPACE
LIVE
ROXX NEWS
ROXXON METEOROLOGICAL EMER
Christine Sohn, Weathernaut
4:37 PM ET
MIDAS FOUNDATION FACES INDICTM
AH, APOLOGIES TO OUR VIEWERS, BUT IT APPEARS OUR WEATHER STATION IS EXPERIENCING SOME MINOR TECHNICAL DIFFICULTIES.
LET'S GO INSTEAD TO THE ROXXOR BEER HOLOGRAPHIC MAN-HUB FOR THE ROXX AND JOCKS SPORTS REPORT.
WELL.
MAYBE NEXT TIME.
MJOLNIR.

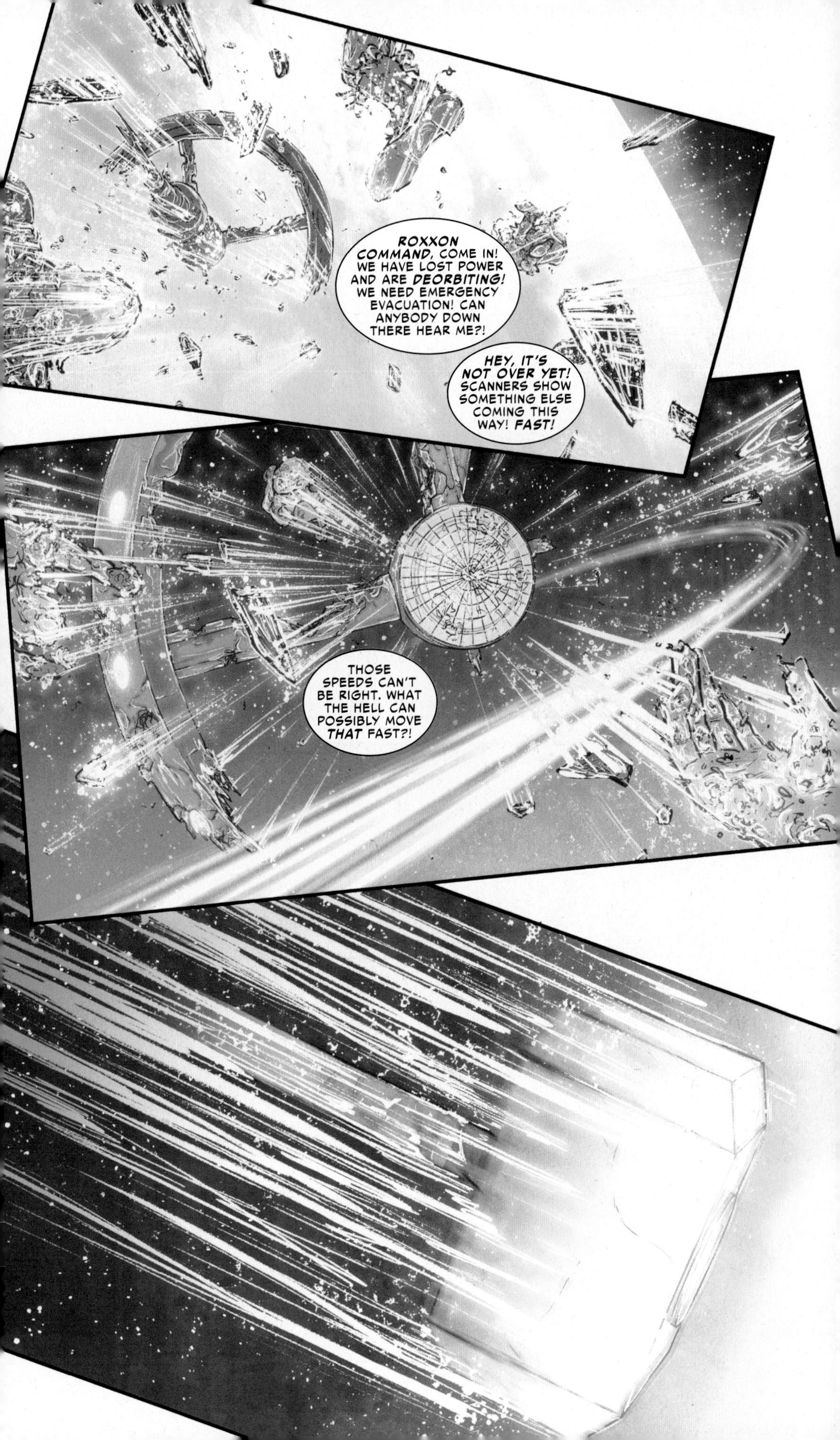
ROXXON COMMAND, COME IN! WE HAVE LOST POWER AND ARE DEORBITING! WE NEED EMERGENCY EVACUATION! CAN ANYBODY DOWN THERE HEAR ME?!
HEY, IT'S NOT OVER YET! SCANNERS SHOW SOMETHING ELSE COMING THIS WAY! FAST!
THOSE SPEEDS CAN'T BE RIGHT. WHAT THE HELL CAN POSSIBLY MOVE THAT FAST?!

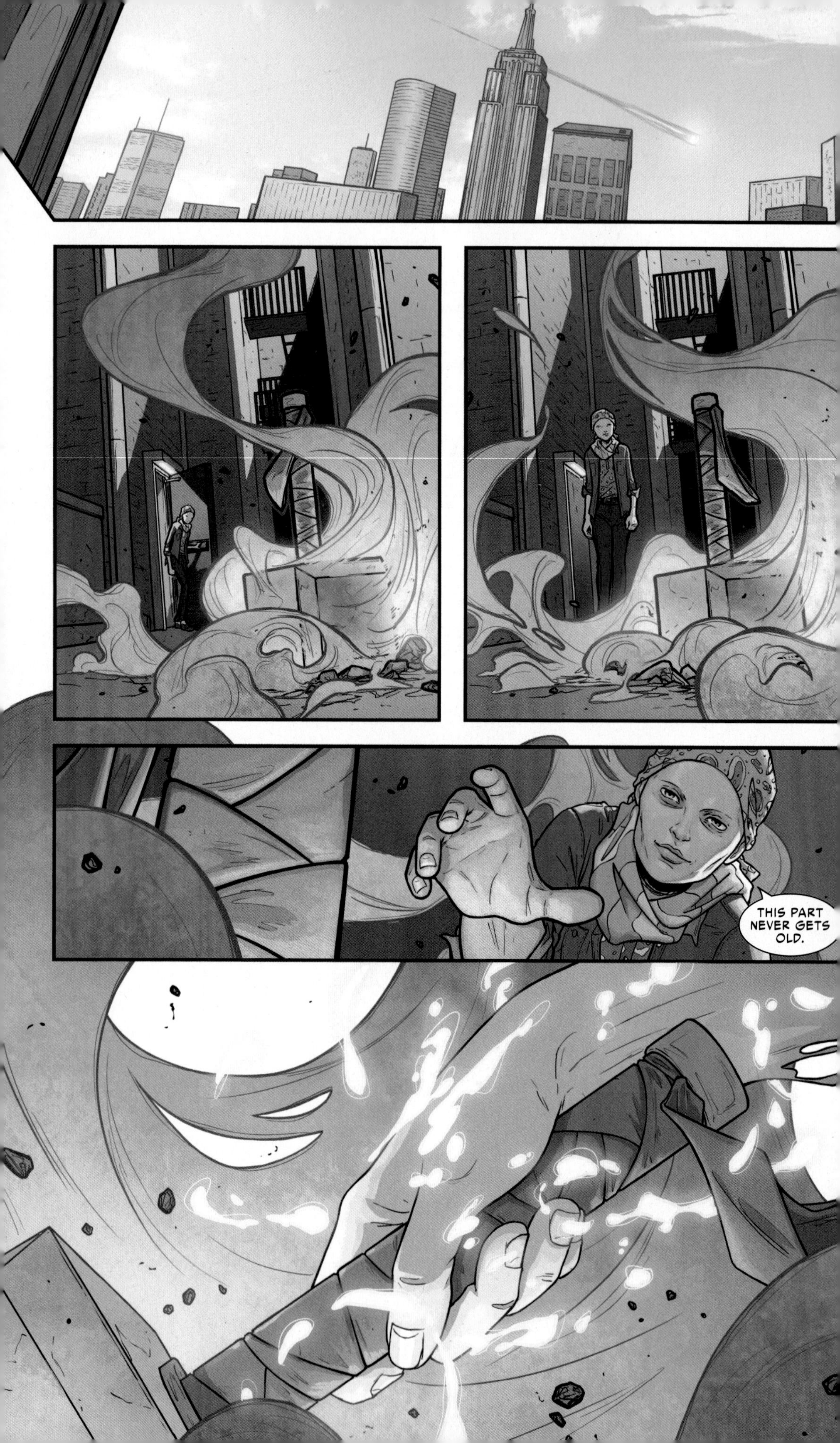
THIS PART NEVER GETS OLD.

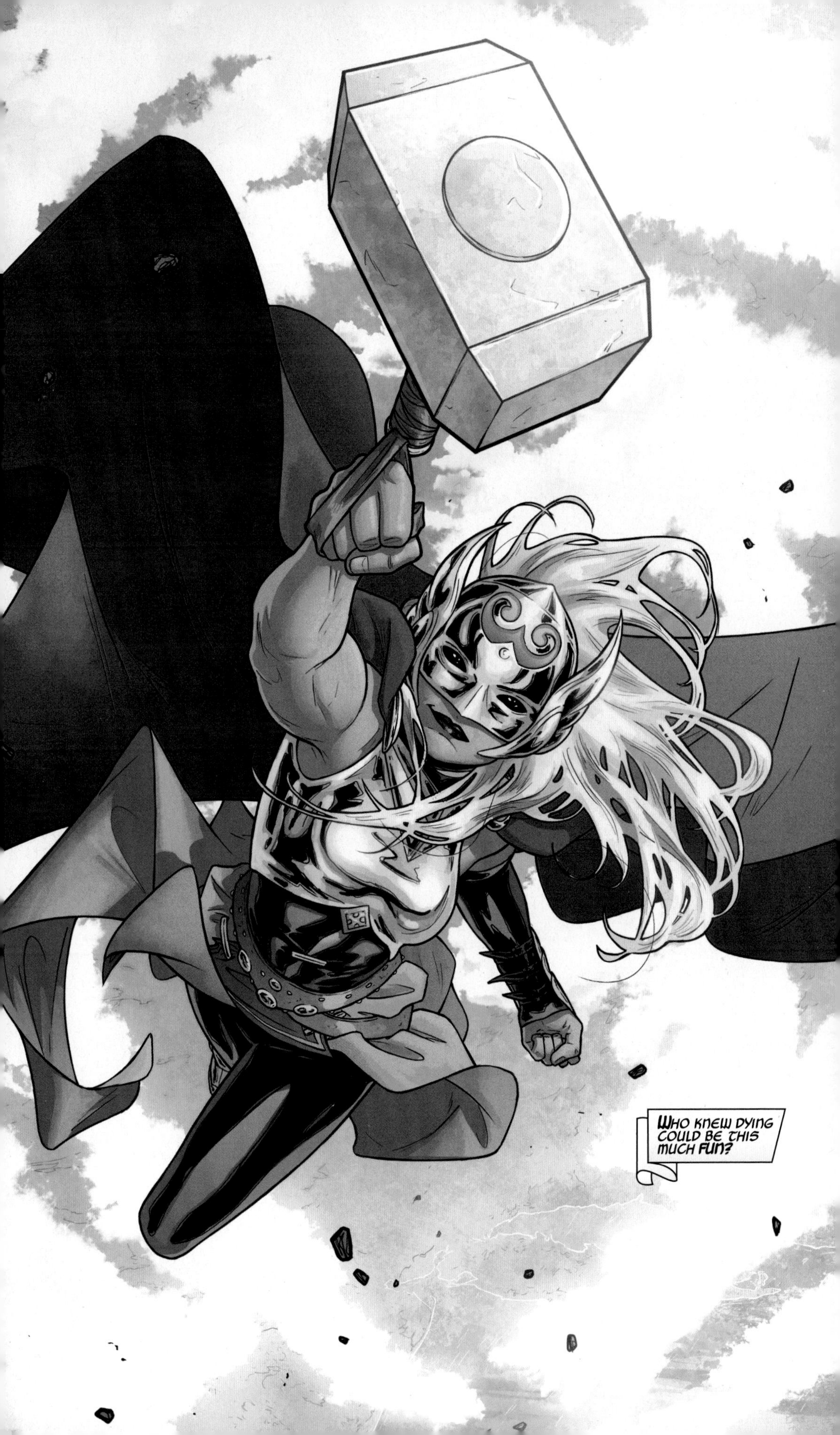
WHO KNEW DYING COULD BE THIS MUCH FUN?

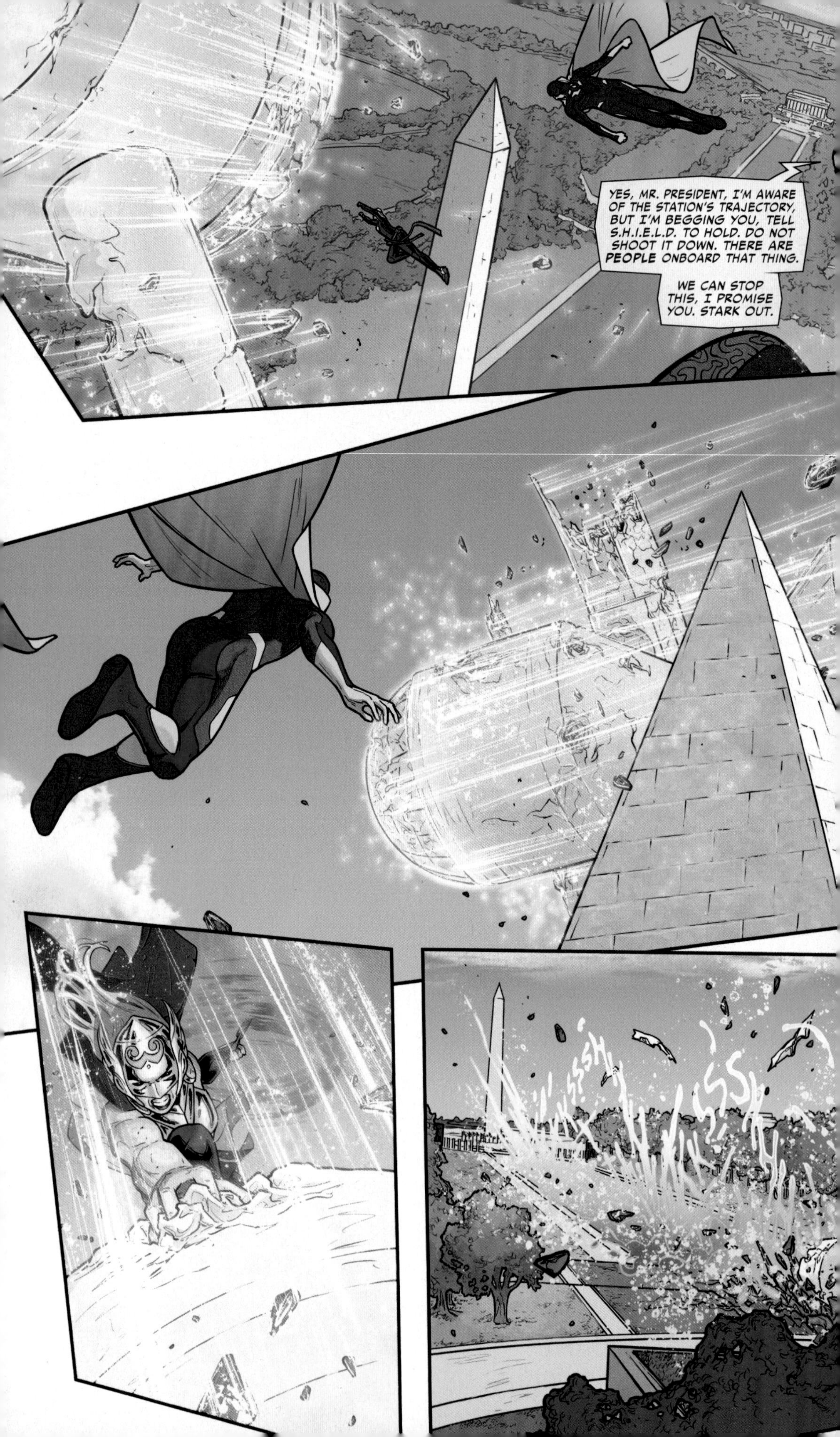
YES, MR. PRESIDENT, I'M AWARE OF THE STATION'S TRAJECTORY, BUT I'M BEGGING YOU, TELL S.H.I.E.L.D. TO HOLD. DO NOT SHOOT IT DOWN. THERE ARE PEOPLE ONBOARD THAT THING.
WE CAN STOP THIS, I PROMISE YOU. STARK OUT.
KSSSH
KSSH

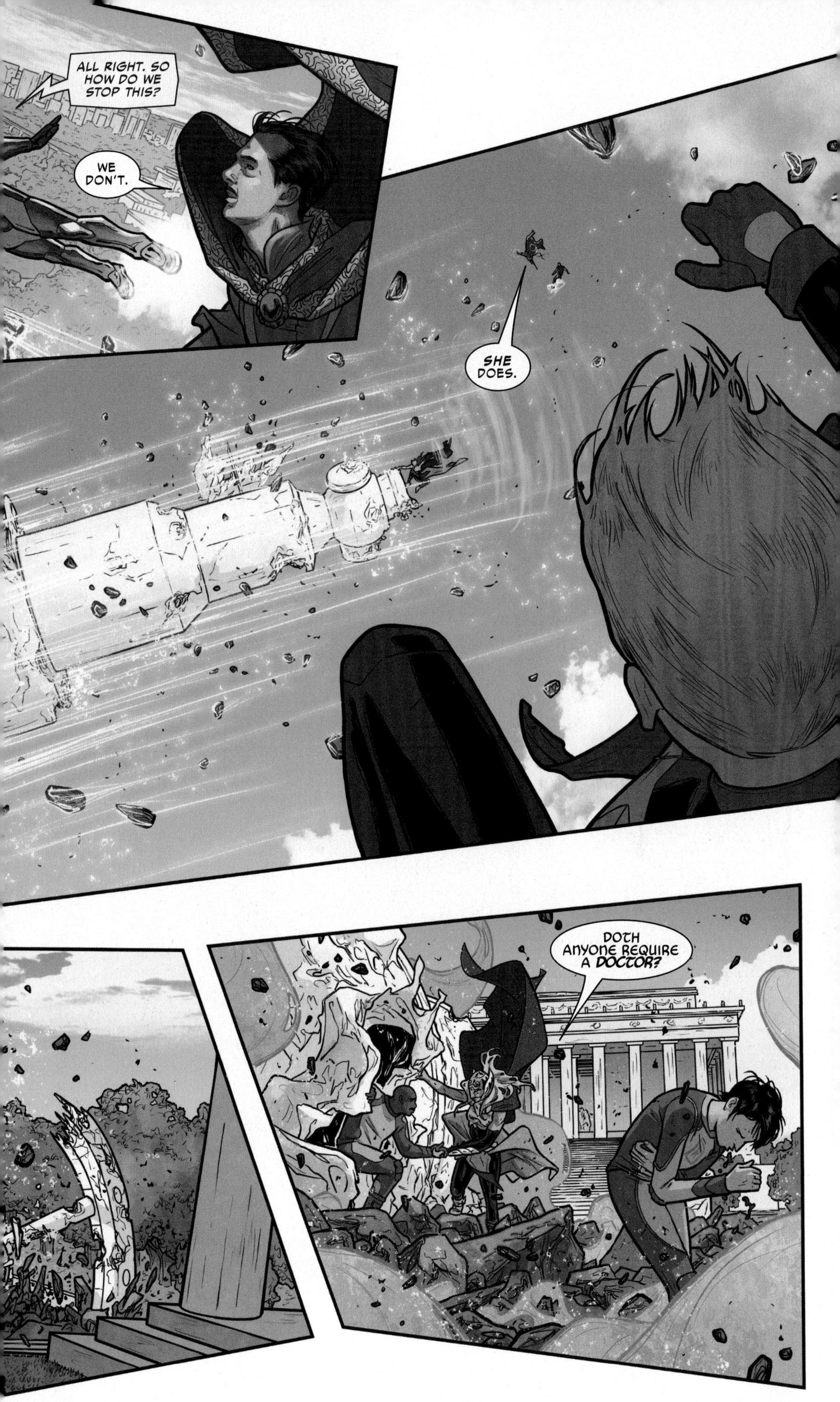
ALL RIGHT. SO HOW DO WE STOP THIS?
WE DON'T.
SHE DOES.
DOTH ANYONE REQUIRE A DOCTOR?

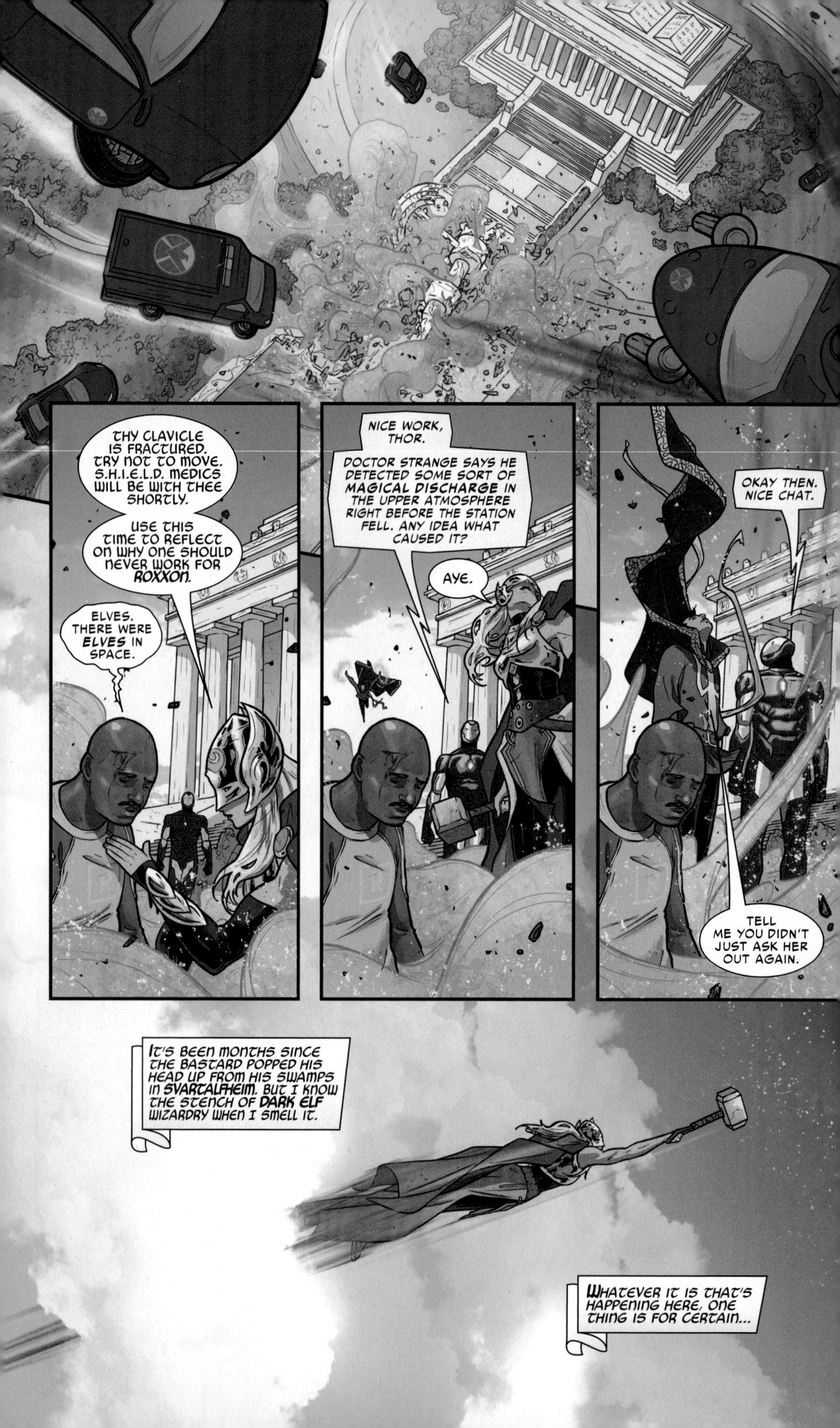
THY CLAVICLE IS FRACTURED. TRY NOT TO MOVE. S.H.I.E.L.D. MEDICS WILL BE WITH THEE SHORTLY.
USE THIS TIME TO REFLECT ON WHY ONE SHOULD NEVER WORK FOR ROXXON.
ELVES. THERE WERE ELVES IN SPACE.
NICE WORK, THOR.
DOCTOR STRANGE SAYS HE DETECTED SOME SORT OF MAGICAL DISCHARGE IN THE UPPER ATMOSPHERE RIGHT BEFORE THE STATION FELL. ANY IDEA WHAT CAUSED IT?
AYE.
OKAY THEN. NICE CHAT.
TELL ME YOU DIDN'T JUST ASK HER OUT AGAIN.
IT'S BEEN MONTHS SINCE THE BASTARD POPPED HIS HEAD UP FROM HIS SWAMPS IN SVARTALFHEIM. BUT I KNOW THE STENCH OF DARK ELF WIZARDRY WHEN I SMELL IT.
WHATEVER IT IS THAT'S HAPPENING HERE, ONE THING IS FOR CERTAIN...

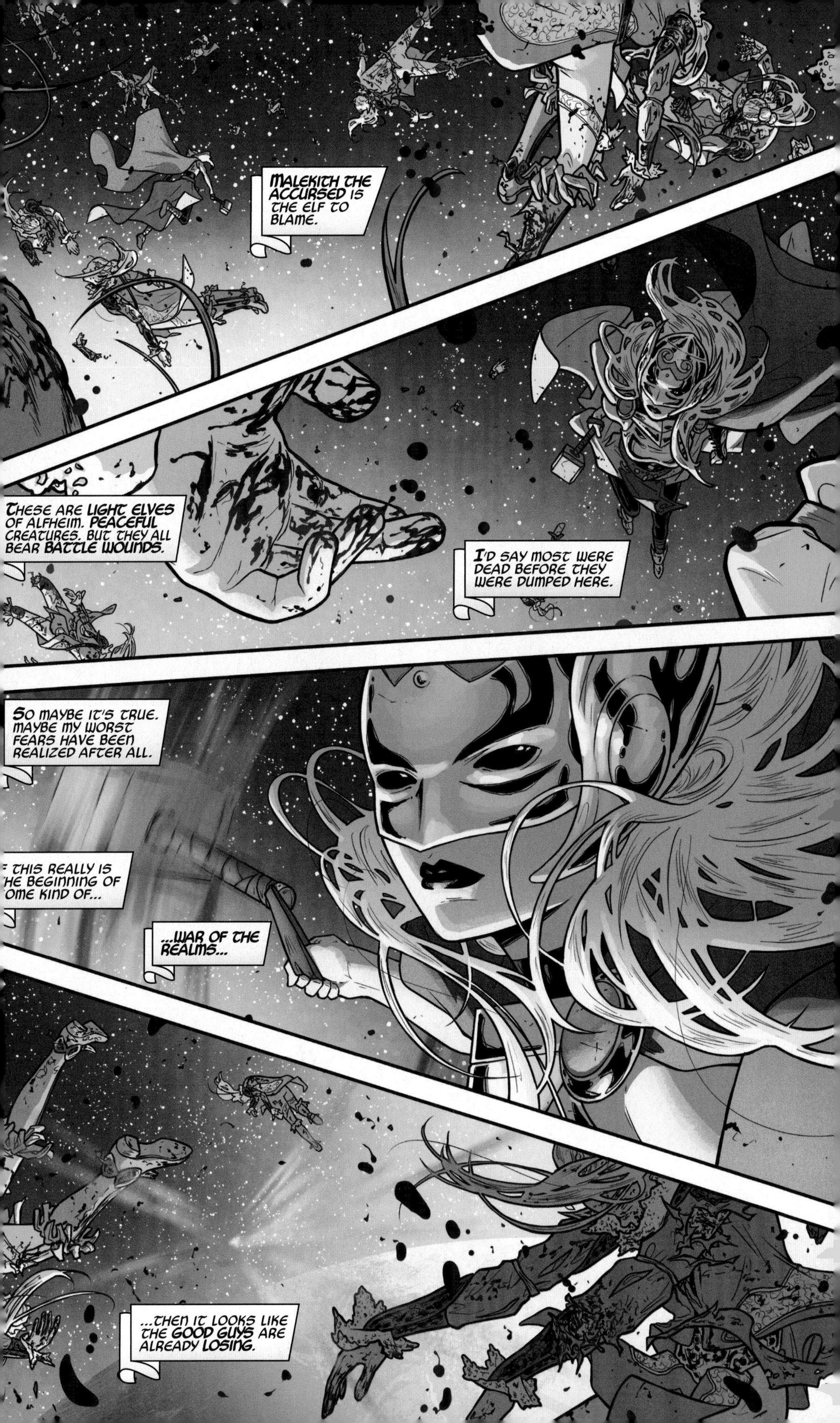
MALEKITH THE ACCURSED IS THE ELF TO BLAME.
THESE ARE LIGHT ELVES OF ALFHEIM. PEACEFUL CREATURES. BUT THEY ALL BEAR BATTLE WOUNDS.
I'D SAY MOST WERE DEAD BEFORE THEY WERE DUMPED HERE.
SO MAYBE IT'S TRUE. MAYBE MY WORST FEARS HAVE BEEN REALIZED AFTER ALL.
F THIS REALLY IS HE BEGINNING OF OME KIND OF...
...WAR OF THE REALMS...
...THEN IT LOOKS LIKE THE GOOD GUYS ARE ALREADY LOSING.

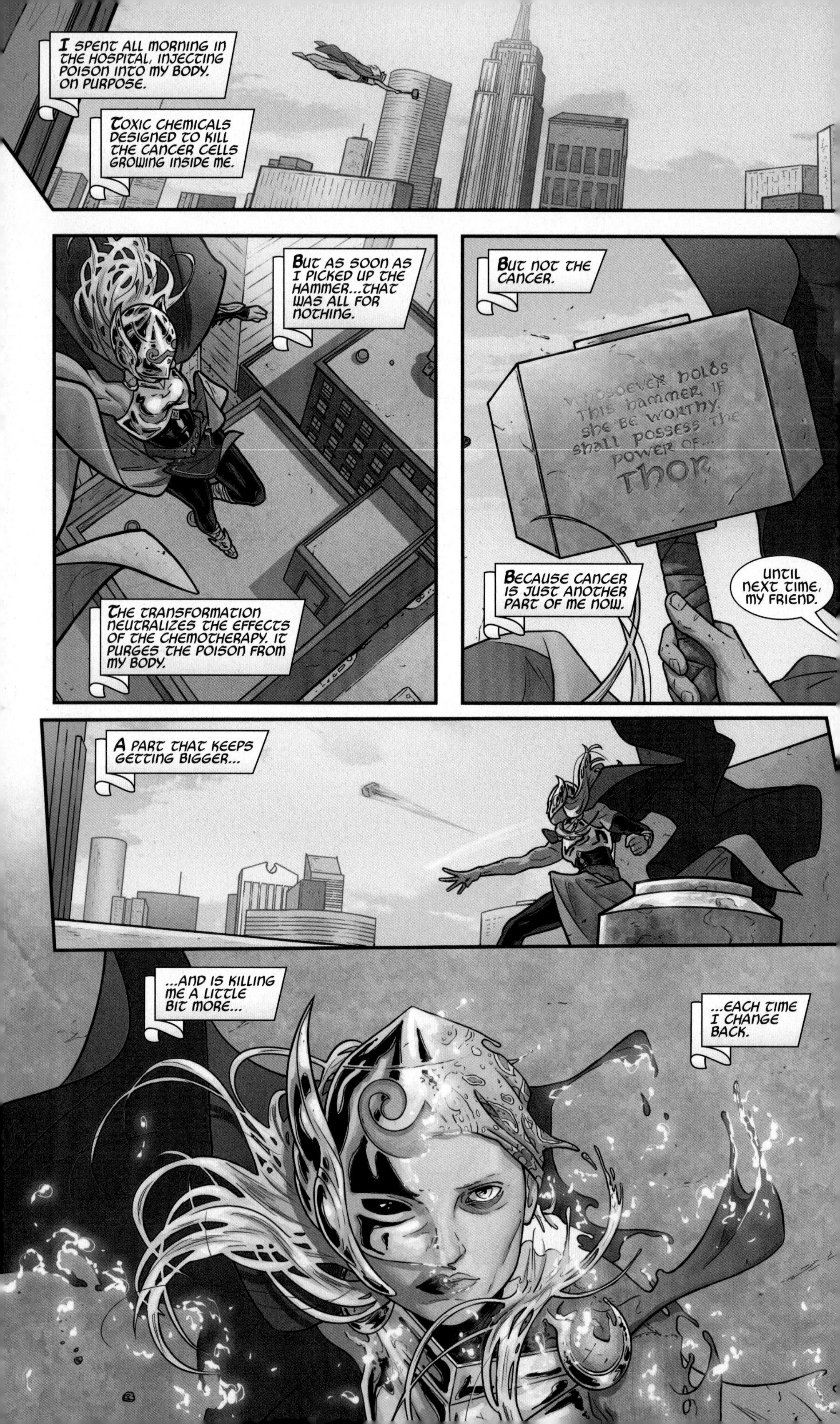

I SPENT ALL MORNING IN THE HOSPITAL, INJECTING POISON INTO MY BODY. ON PURPOSE.
TOXIC CHEMICALS DESIGNED TO KILL THE CANCER CELLS GROWING INSIDE ME.
BUT AS SOON AS I PICKED UP THE HAMMER...THAT WAS ALL FOR NOTHING.
THE TRANSFORMATION NEUTRALIZES THE EFFECTS OF THE CHEMOTHERAPY. IT PURGES THE POISON FROM MY BODY.
BUT NOT THE CANCER.
WHOSOEVER HOLDS THIS HAMMER, IF SHE BE WORTHY, SHALL POSSESS THE POWER OF... THOR
BECAUSE CANCER IS JUST ANOTHER PART OF ME NOW.
UNTIL NEXT TIME, MY FRIEND.
A PART THAT KEEPS GETTING BIGGER...
...AND IS KILLING ME A LITTLE BIT MORE...
...EACH TIME I CHANGE BACK.

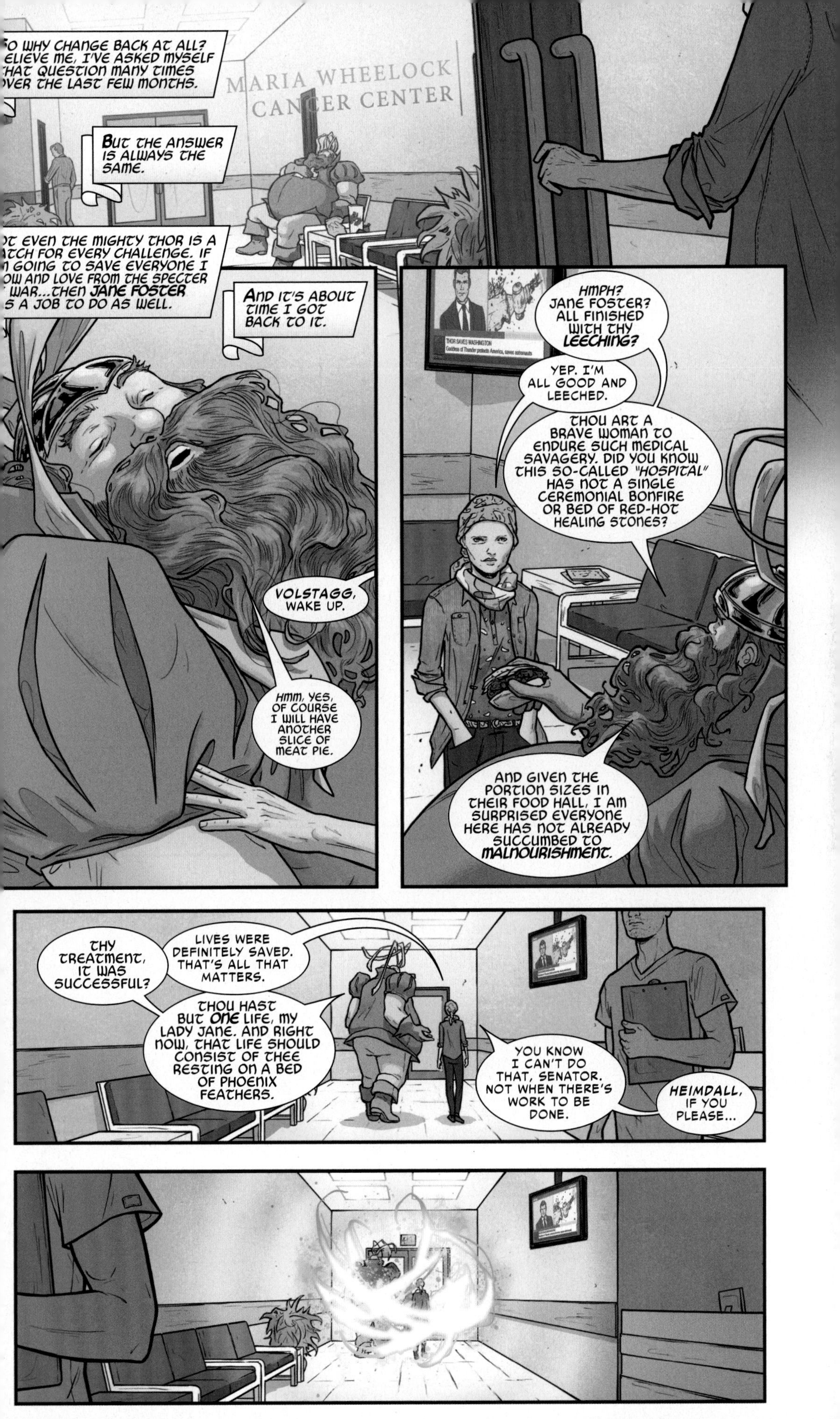
O WHY CHANGE BACK AT ALL? ELIEVE ME, I'VE ASKED MYSELF HAT QUESTION MANY TIMES VER THE LAST FEW MONTHS.
MARIA WHEELOCK CANCER CENTER
BUT THE ANSWER IS ALWAYS THE SAME.
OT EVEN THE MIGHTY THOR IS A ATCH FOR EVERY CHALLENGE. IF N GOING TO SAVE EVERYONE I OW AND LOVE FROM THE SPECTER WAR...THEN JANE FOSTER S A JOB TO DO AS WELL.
AND IT'S ABOUT TIME I GOT BACK TO IT.
VOLSTAGG, WAKE UP.
HMM, YES, OF COURSE I WILL HAVE ANOTHER SLICE OF MEAT PIE.
THOR SAVES WASHINGTON
Goddess of Thunder protects America, saves astronauts
HMPH? JANE FOSTER? ALL FINISHED WITH THY LEECHING?
YEP. I'M ALL GOOD AND LEECHED.
THOU ART A BRAVE WOMAN TO ENDURE SUCH MEDICAL SAVAGERY. DID YOU KNOW THIS SO-CALLED "HOSPITAL" HAS NOT A SINGLE CEREMONIAL BONFIRE OR BED OF RED-HOT HEALING STONES?
AND GIVEN THE PORTION SIZES IN THEIR FOOD HALL, I AM SURPRISED EVERYONE HERE HAS NOT ALREADY SUCCUMBED TO MALNOURISHMENT.
THY TREATMENT, IT WAS SUCCESSFUL?
LIVES WERE DEFINITELY SAVED. THAT'S ALL THAT MATTERS.
THOU HAST BUT ONE LIFE, MY LADY JANE. AND RIGHT NOW, THAT LIFE SHOULD CONSIST OF THEE RESTING ON A BED OF PHOENIX FEATHERS.
YOU KNOW I CAN'T DO THAT, SENATOR. NOT WHEN THERE'S WORK TO BE DONE.
HEIMDALL, IF YOU PLEASE...

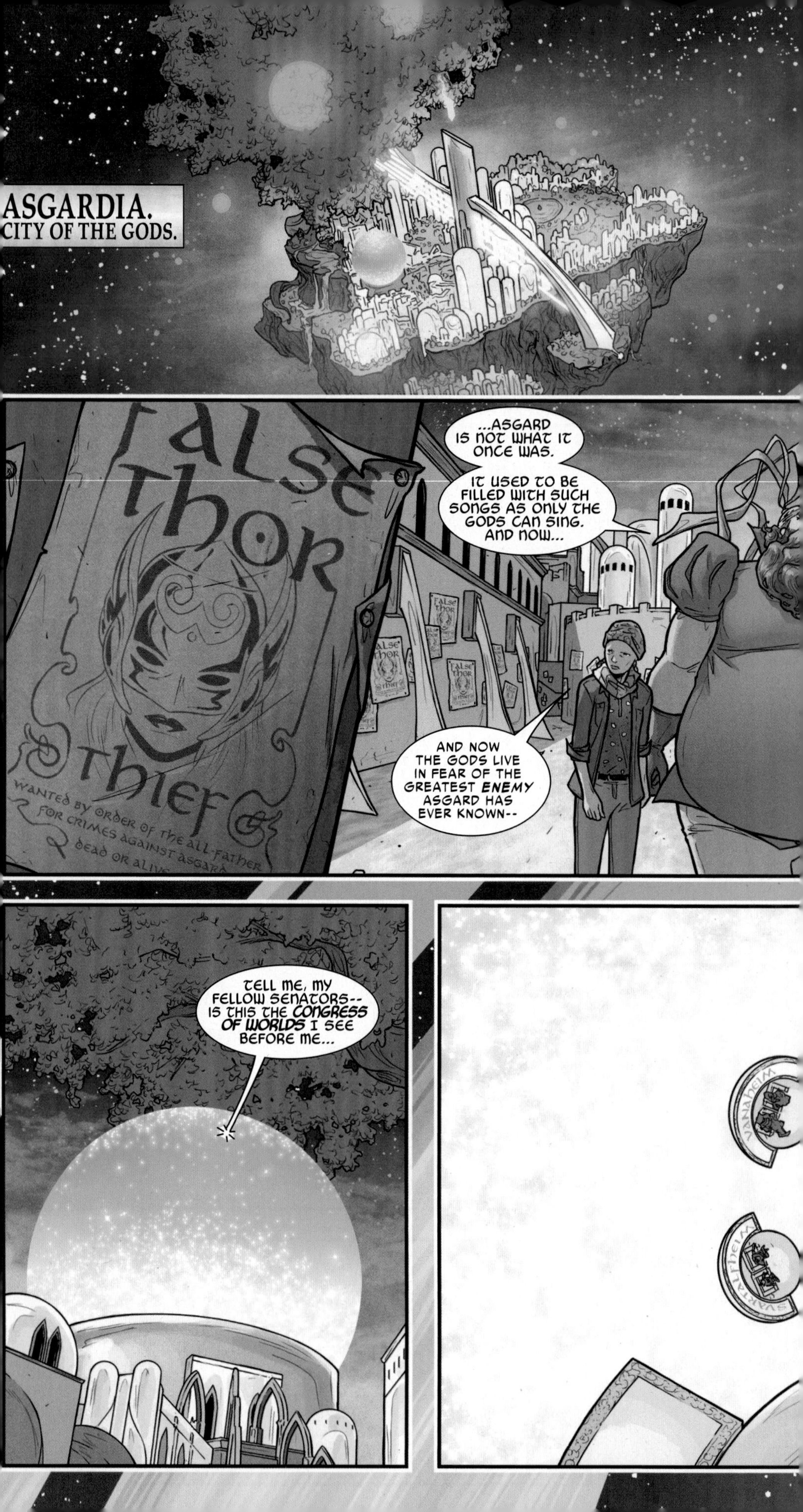

ASGARDIA.
CITY OF THE GODS.
FALSE THOR
THIEF
WANTED BY ORDER OF THE ALL-FATHER FOR CRIMES AGAINST ASGARD
...ASGARD IS NOT WHAT IT ONCE WAS.
IT USED TO BE FILLED WITH SUCH SONGS AS ONLY THE GODS CAN SING. AND NOW...
AND NOW THE GODS LIVE IN FEAR OF THE GREATEST ENEMY ASGARD HAS EVER KNOWN--
TELL ME, MY FELLOW SENATORS-- IS THIS THE CONGRESS OF WORLDS I SEE BEFORE ME...
VANAHEIM
SVARTALFHEIM

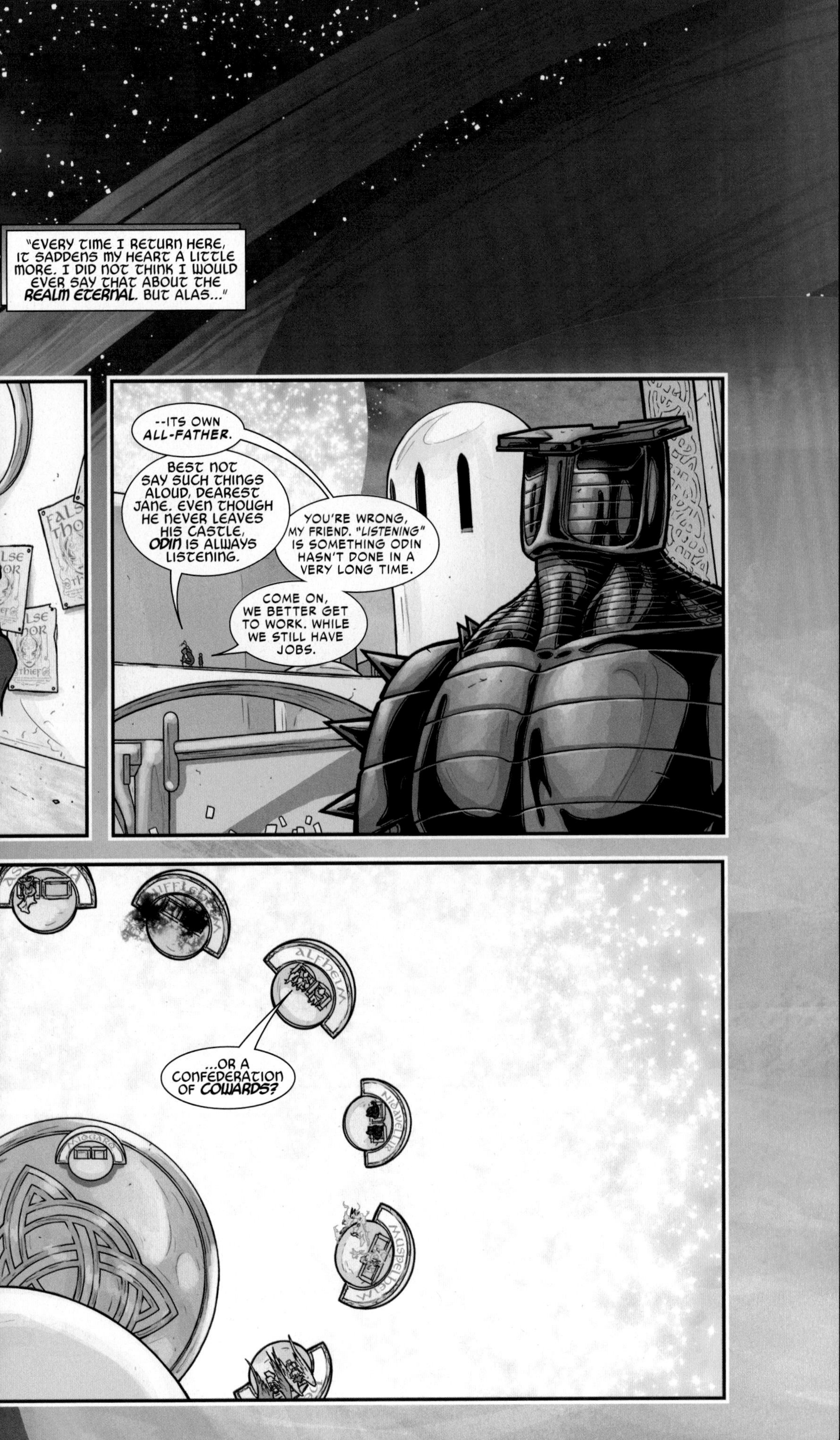
"EVERY TIME I RETURN HERE, IT SADDENS MY HEART A LITTLE MORE. I DID NOT THINK I WOULD EVER SAY THAT ABOUT THE **REALM ETERNAL**. BUT ALAS..."
--ITS OWN **ALL-FATHER**.
BEST NOT SAY SUCH THINGS ALOUD, DEAREST JANE. EVEN THOUGH HE NEVER LEAVES HIS CASTLE, **ODIN** IS ALWAYS LISTENING.
YOU'RE WRONG, MY FRIEND. "*LISTENING*" IS SOMETHING ODIN HASN'T DONE IN A VERY LONG TIME.
COME ON, WE BETTER GET TO WORK. WHILE WE STILL HAVE JOBS.
...OR A CONFEDERATION OF **COWARDS?**

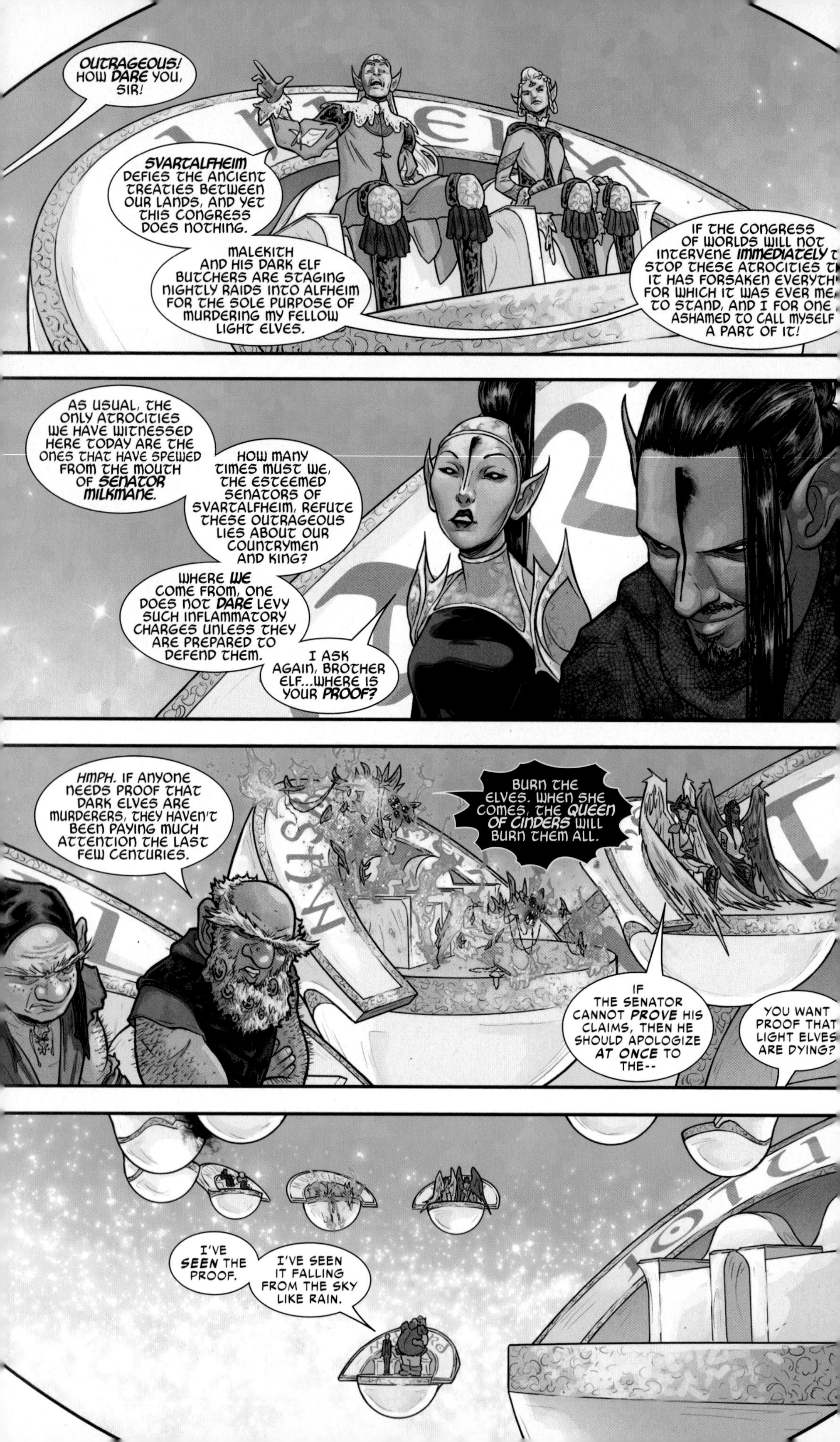
OUTRAGEOUS! HOW DARE YOU, SIR!
SVARTALFHEIM DEFIES THE ANCIENT TREATIES BETWEEN OUR LANDS, AND YET THIS CONGRESS DOES NOTHING.
MALEKITH AND HIS DARK ELF BUTCHERS ARE STAGING NIGHTLY RAIDS INTO ALFHEIM FOR THE SOLE PURPOSE OF MURDERING MY FELLOW LIGHT ELVES.
IF THE CONGRESS OF WORLDS WILL NOT INTERVENE IMMEDIATELY T STOP THESE ATROCITIES T IT HAS FORSAKEN EVERYTH FOR WHICH IT WAS EVER ME TO STAND, AND I FOR ONE ASHAMED TO CALL MYSELF A PART OF IT!
AS USUAL, THE ONLY ATROCITIES WE HAVE WITNESSED HERE TODAY ARE THE ONES THAT HAVE SPEWED FROM THE MOUTH OF SENATOR MILKMANE.
HOW MANY TIMES MUST WE, THE ESTEEMED SENATORS OF SVARTALFHEIM, REFUTE THESE OUTRAGEOUS LIES ABOUT OUR COUNTRYMEN AND KING?
WHERE WE COME FROM, ONE DOES NOT DARE LEVY SUCH INFLAMMATORY CHARGES UNLESS THEY ARE PREPARED TO DEFEND THEM.
I ASK AGAIN, BROTHER ELF...WHERE IS YOUR PROOF?
HMPH. IF ANYONE NEEDS PROOF THAT DARK ELVES ARE MURDERERS, THEY HAVEN'T BEEN PAYING MUCH ATTENTION THE LAST FEW CENTURIES.
BURN THE ELVES. WHEN SHE COMES, THE QUEEN OF CINDERS WILL BURN THEM ALL.
IF THE SENATOR CANNOT PROVE HIS CLAIMS, THEN HE SHOULD APOLOGIZE AT ONCE TO THE--
YOU WANT PROOF THAT LIGHT ELVES ARE DYING?
I'VE SEEN THE PROOF.
I'VE SEEN IT FALLING FROM THE SKY LIKE RAIN.

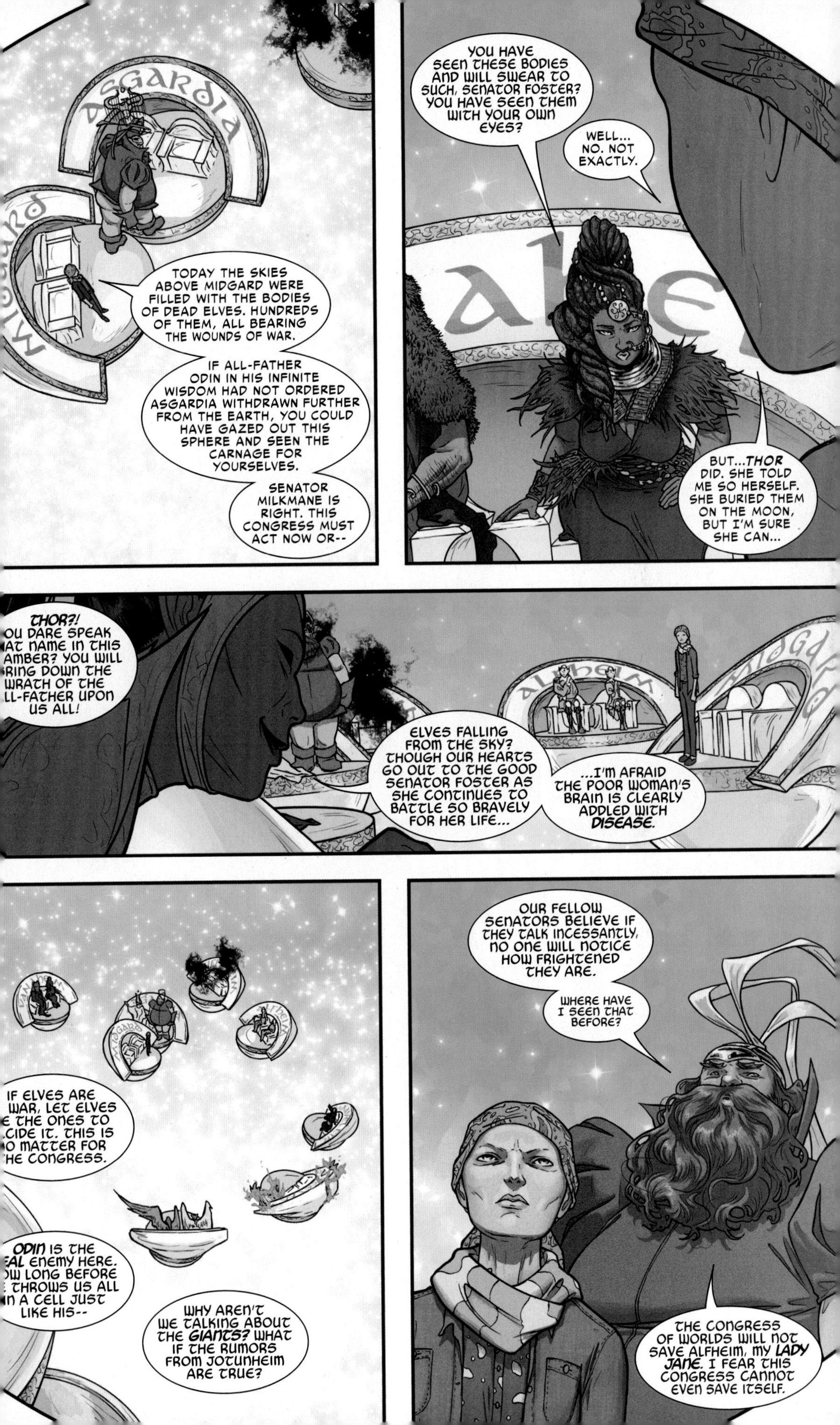

ASGARDIA
TODAY THE SKIES ABOVE MIDGARD WERE FILLED WITH THE BODIES OF DEAD ELVES. HUNDREDS OF THEM, ALL BEARING THE WOUNDS OF WAR.
IF ALL-FATHER ODIN IN HIS INFINITE WISDOM HAD NOT ORDERED ASGARDIA WITHDRAWN FURTHER FROM THE EARTH, YOU COULD HAVE GAZED OUT THIS SPHERE AND SEEN THE CARNAGE FOR YOURSELVES.
SENATOR MILKMANE IS RIGHT. THIS CONGRESS MUST ACT NOW OR--
YOU HAVE SEEN THESE BODIES AND WILL SWEAR TO SUCH, SENATOR FOSTER? YOU HAVE SEEN THEM WITH YOUR OWN EYES?
WELL... NO. NOT EXACTLY.
BUT...THOR DID. SHE TOLD ME SO HERSELF. SHE BURIED THEM ON THE MOON, BUT I'M SURE SHE CAN...
THOR?! OU DARE SPEAK AT NAME IN THIS AMBER? YOU WILL RING DOWN THE WRATH OF THE LL-FATHER UPON US ALL!
ELVES FALLING FROM THE SKY? THOUGH OUR HEARTS GO OUT TO THE GOOD SENATOR FOSTER AS SHE CONTINUES TO BATTLE SO BRAVELY FOR HER LIFE...
...I'M AFRAID THE POOR WOMAN'S BRAIN IS CLEARLY ADDLED WITH DISEASE.
IF ELVES ARE WAR, LET ELVES E THE ONES TO CIDE IT. THIS IS O MATTER FOR HE CONGRESS.
ODIN IS THE EAL ENEMY HERE. OW LONG BEFORE E THROWS US ALL N A CELL JUST LIKE HIS--
WHY AREN'T WE TALKING ABOUT THE GIANTS? WHAT IF THE RUMORS FROM JOTUNHEIM ARE TRUE?
OUR FELLOW SENATORS BELIEVE IF THEY TALK INCESSANTLY, NO ONE WILL NOTICE HOW FRIGHTENED THEY ARE.
WHERE HAVE I SEEN THAT BEFORE?
THE CONGRESS OF WORLDS WILL NOT SAVE ALFHEIM, MY LADY JANE. I FEAR THIS CONGRESS CANNOT EVEN SAVE ITSELF.

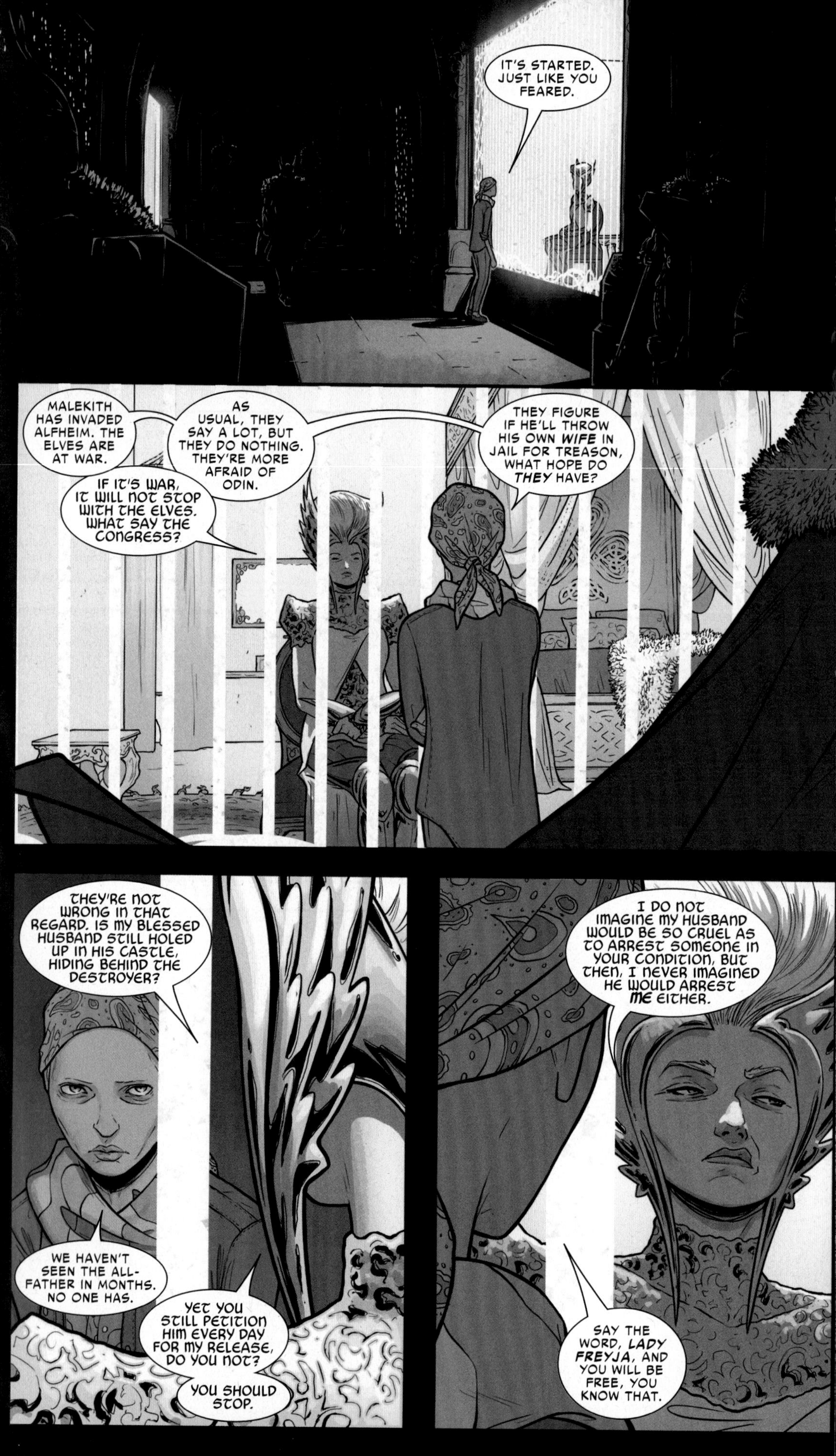
IT'S STARTED. JUST LIKE YOU FEARED.
MALEKITH HAS INVADED ALFHEIM. THE ELVES ARE AT WAR.
IF IT'S WAR, IT WILL NOT STOP WITH THE ELVES. WHAT SAY THE CONGRESS?
AS USUAL, THEY SAY A LOT, BUT THEY DO NOTHING. THEY'RE MORE AFRAID OF ODIN.
THEY FIGURE IF HE'LL THROW HIS OWN WIFE IN JAIL FOR TREASON, WHAT HOPE DO THEY HAVE?
THEY'RE NOT WRONG IN THAT REGARD. IS MY BLESSED HUSBAND STILL HOLED UP IN HIS CASTLE, HIDING BEHIND THE DESTROYER?
WE HAVEN'T SEEN THE ALL-FATHER IN MONTHS. NO ONE HAS.
YET YOU STILL PETITION HIM EVERY DAY FOR MY RELEASE, DO YOU NOT?
YOU SHOULD STOP.
I DO NOT IMAGINE MY HUSBAND WOULD BE SO CRUEL AS TO ARREST SOMEONE IN YOUR CONDITION, BUT THEN, I NEVER IMAGINED HE WOULD ARREST ME EITHER.
SAY THE WORD, LADY FREYJA, AND YOU WILL BE FREE, YOU KNOW THAT.

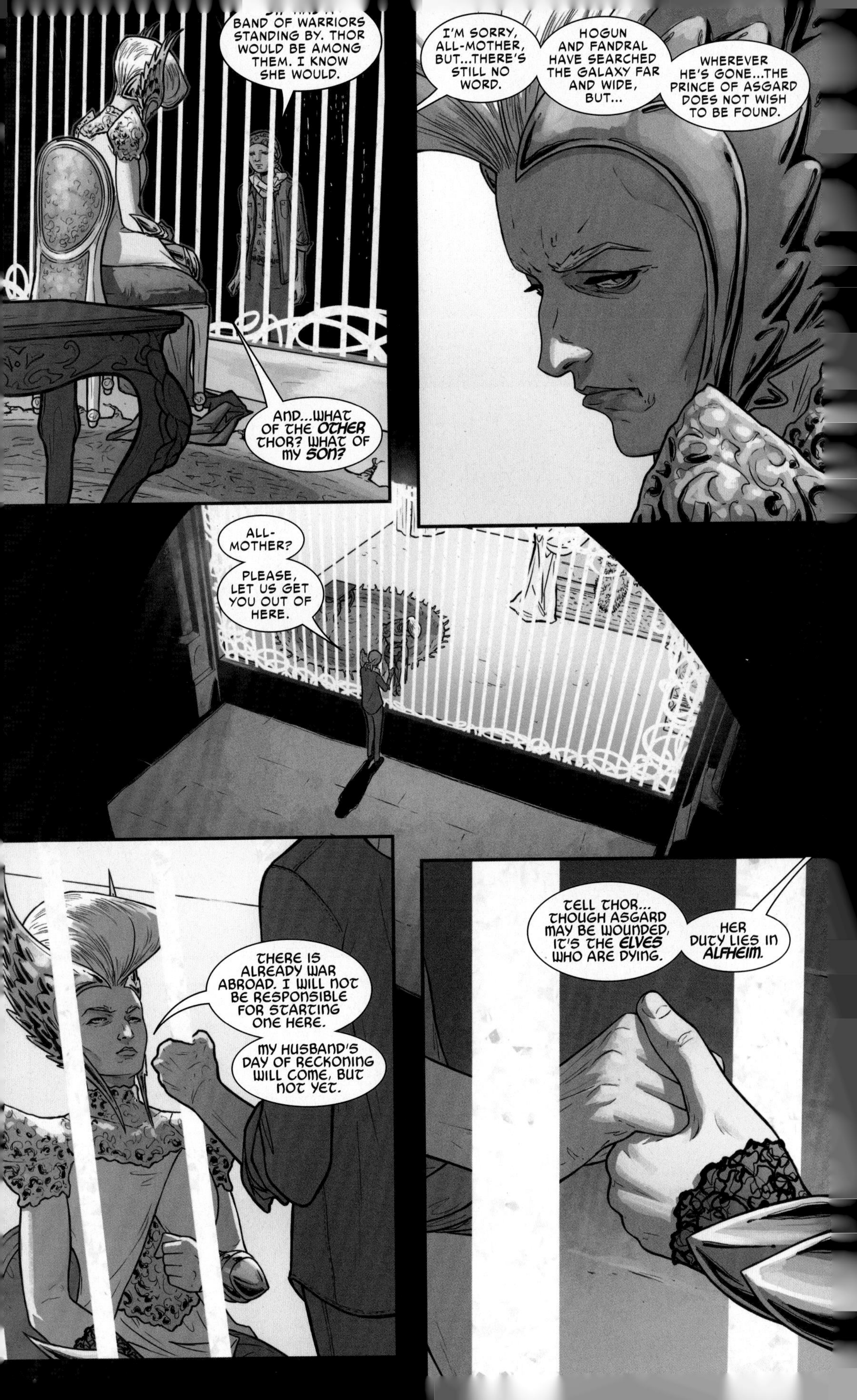
BAND OF WARRIORS STANDING BY. THOR WOULD BE AMONG THEM. I KNOW SHE WOULD.
AND...WHAT OF THE OTHER THOR? WHAT OF MY SON?
I'M SORRY, ALL-MOTHER, BUT...THERE'S STILL NO WORD.
HOGUN AND FANDRAL HAVE SEARCHED THE GALAXY FAR AND WIDE, BUT...
WHEREVER HE'S GONE...THE PRINCE OF ASGARD DOES NOT WISH TO BE FOUND.
ALL-MOTHER?
PLEASE, LET US GET YOU OUT OF HERE.
THERE IS ALREADY WAR ABROAD. I WILL NOT BE RESPONSIBLE FOR STARTING ONE HERE.
MY HUSBAND'S DAY OF RECKONING WILL COME, BUT NOT YET.
TELL THOR... THOUGH ASGARD MAY BE WOUNDED, IT'S THE ELVES WHO ARE DYING.
HER DUTY LIES IN ALFHEIM.

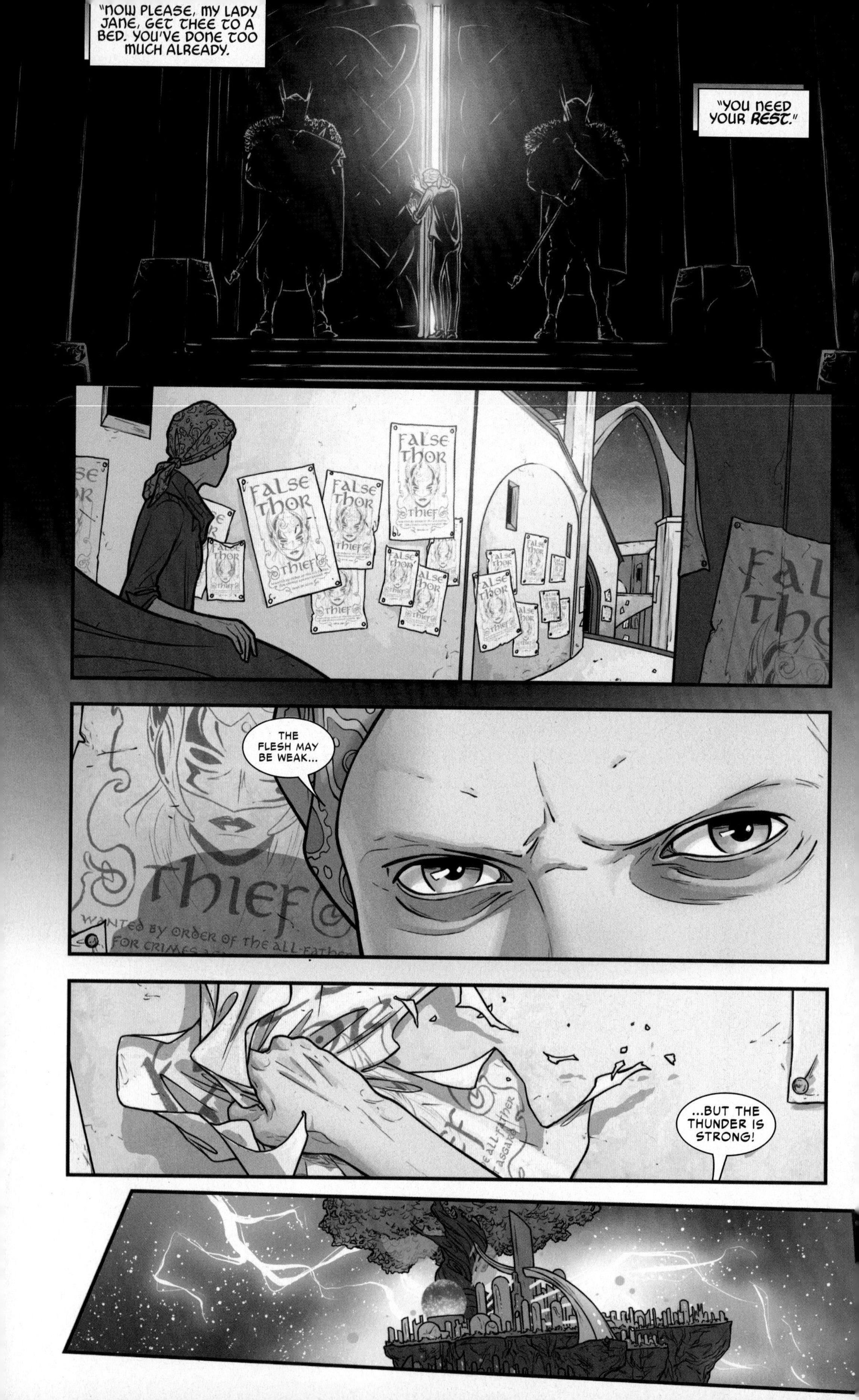
"NOW PLEASE, MY LADY JANE, GET THEE TO A BED. YOU'VE DONE TOO MUCH ALREADY.
"YOU NEED YOUR REST."
FALSE THOR
THIEF
THE FLESH MAY BE WEAK...
WANTED BY ORDER OF THE ALL-FATHER
...BUT THE THUNDER IS STRONG!

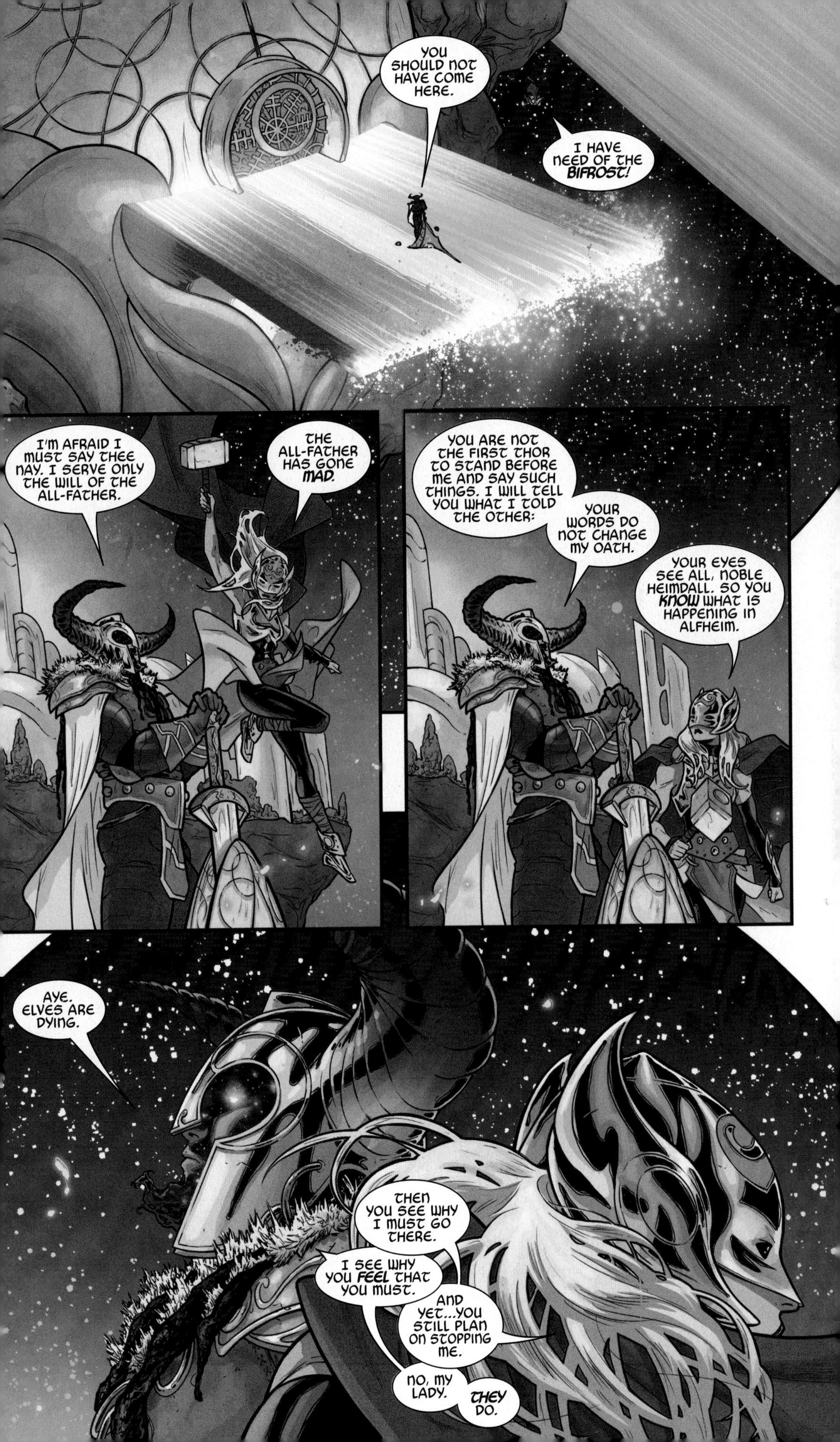
YOU SHOULD NOT HAVE COME HERE.
I HAVE NEED OF THE BIFROST!
I'M AFRAID I MUST SAY THEE NAY. I SERVE ONLY THE WILL OF THE ALL-FATHER.
THE ALL-FATHER HAS GONE MAD.
YOU ARE NOT THE FIRST THOR TO STAND BEFORE ME AND SAY SUCH THINGS. I WILL TELL YOU WHAT I TOLD THE OTHER:
YOUR WORDS DO NOT CHANGE MY OATH.
YOUR EYES SEE ALL, NOBLE HEIMDALL. SO YOU KNOW WHAT IS HAPPENING IN ALFHEIM.
AYE. ELVES ARE DYING.
THEN YOU SEE WHY I MUST GO THERE.
I SEE WHY YOU FEEL THAT YOU MUST.
AND YET...YOU STILL PLAN ON STOPPING ME.
NO, MY LADY.
THEY DO.

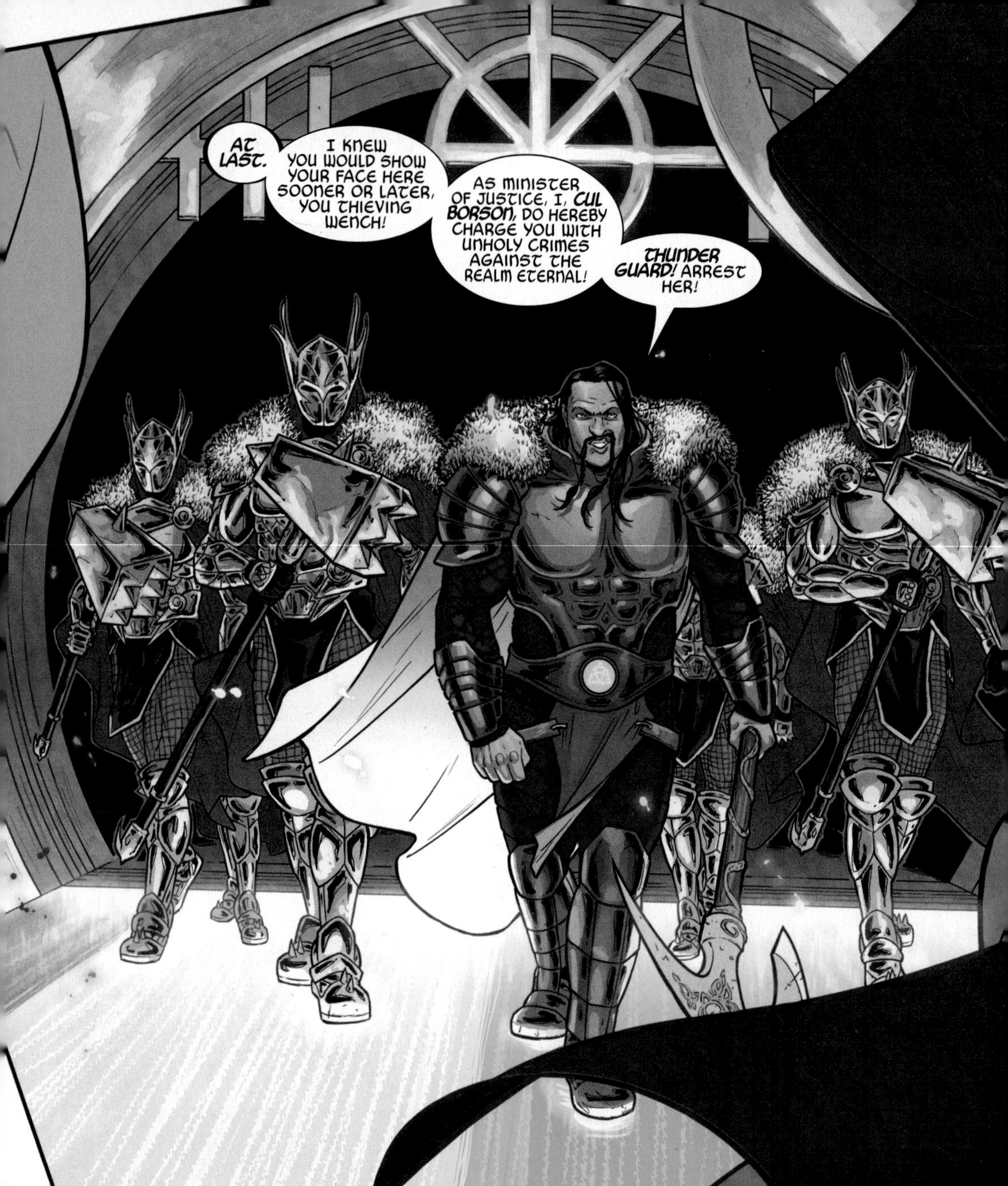
AT LAST.
I KNEW YOU WOULD SHOW YOUR FACE HERE SOONER OR LATER, YOU THIEVING WENCH!
AS MINISTER OF JUSTICE, I, CUL BORSON, DO HEREBY CHARGE YOU WITH UNHOLY CRIMES AGAINST THE REALM ETERNAL!
THUNDER GUARD! ARREST HER!

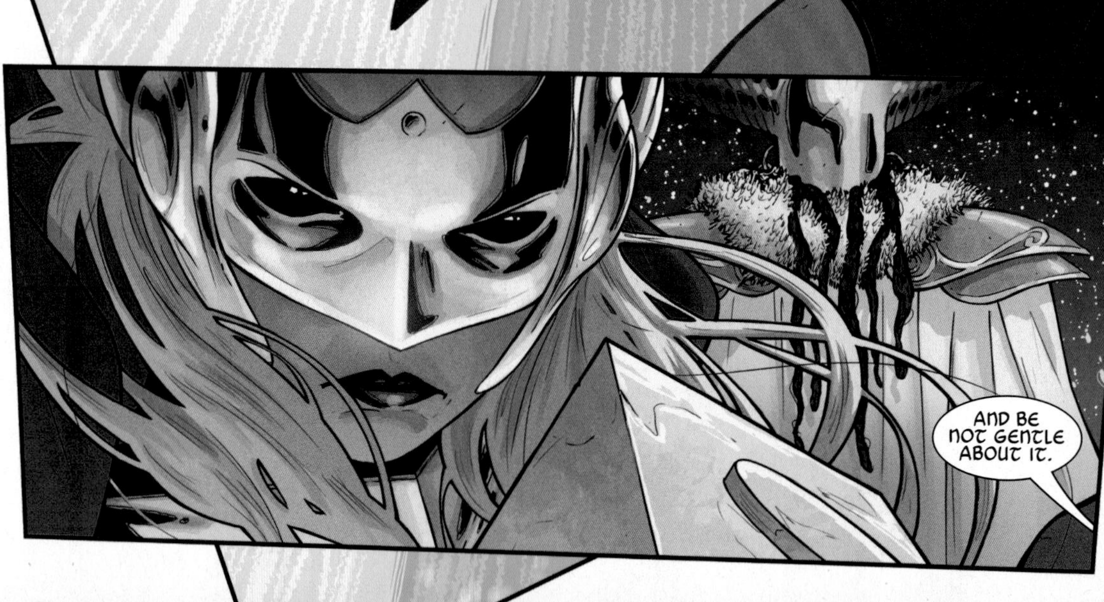
AND BE NOT GENTLE ABOUT IT.

"IT HAS *BEGUN.* JUST AS I PROMISED."

AS WE SPEAK, THE ELVES OF ALFHEIM ARE BLEEDING AND BURNING. PARENTS ARE BURYING THEIR CHILDREN. INFANTS CRY FOR MOTHERS WHO WILL NEVER COME.

SHALL WE DRINK A TOAST, MY FRIENDS?

TO THE PLEASURES OF *WAR.*

PARDON ME IF I'M NOT IN THE MOOD, BUT I DON'T TAKE MUCH PLEASURE FROM THE *LOSSES* I'VE SUFFERED TODAY.

NAMELY, *TWO HUNDRED BILLION DOLLARS'* WORTH OF LOSSES.

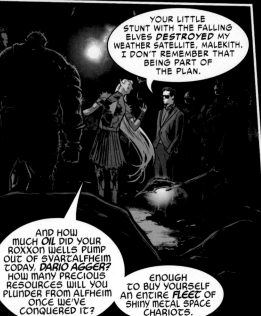

YOUR LITTLE STUNT WITH THE FALLING ELVES *DESTROYED* MY WEATHER SATELLITE, MALEKITH. I DON'T REMEMBER THAT BEING PART OF THE PLAN.

AND HOW MUCH *OIL* DID YOUR ROXXON WELLS PUMP OUT OF SVARTALFHEIM TODAY, *DARIO AGGER?* HOW MANY PRECIOUS RESOURCES WILL YOU PLUNDER FROM ALFHEIM ONCE WE'VE CONQUERED IT?

ENOUGH TO BUY YOURSELF AN ENTIRE *FLEET* OF SHINY METAL SPACE CHARIOTS.

DUMPING HUNDREDS OF BODIES INTO THE SKIES OF ANOTHER REALM WAS BOUND TO RESULT IN SOME...COLLATERAL DAMAGE. BUT WE ALL AGREED IT WAS A NECESSARY STEP.

THOR WILL COME TO US NOW. THE QUESTION BEFORE US TODAY IS...HOW WOULD THIS COUNCIL LIKE TO *GREET* HER?

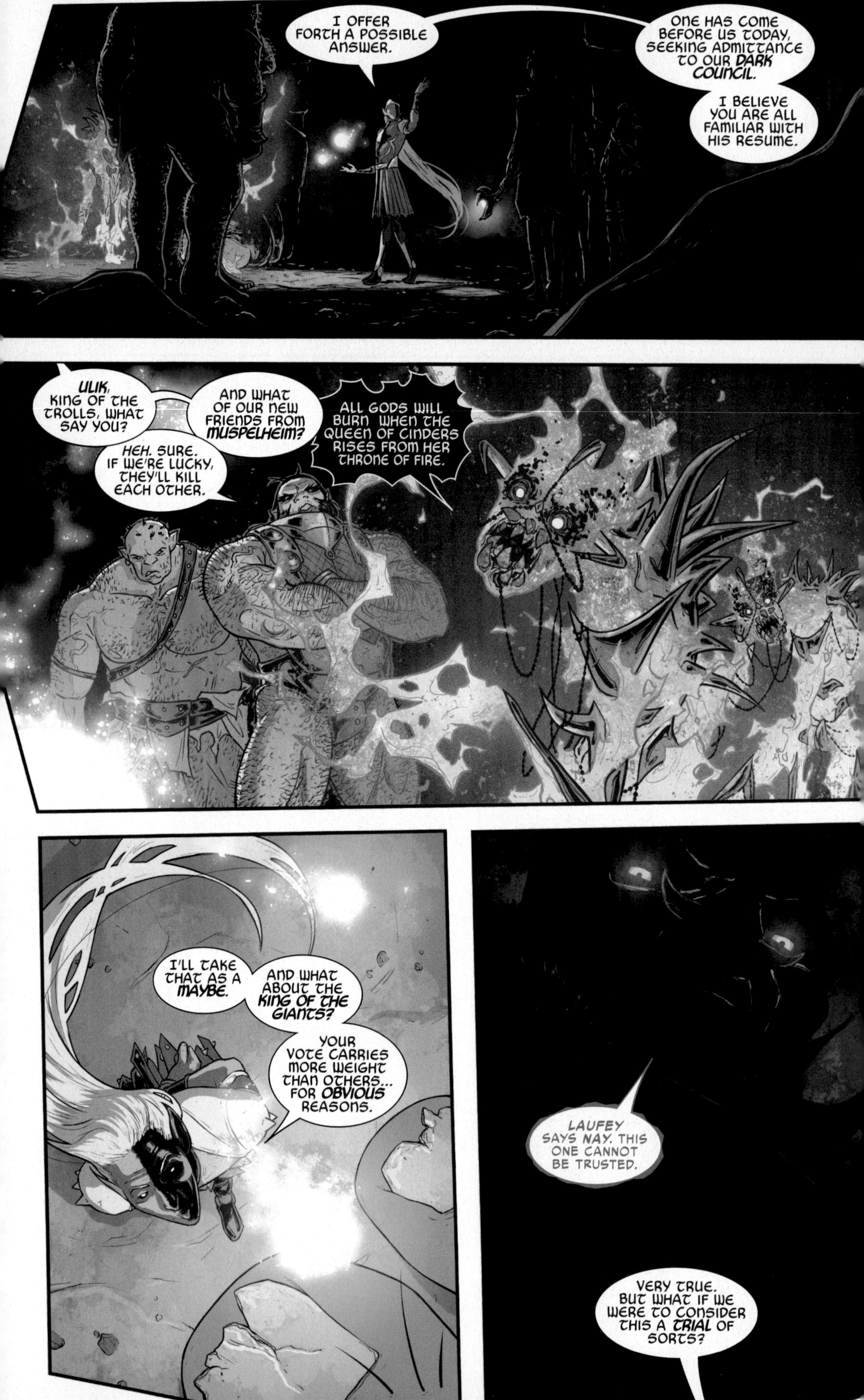

I OFFER FORTH A POSSIBLE ANSWER.
ONE HAS COME BEFORE US TODAY, SEEKING ADMITTANCE TO OUR DARK COUNCIL.
I BELIEVE YOU ARE ALL FAMILIAR WITH HIS RESUME.
ULIK, KING OF THE TROLLS, WHAT SAY YOU?
HEH. SURE. IF WE'RE LUCKY, THEY'LL KILL EACH OTHER.
AND WHAT OF OUR NEW FRIENDS FROM MUSPELHEIM?
ALL GODS WILL BURN WHEN THE QUEEN OF CINDERS RISES FROM HER THRONE OF FIRE.
I'LL TAKE THAT AS A MAYBE.
AND WHAT ABOUT THE KING OF THE GIANTS?
YOUR VOTE CARRIES MORE WEIGHT THAN OTHERS... FOR OBVIOUS REASONS.
LAUFEY SAYS NAY. THIS ONE CANNOT BE TRUSTED.
VERY TRUE. BUT WHAT IF WE WERE TO CONSIDER THIS A TRIAL OF SORTS?

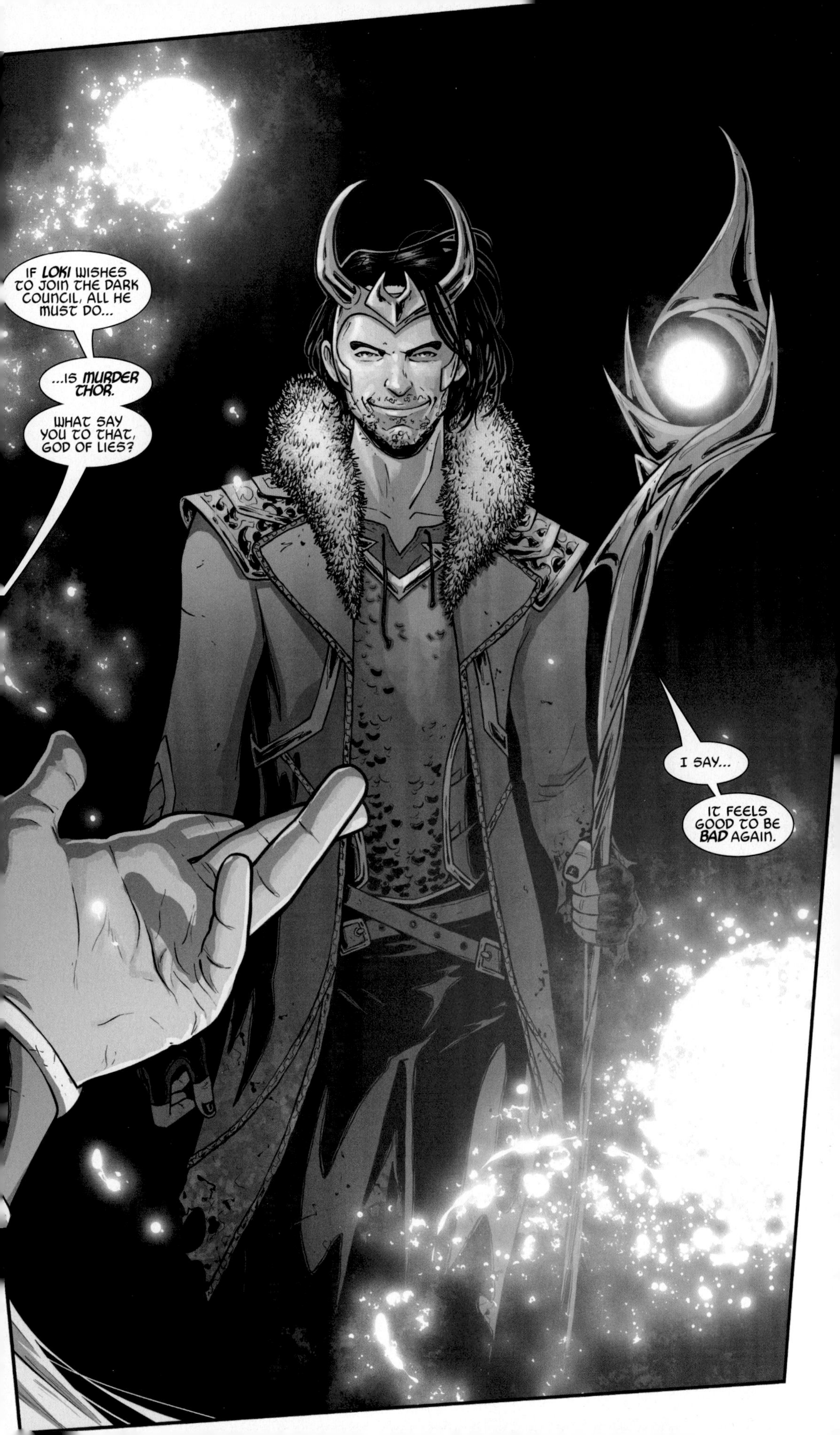
IF LOKI WISHES TO JOIN THE DARK COUNCIL, ALL HE MUST DO...
...IS MURDER THOR.
WHAT SAY YOU TO THAT, GOD OF LIES?
I SAY...
IT FEELS GOOD TO BE BAD AGAIN.

— 2 —

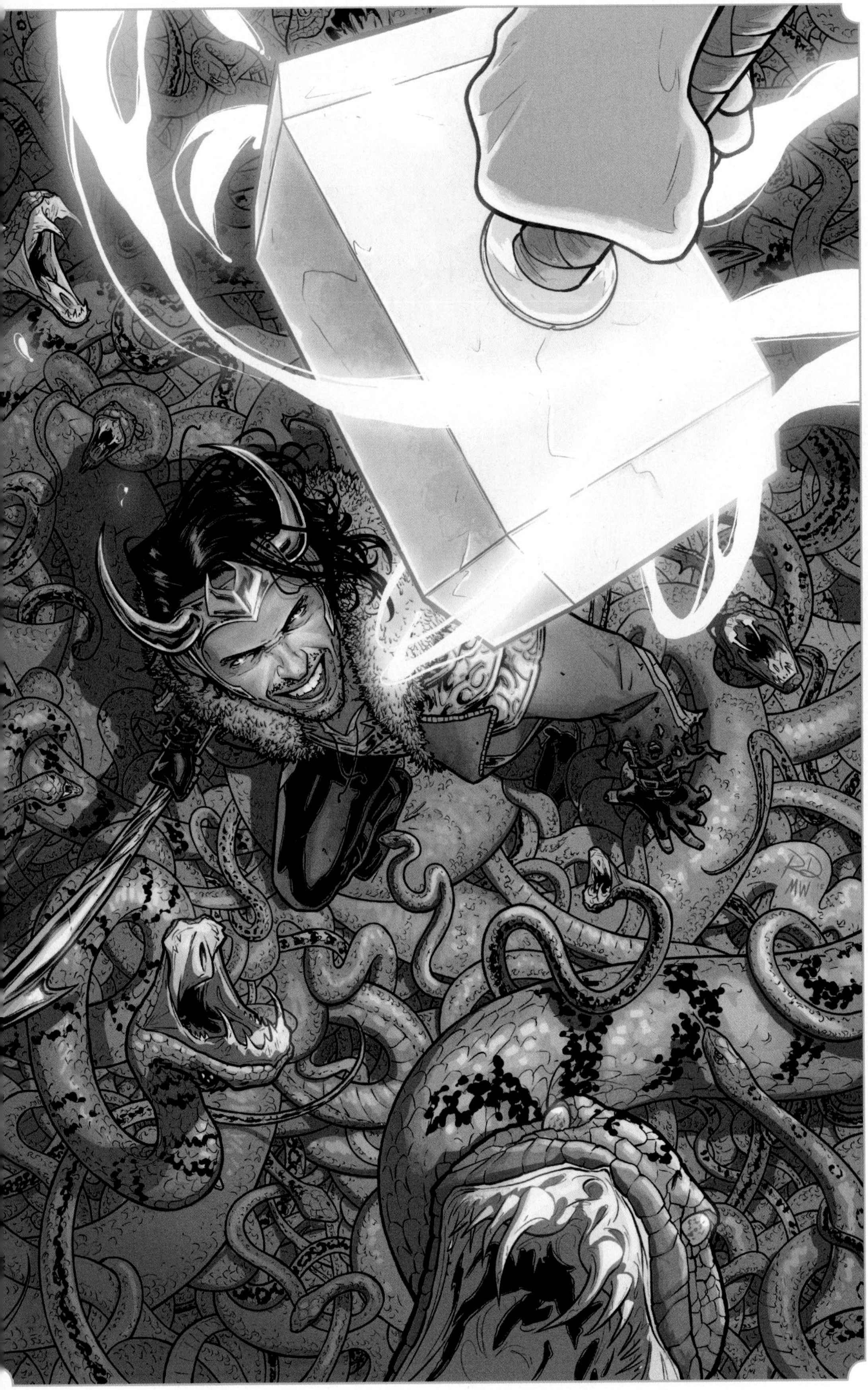

THE WAR OF THE ELVES

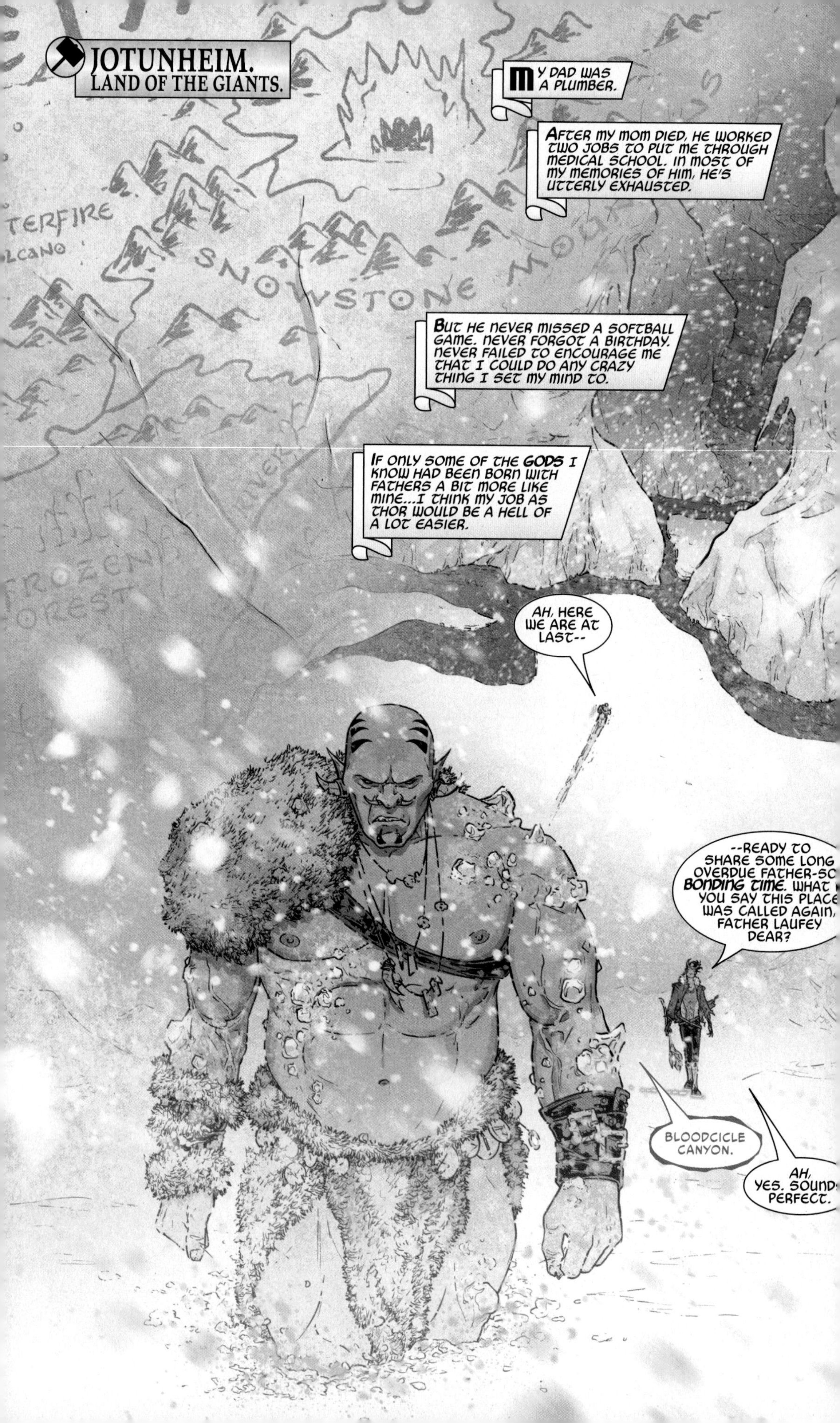
JOTUNHEIM. LAND OF THE GIANTS.
MY DAD WAS A PLUMBER.
AFTER MY MOM DIED, HE WORKED TWO JOBS TO PUT ME THROUGH MEDICAL SCHOOL. IN MOST OF MY MEMORIES OF HIM, HE'S UTTERLY EXHAUSTED.
TERFIRE
LCANO
SNOWSTONE MOU
BUT HE NEVER MISSED A SOFTBALL GAME. NEVER FORGOT A BIRTHDAY. NEVER FAILED TO ENCOURAGE ME THAT I COULD DO ANY CRAZY THING I SET MY MIND TO.
IF ONLY SOME OF THE GODS I KNOW HAD BEEN BORN WITH FATHERS A BIT MORE LIKE MINE...I THINK MY JOB AS THOR WOULD BE A HELL OF A LOT EASIER.
FROZEN
OREST
AH, HERE WE ARE AT LAST--
--READY TO SHARE SOME LONG OVERDUE FATHER-SO BONDING TIME. WHAT YOU SAY THIS PLACE WAS CALLED AGAIN, FATHER LAUFEY DEAR?
BLOODCICLE CANYON.
AH, YES. SOUND PERFECT.

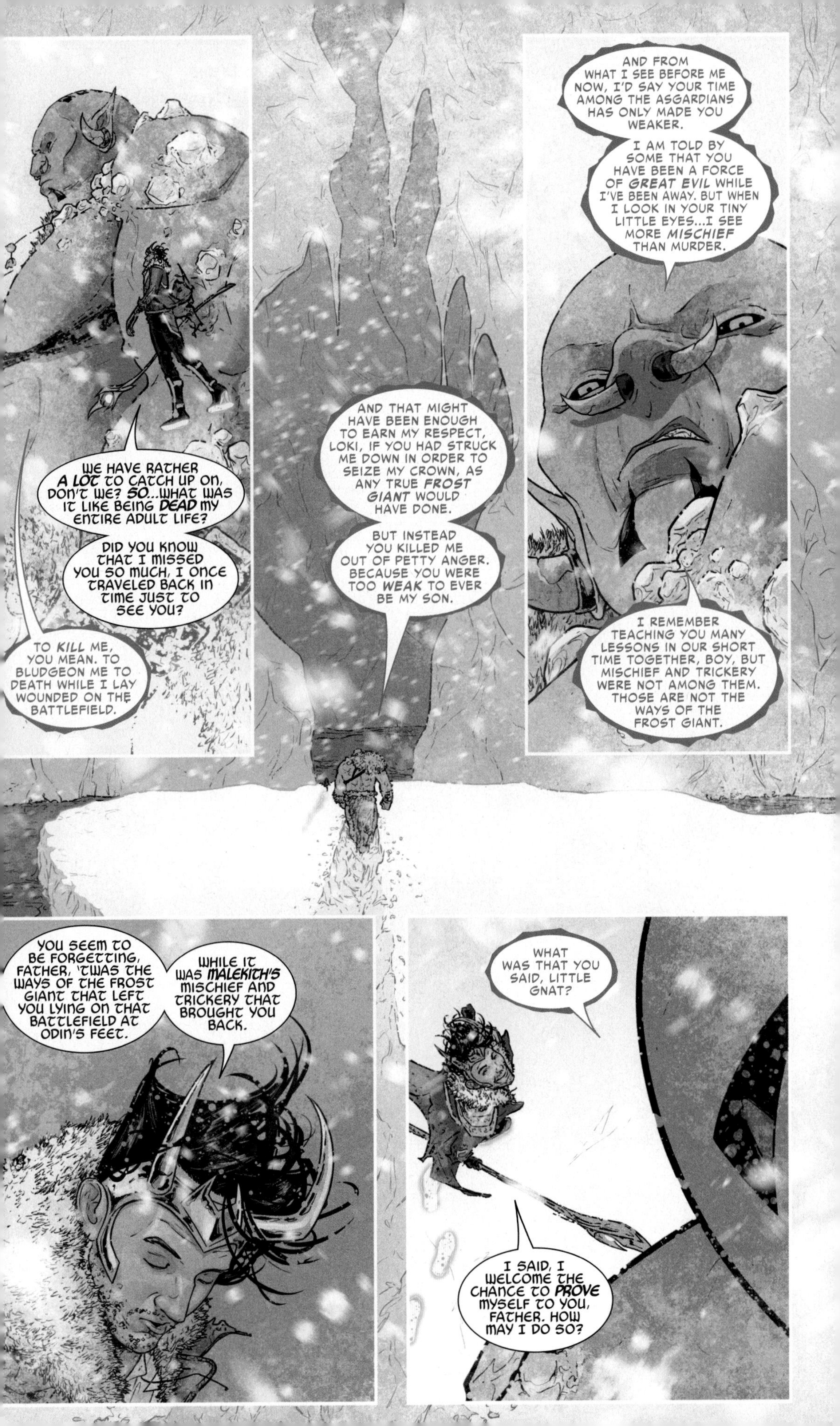
WE HAVE RATHER A LOT TO CATCH UP ON, DON'T WE? SO...WHAT WAS IT LIKE BEING DEAD MY ENTIRE ADULT LIFE?
DID YOU KNOW THAT I MISSED YOU SO MUCH, I ONCE TRAVELED BACK IN TIME JUST TO SEE YOU?
TO KILL ME, YOU MEAN. TO BLUDGEON ME TO DEATH WHILE I LAY WOUNDED ON THE BATTLEFIELD.
AND THAT MIGHT HAVE BEEN ENOUGH TO EARN MY RESPECT, LOKI, IF YOU HAD STRUCK ME DOWN IN ORDER TO SEIZE MY CROWN, AS ANY TRUE FROST GIANT WOULD HAVE DONE.
BUT INSTEAD YOU KILLED ME OUT OF PETTY ANGER. BECAUSE YOU WERE TOO WEAK TO EVER BE MY SON.
AND FROM WHAT I SEE BEFORE ME NOW, I'D SAY YOUR TIME AMONG THE ASGARDIANS HAS ONLY MADE YOU WEAKER.
I AM TOLD BY SOME THAT YOU HAVE BEEN A FORCE OF GREAT EVIL WHILE I'VE BEEN AWAY. BUT WHEN I LOOK IN YOUR TINY LITTLE EYES...I SEE MORE MISCHIEF THAN MURDER.
I REMEMBER TEACHING YOU MANY LESSONS IN OUR SHORT TIME TOGETHER, BOY, BUT MISCHIEF AND TRICKERY WERE NOT AMONG THEM. THOSE ARE NOT THE WAYS OF THE FROST GIANT.
YOU SEEM TO BE FORGETTING, FATHER, 'TWAS THE WAYS OF THE FROST GIANT THAT LEFT YOU LYING ON THAT BATTLEFIELD AT ODIN'S FEET.
WHILE IT WAS MALEKITH'S MISCHIEF AND TRICKERY THAT BROUGHT YOU BACK.
WHAT WAS THAT YOU SAID, LITTLE GNAT?
I SAID, I WELCOME THE CHANCE TO PROVE MYSELF TO YOU, FATHER. HOW MAY I DO SO?

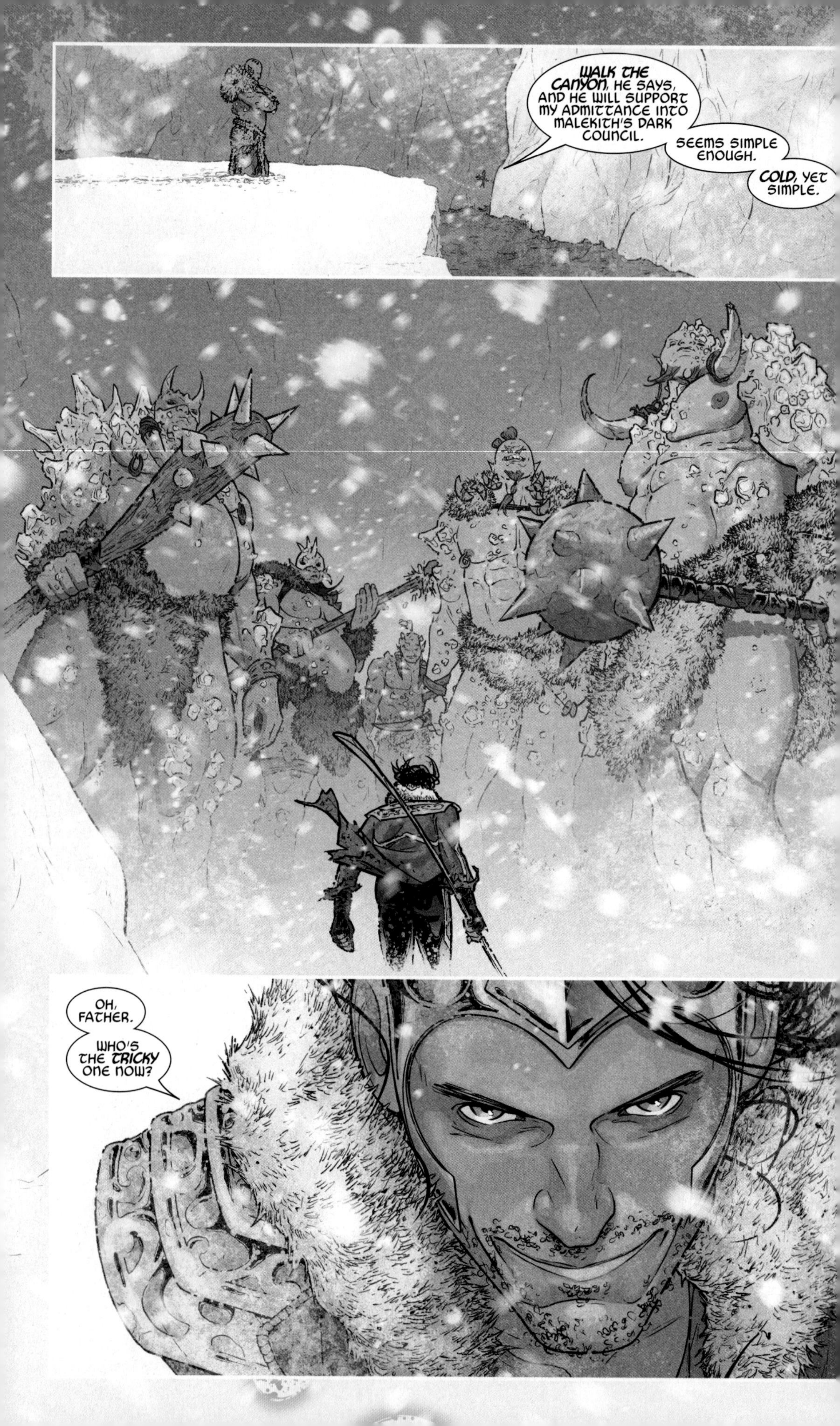
WALK THE CANYON, HE SAYS, AND HE WILL SUPPORT MY ADMITTANCE INTO MALEKITH'S DARK COUNCIL.
SEEMS SIMPLE ENOUGH.
COLD, YET SIMPLE.
OH, FATHER.
WHO'S THE TRICKY ONE NOW?

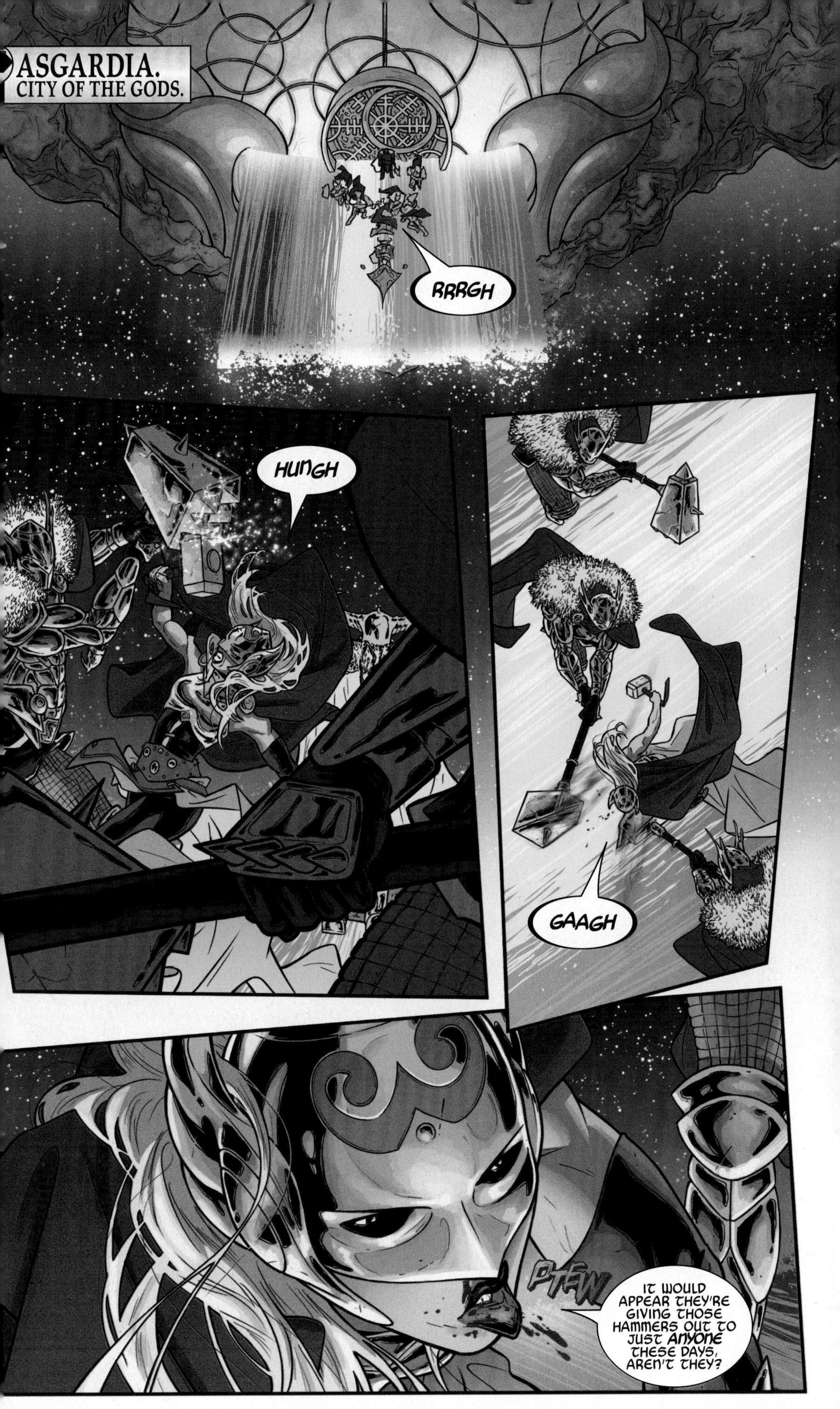
ASGARDIA.
CITY OF THE GODS.
RRRGH
HUNGH
GAAGH
PTEW
IT WOULD APPEAR THEY'RE GIVING THOSE HAMMERS OUT TO JUST *ANYONE* THESE DAYS, AREN'T THEY?

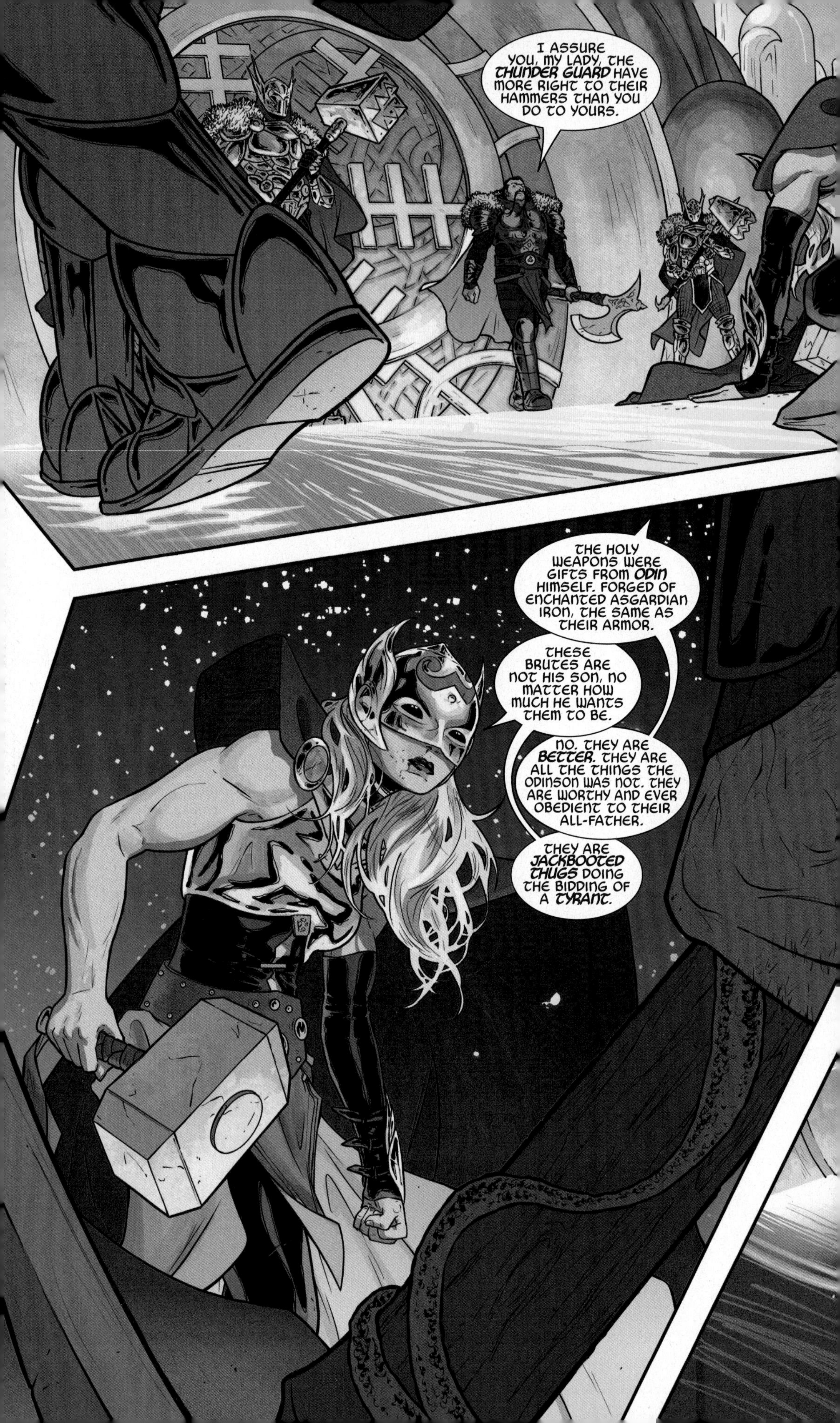
I ASSURE YOU, MY LADY, THE THUNDER GUARD HAVE MORE RIGHT TO THEIR HAMMERS THAN YOU DO TO YOURS.
THE HOLY WEAPONS WERE GIFTS FROM ODIN HIMSELF. FORGED OF ENCHANTED ASGARDIAN IRON, THE SAME AS THEIR ARMOR.
THESE BRUTES ARE NOT HIS SON, NO MATTER HOW MUCH HE WANTS THEM TO BE.
NO. THEY ARE BETTER. THEY ARE ALL THE THINGS THE ODINSON WAS NOT. THEY ARE WORTHY AND EVER OBEDIENT TO THEIR ALL-FATHER.
THEY ARE JACKBOOTED THUGS DOING THE BIDDING OF A TYRANT.

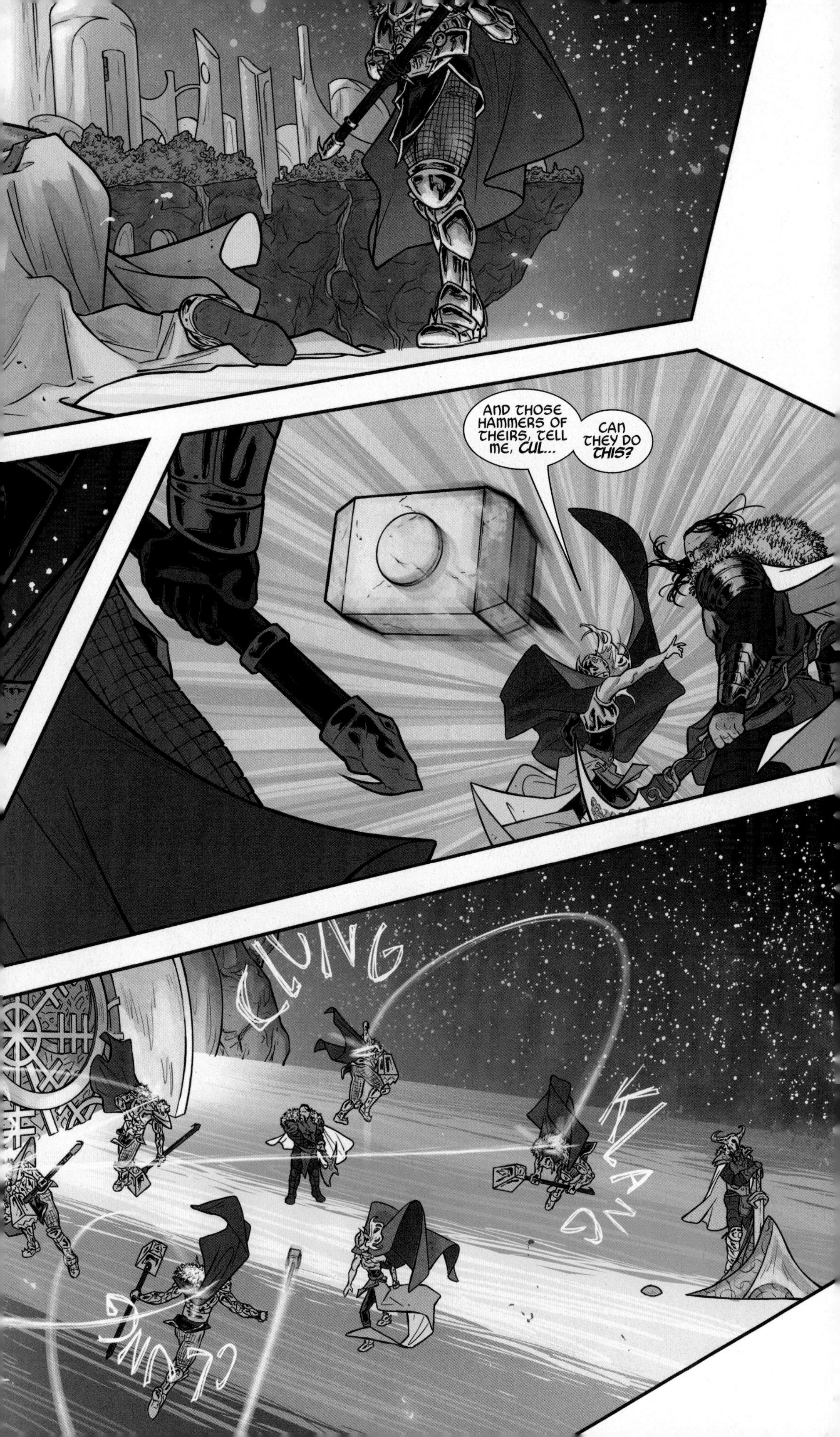
AND THOSE HAMMERS OF THEIRS, TELL ME, CUL...
CAN THEY DO THIS?
CLUNG
KLANG
CLUNG

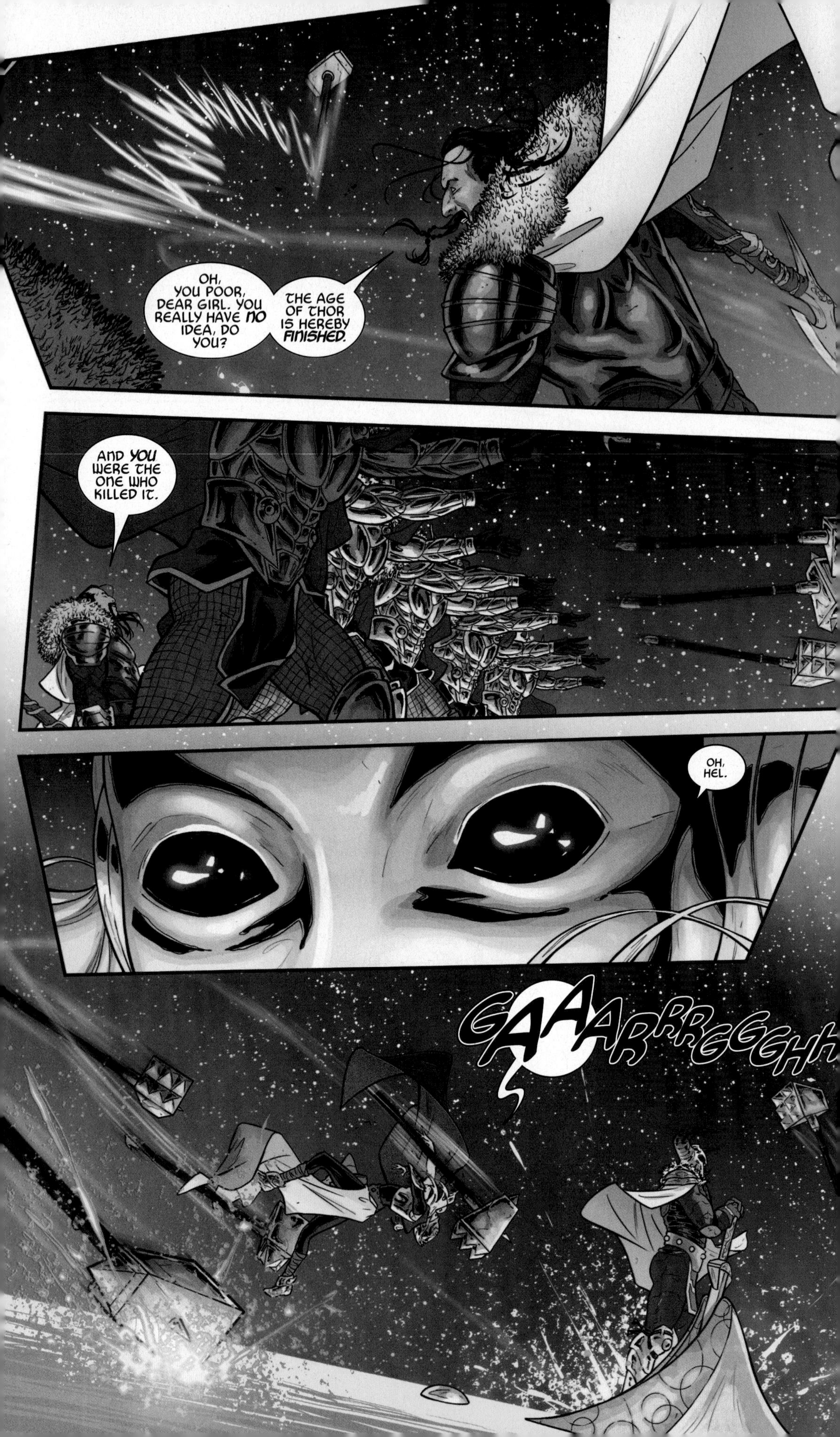
OH, YOU POOR, DEAR GIRL. YOU REALLY HAVE NO IDEA, DO YOU?
THE AGE OF THOR IS HEREBY FINISHED.
AND YOU WERE THE ONE WHO KILLED IT.
OH, HEL.
GAAARRRGGGHH

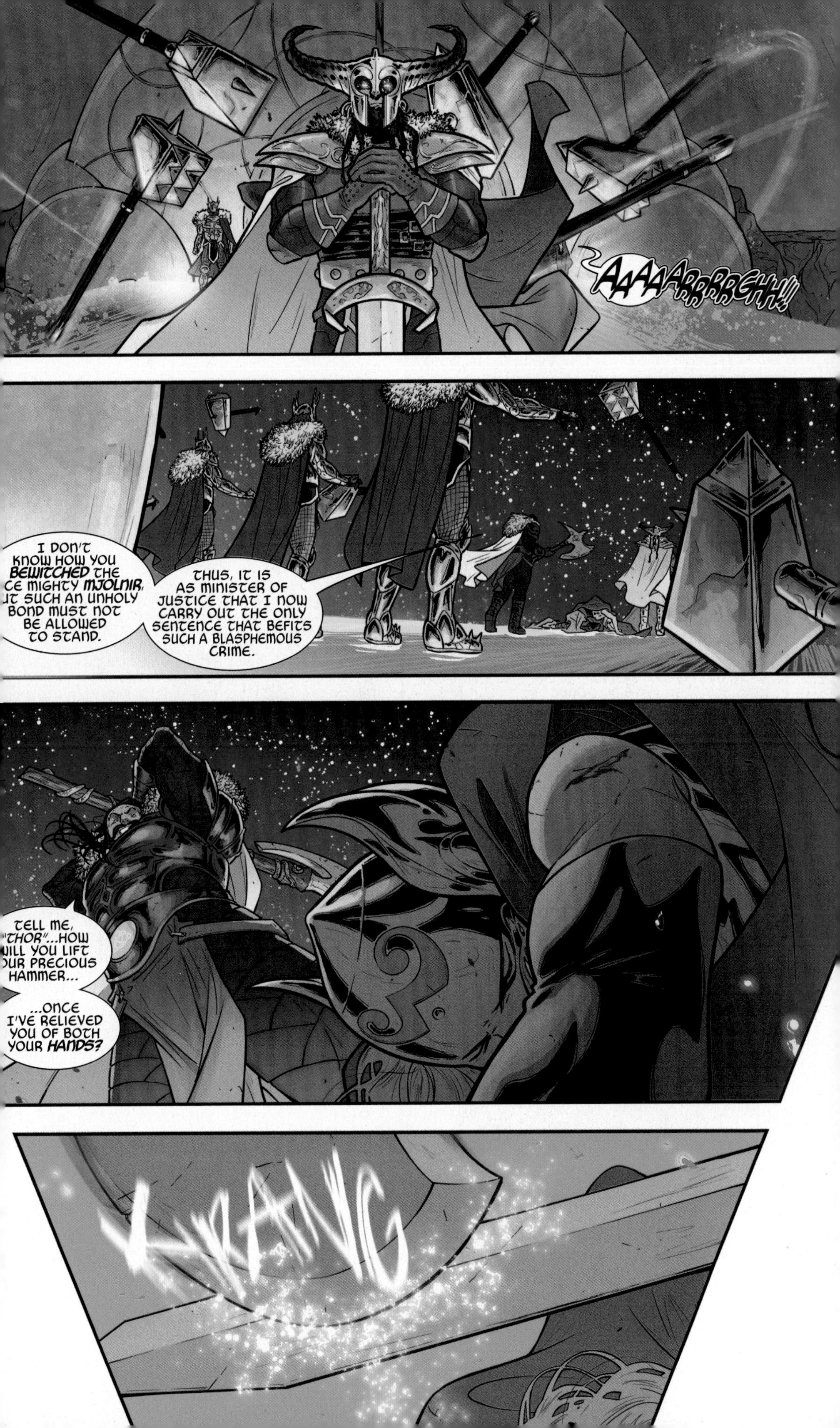
AAAAARRRRRGHH!!
I DON'T KNOW HOW YOU BEWITCHED THE
CE MIGHTY MJOLNIR,
UT SUCH AN UNHOLY BOND MUST NOT BE ALLOWED TO STAND.
THUS, IT IS AS MINISTER OF JUSTICE THAT I NOW CARRY OUT THE ONLY SENTENCE THAT BEFITS SUCH A BLASPHEMOUS CRIME.
TELL ME, "THOR"...HOW
ILL YOU LIFT
UR PRECIOUS HAMMER...
...ONCE I'VE RELIEVED YOU OF BOTH YOUR HANDS?
KRANG

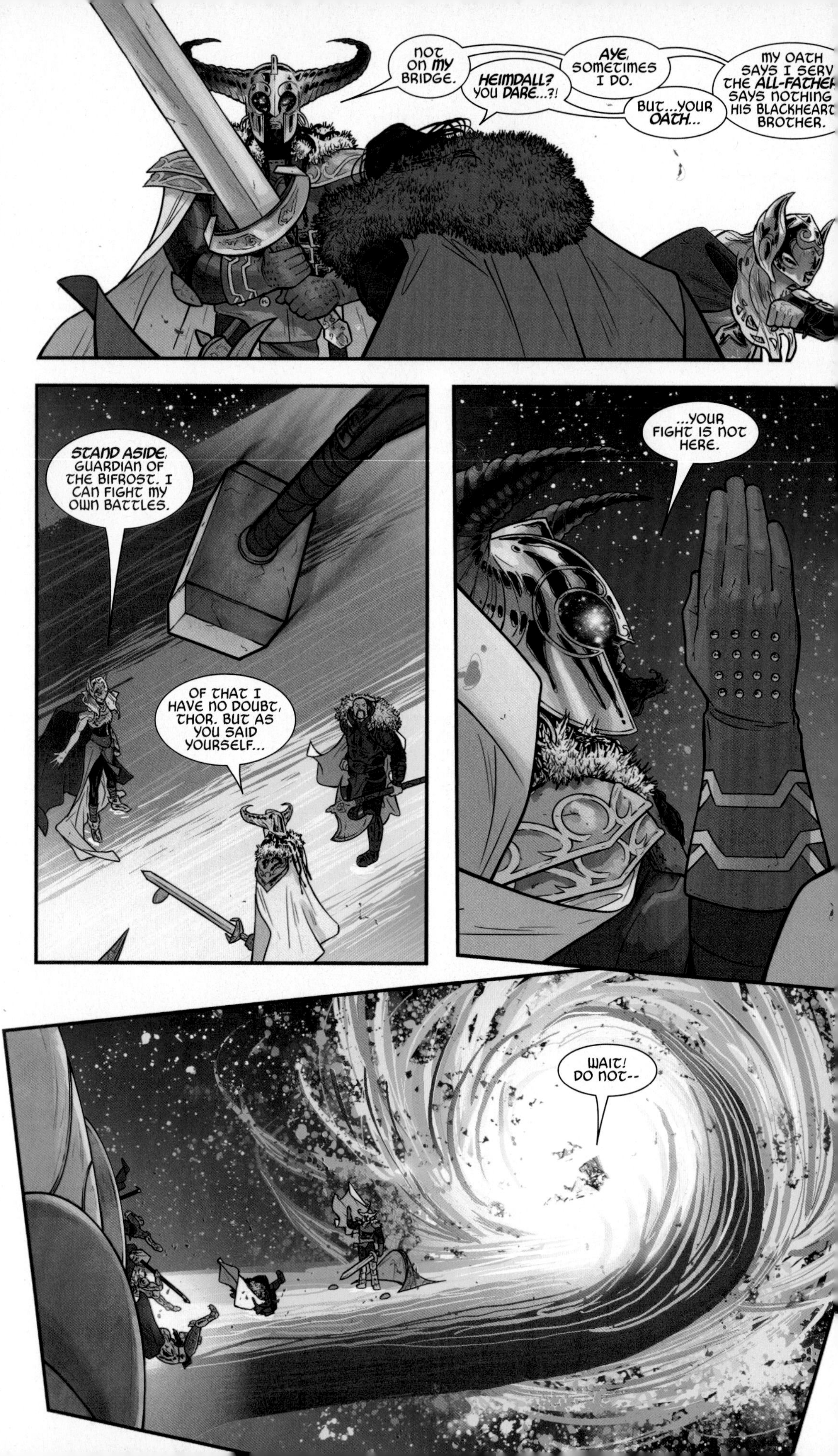

NOT ON MY BRIDGE.
HEIMDALL? YOU DARE...?!
AYE, SOMETIMES I DO.
BUT...YOUR OATH...
MY OATH SAYS I SERV THE ALL-FATHE SAYS NOTHING HIS BLACKHEART BROTHER.
STAND ASIDE, GUARDIAN OF THE BIFROST. I CAN FIGHT MY OWN BATTLES.
OF THAT I HAVE NO DOUBT, THOR. BUT AS YOU SAID YOURSELF...
...YOUR FIGHT IS NOT HERE.
WAIT! DO NOT--

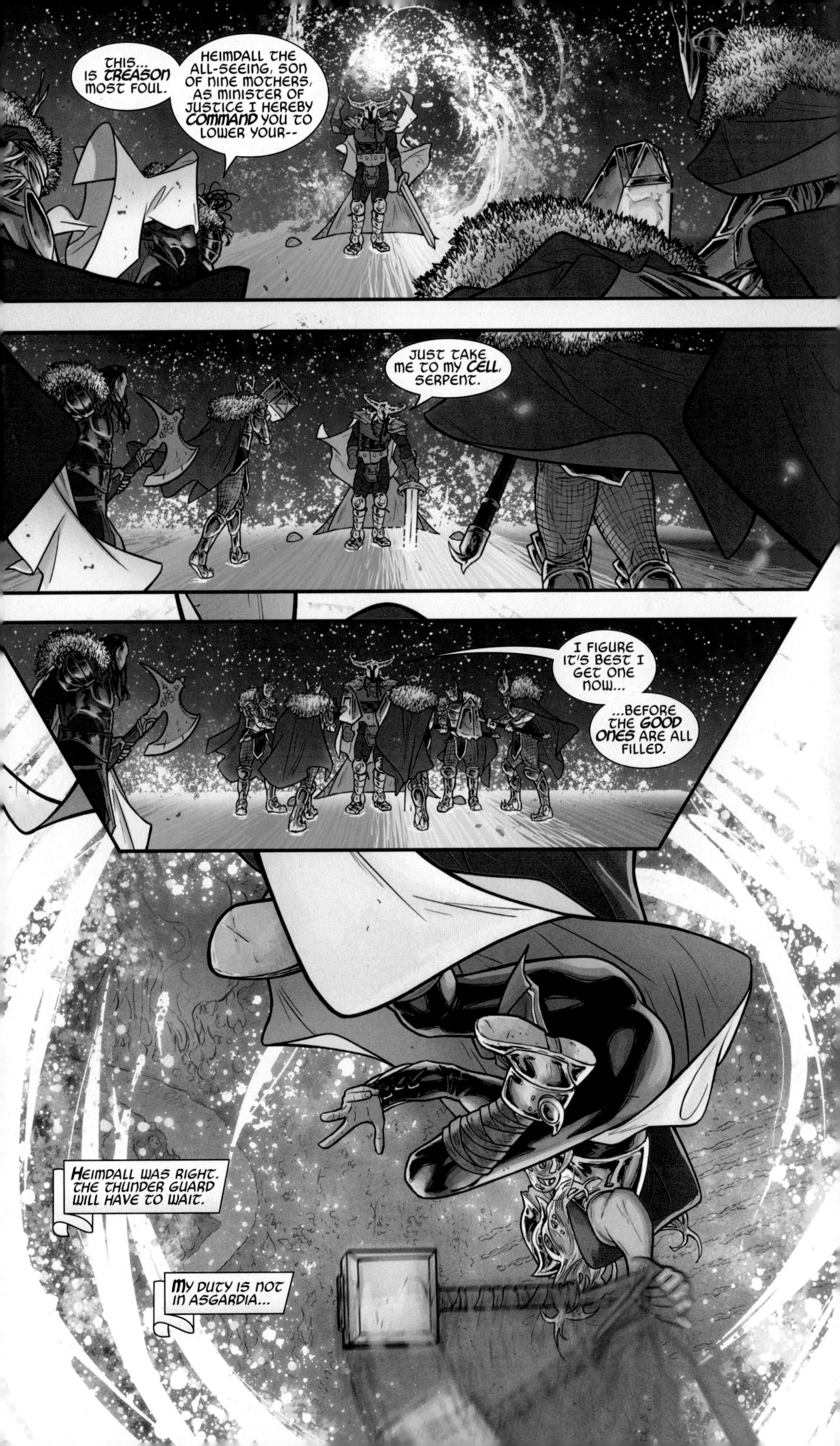
THIS... IS TREASON MOST FOUL.
HEIMDALL THE ALL-SEEING, SON OF NINE MOTHERS, AS MINISTER OF JUSTICE I HEREBY COMMAND YOU TO LOWER YOUR--
JUST TAKE ME TO MY CELL, SERPENT.
I FIGURE IT'S BEST I GET ONE NOW...
...BEFORE THE GOOD ONES ARE ALL FILLED.
HEIMDALL WAS RIGHT. THE THUNDER GUARD WILL HAVE TO WAIT.
MY DUTY IS NOT IN ASGARDIA...

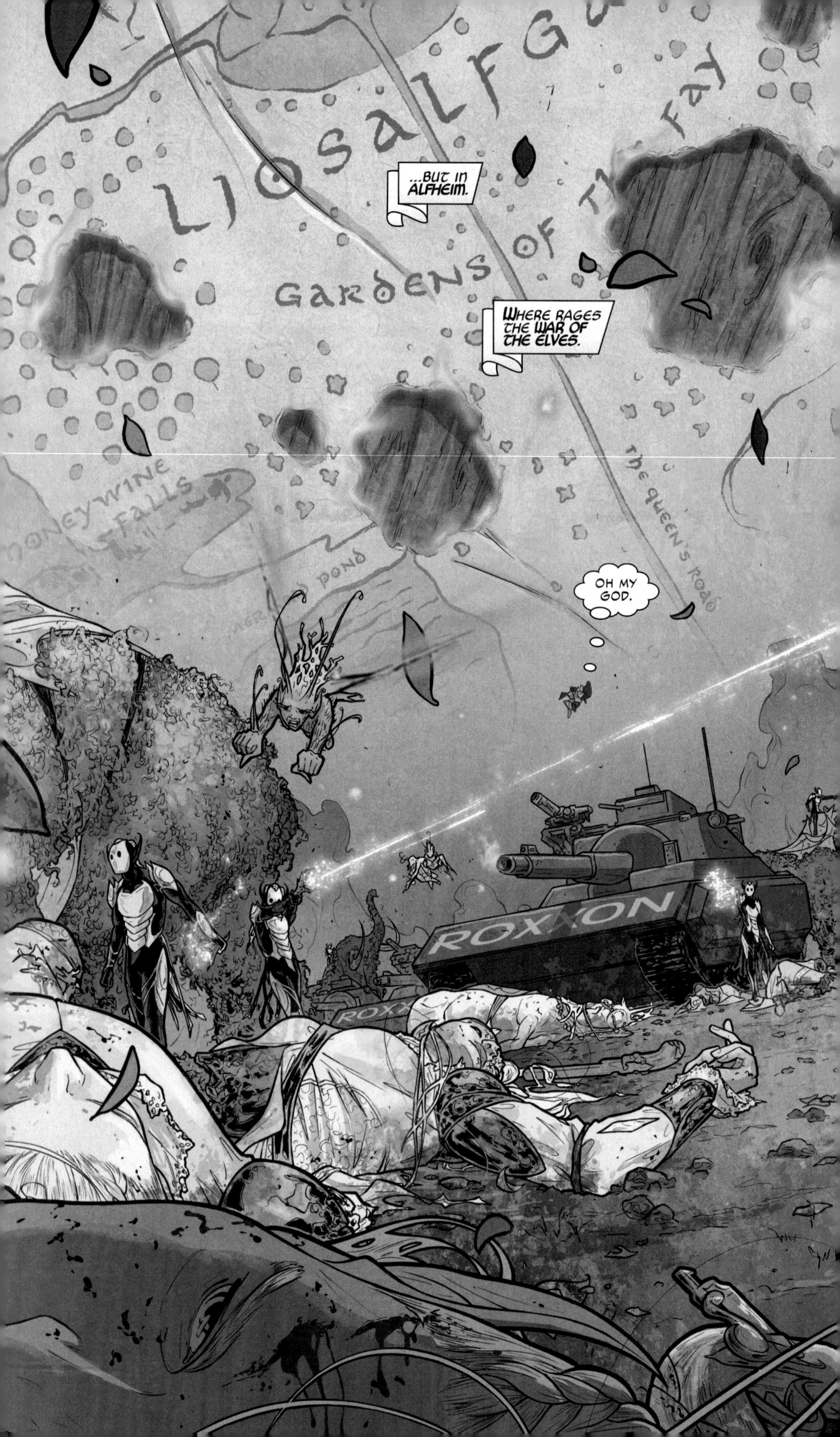

LJOSALFG
GARDENS OF TH
FAT
...BUT IN ALFHEIM.
WHERE RAGES THE WAR OF THE ELVES.
HONEYWINE FALLS
THE QUEEN'S ROAD
POND
OH MY GOD.
ROXXON

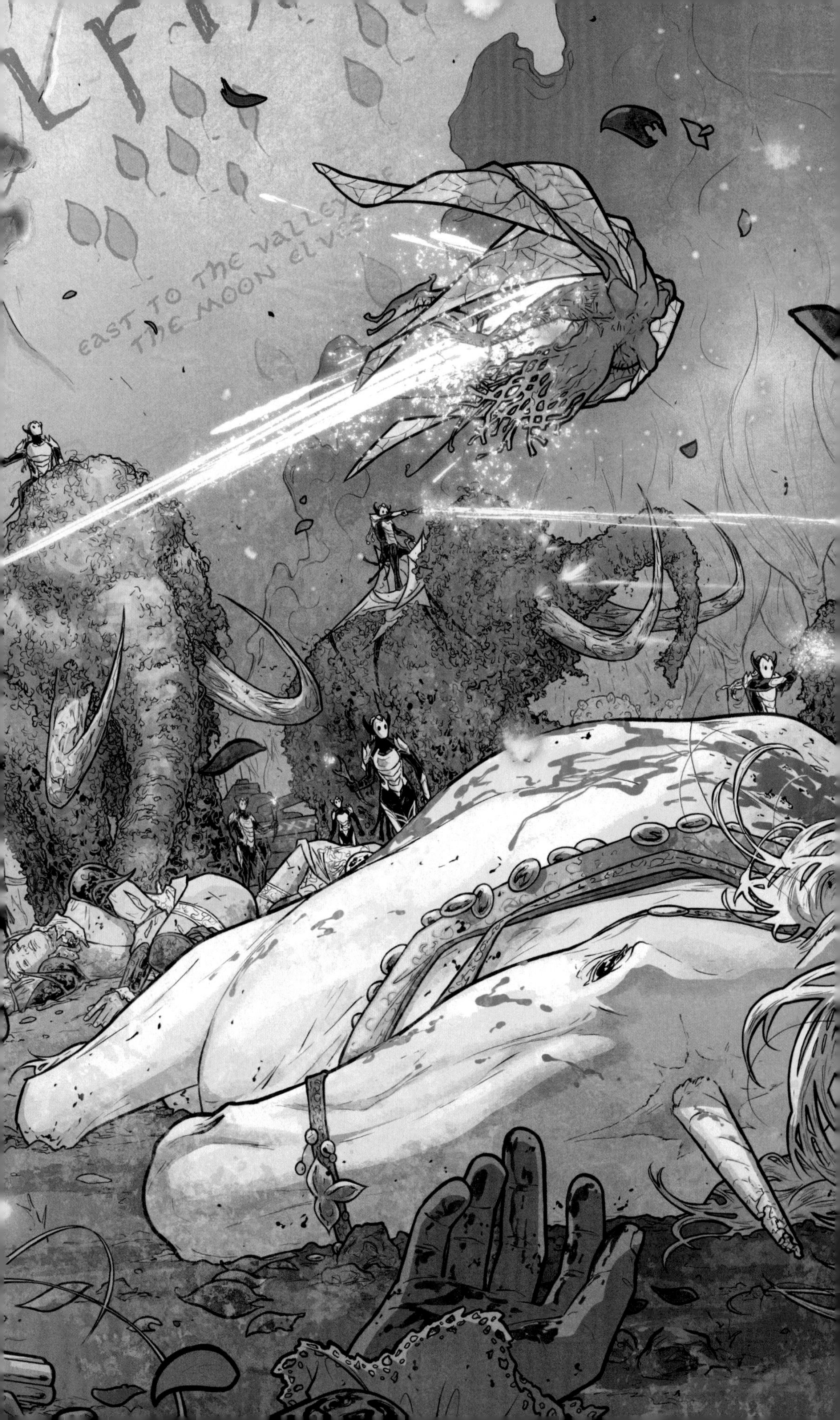
EAST TO THE VALLEY OF
THE MOON ELVES

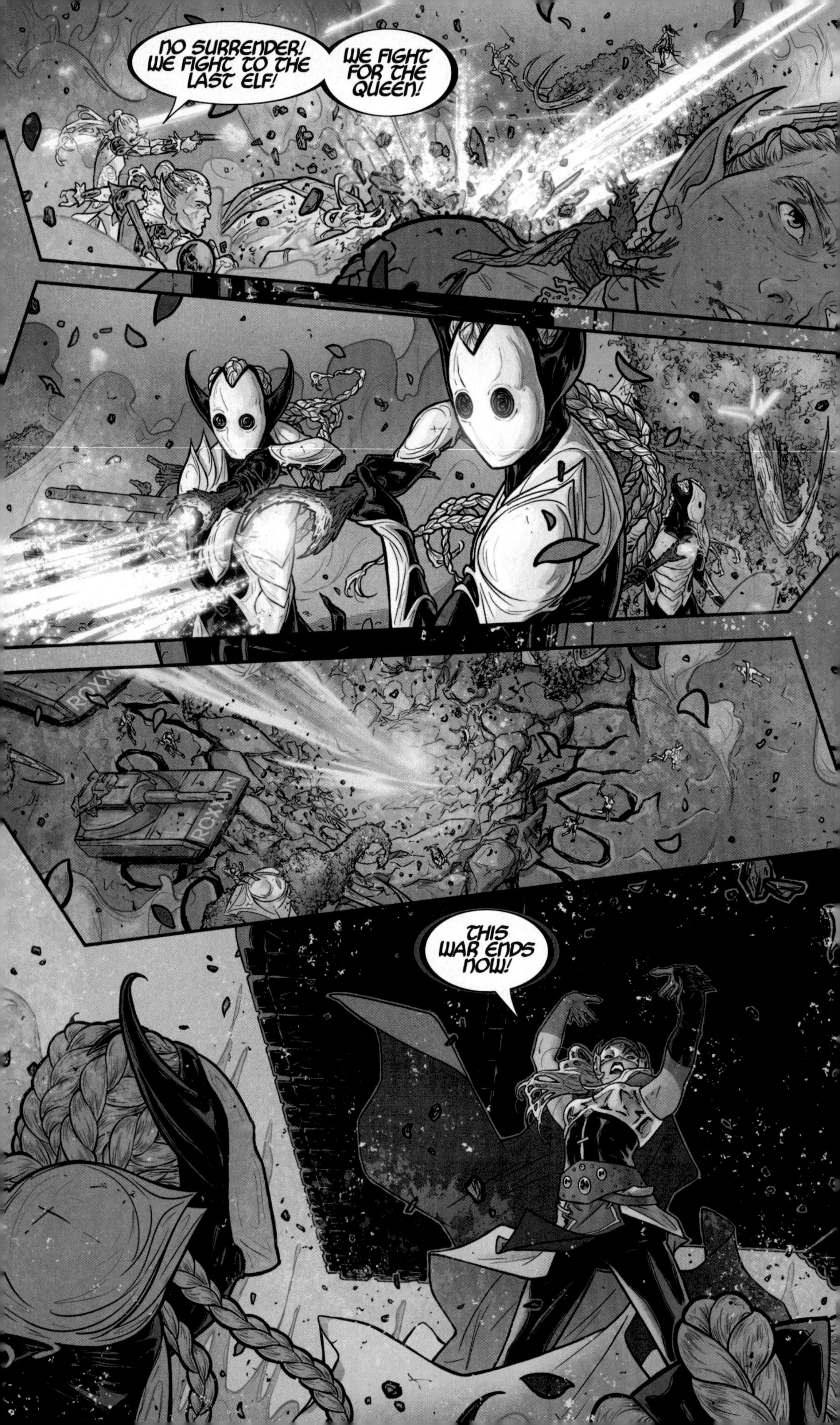
NO SURRENDER! WE FIGHT TO THE LAST ELF!
WE FIGHT FOR THE QUEEN!
ROXXON
ROXXON
THIS WAR ENDS NOW!

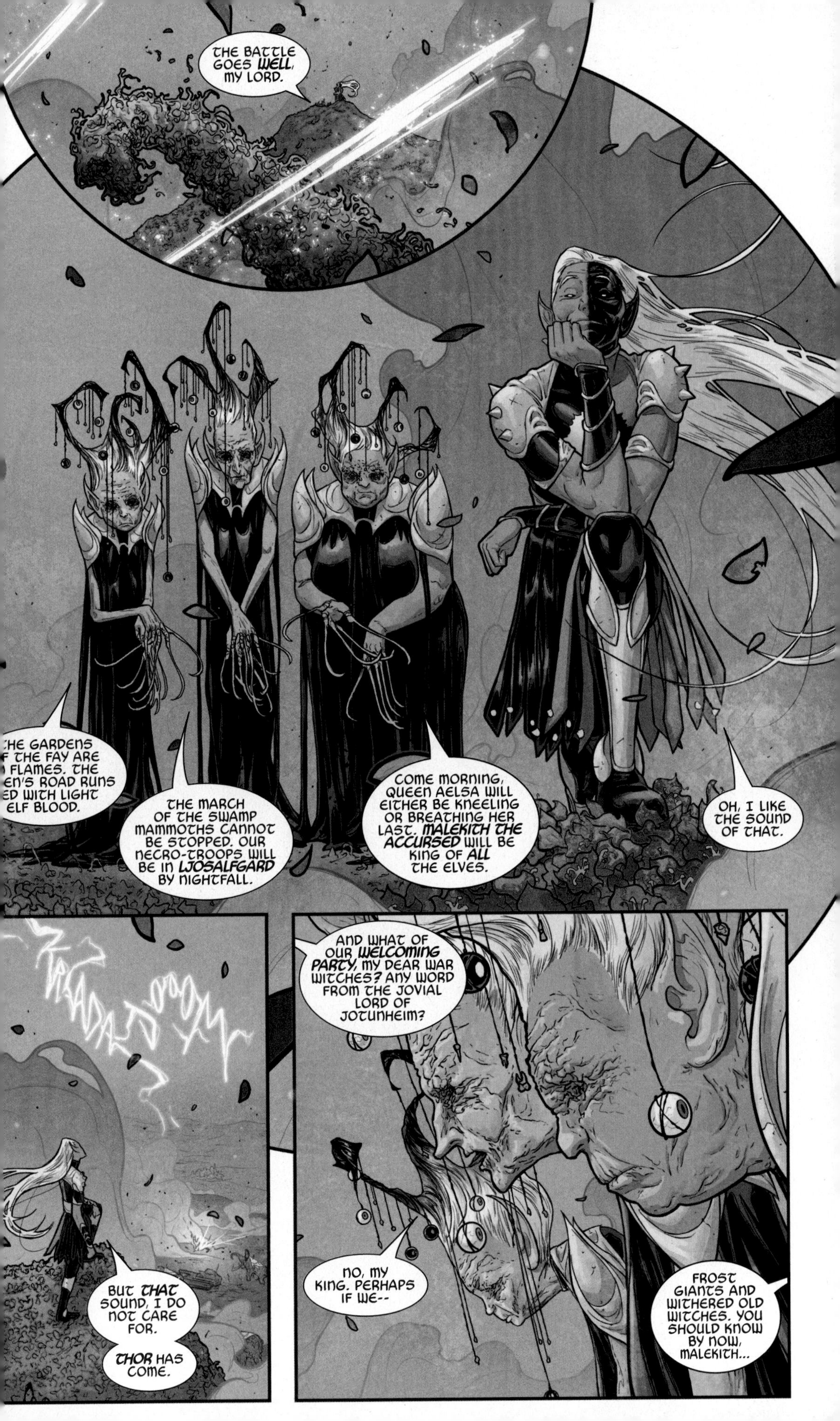
THE BATTLE GOES WELL, MY LORD.
THE GARDENS F THE FAY ARE FLAMES. THE EN'S ROAD RUNS ED WITH LIGHT ELF BLOOD.
THE MARCH OF THE SWAMP MAMMOTHS CANNOT BE STOPPED. OUR NECRO-TROOPS WILL BE IN LJOSALFGARD BY NIGHTFALL.
COME MORNING, QUEEN AELSA WILL EITHER BE KNEELING OR BREATHING HER LAST. MALEKITH THE ACCURSED WILL BE KING OF ALL THE ELVES.
OH, I LIKE THE SOUND OF THAT.
BUT THAT SOUND, I DO NOT CARE FOR.
THOR HAS COME.
AND WHAT OF OUR WELCOMING PARTY, MY DEAR WAR WITCHES? ANY WORD FROM THE JOVIAL LORD OF JOTUNHEIM?
NO, MY KING. PERHAPS IF WE--
FROST GIANTS AND WITHERED OLD WITCHES. YOU SHOULD KNOW BY NOW, MALEKITH...

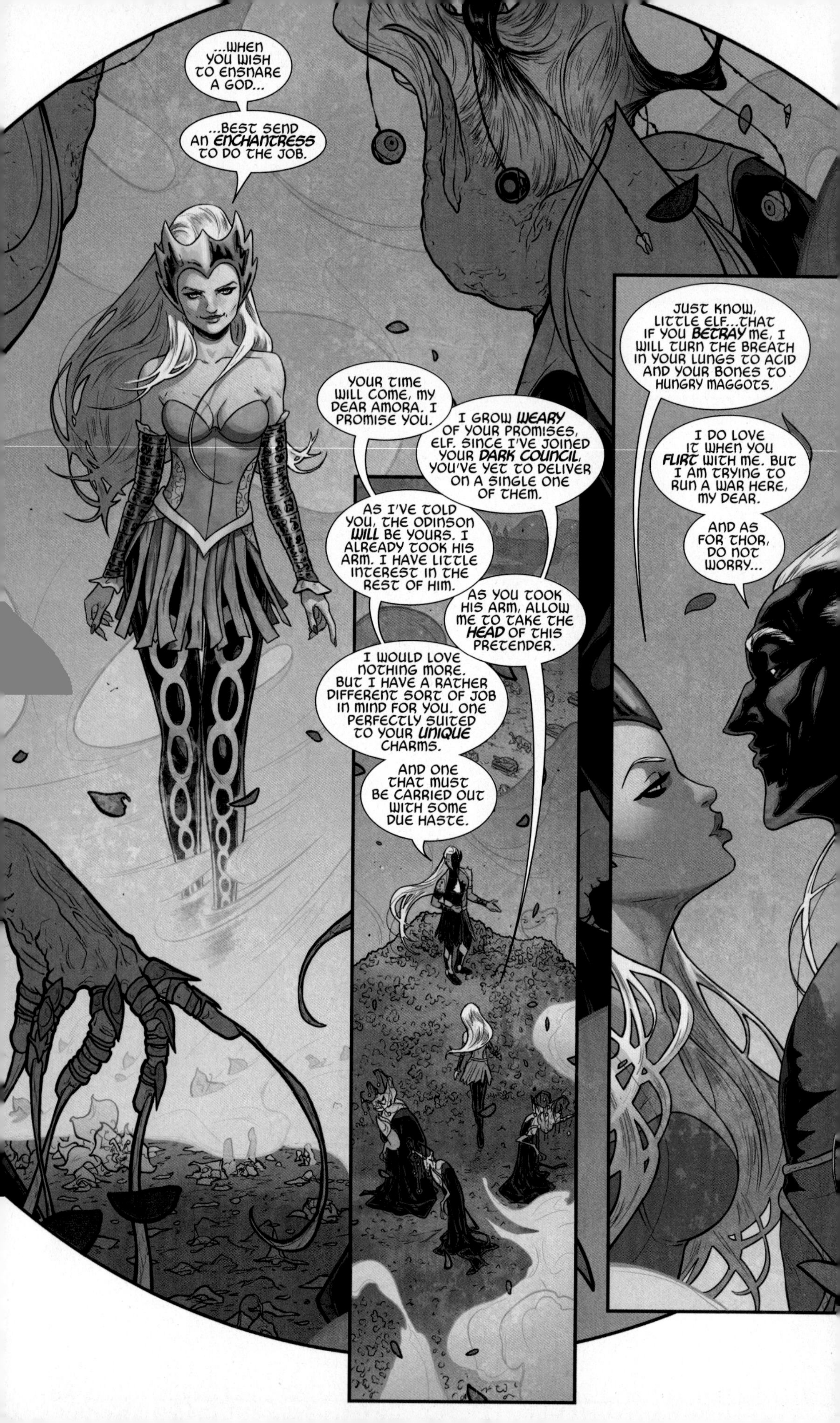
...WHEN YOU WISH TO ENSNARE A GOD...
...BEST SEND AN ENCHANTRESS TO DO THE JOB.
YOUR TIME WILL COME, MY DEAR AMORA. I PROMISE YOU.
I GROW WEARY OF YOUR PROMISES, ELF. SINCE I'VE JOINED YOUR DARK COUNCIL, YOU'VE YET TO DELIVER ON A SINGLE ONE OF THEM.
AS I'VE TOLD YOU, THE ODINSON WILL BE YOURS. I ALREADY TOOK HIS ARM. I HAVE LITTLE INTEREST IN THE REST OF HIM.
AS YOU TOOK HIS ARM, ALLOW ME TO TAKE THE HEAD OF THIS PRETENDER.
I WOULD LOVE NOTHING MORE. BUT I HAVE A RATHER DIFFERENT SORT OF JOB IN MIND FOR YOU. ONE PERFECTLY SUITED TO YOUR UNIQUE CHARMS.
AND ONE THAT MUST BE CARRIED OUT WITH SOME DUE HASTE.
JUST KNOW, LITTLE ELF...THAT IF YOU BETRAY ME, I WILL TURN THE BREATH IN YOUR LUNGS TO ACID AND YOUR BONES TO HUNGRY MAGGOTS.
I DO LOVE IT WHEN YOU FLIRT WITH ME. BUT I AM TRYING TO RUN A WAR HERE, MY DEAR.
AND AS FOR THOR, DO NOT WORRY...

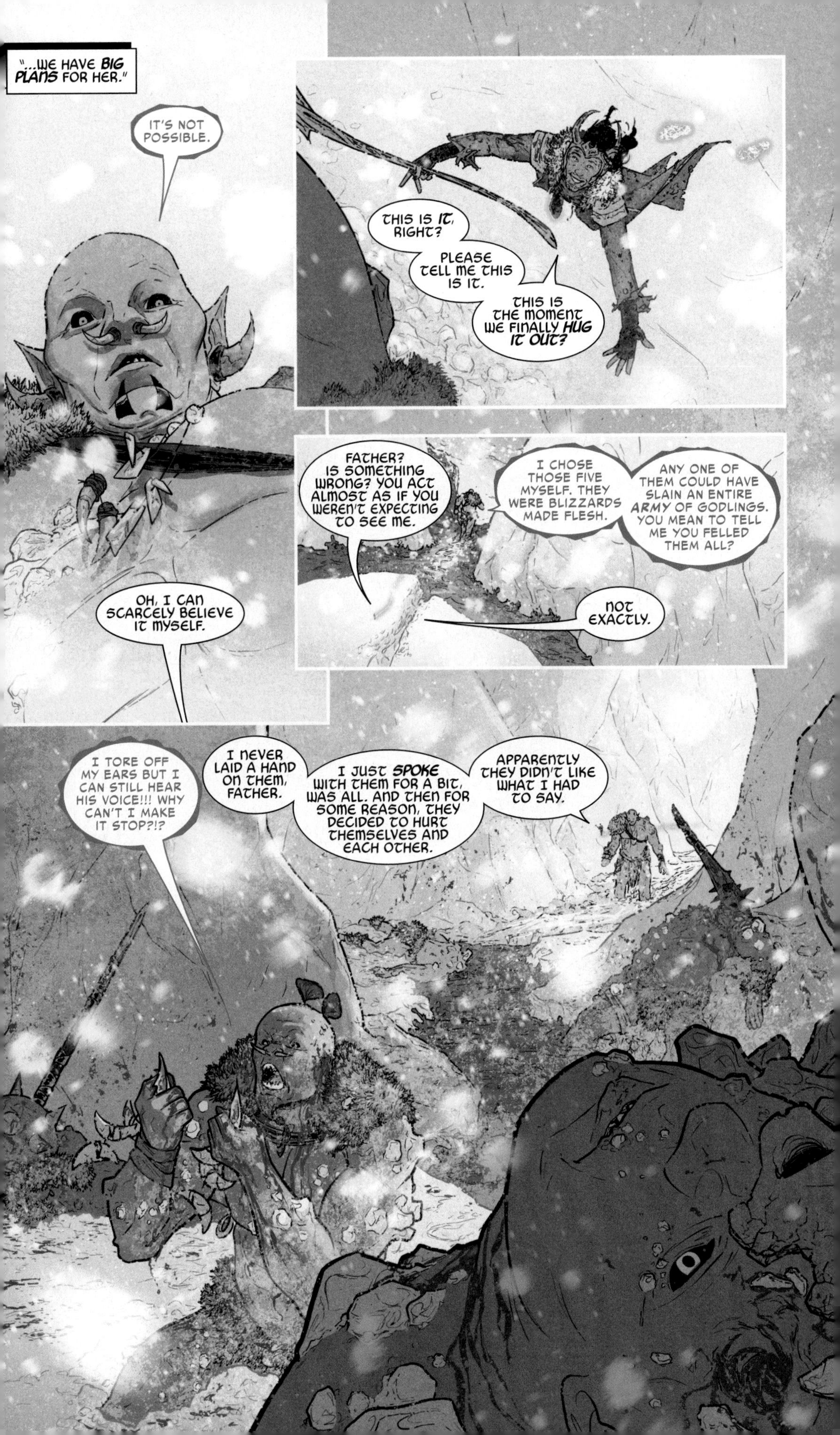
"...WE HAVE BIG PLANS FOR HER."
IT'S NOT POSSIBLE.
THIS IS IT, RIGHT?
PLEASE TELL ME THIS IS IT.
THIS IS THE MOMENT WE FINALLY HUG IT OUT?
OH, I CAN SCARCELY BELIEVE IT MYSELF.
FATHER? IS SOMETHING WRONG? YOU ACT ALMOST AS IF YOU WEREN'T EXPECTING TO SEE ME.
I CHOSE THOSE FIVE MYSELF. THEY WERE BLIZZARDS MADE FLESH.
ANY ONE OF THEM COULD HAVE SLAIN AN ENTIRE ARMY OF GODLINGS. YOU MEAN TO TELL ME YOU FELLED THEM ALL?
NOT EXACTLY.
I TORE OFF MY EARS BUT I CAN STILL HEAR HIS VOICE!!! WHY CAN'T I MAKE IT STOP?!?
I NEVER LAID A HAND ON THEM, FATHER.
I JUST SPOKE WITH THEM FOR A BIT, WAS ALL. AND THEN FOR SOME REASON, THEY DECIDED TO HURT THEMSELVES AND EACH OTHER.
APPARENTLY THEY DIDN'T LIKE WHAT I HAD TO SAY.

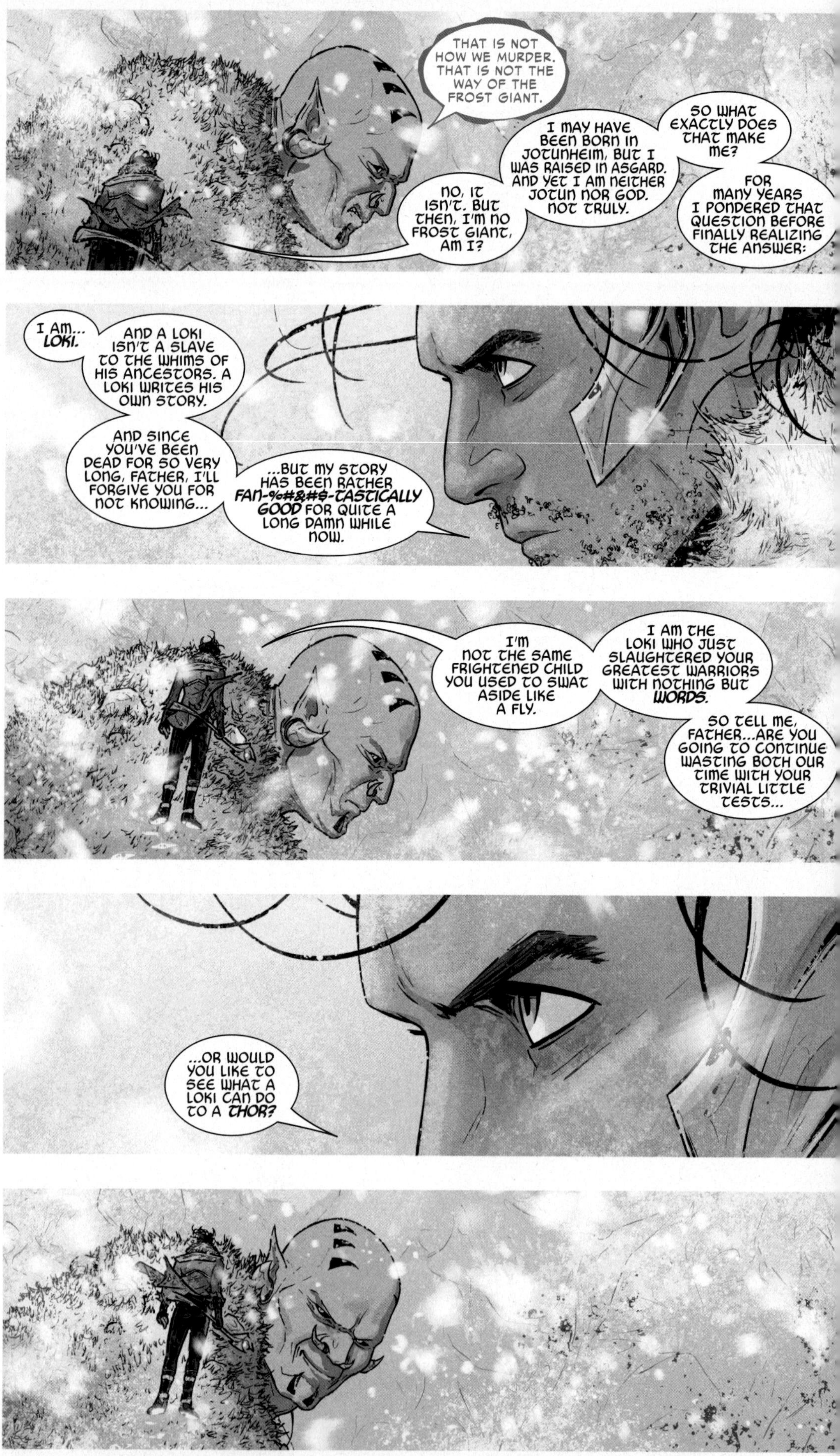
THAT IS NOT HOW WE MURDER. THAT IS NOT THE WAY OF THE FROST GIANT.
NO, IT ISN'T. BUT THEN, I'M NO FROST GIANT, AM I?
I MAY HAVE BEEN BORN IN JOTUNHEIM, BUT I WAS RAISED IN ASGARD. AND YET I AM NEITHER JOTUN NOR GOD. NOT TRULY.
SO WHAT EXACTLY DOES THAT MAKE ME?
FOR MANY YEARS I PONDERED THAT QUESTION BEFORE FINALLY REALIZING THE ANSWER:
I AM... LOKI.
AND A LOKI ISN'T A SLAVE TO THE WHIMS OF HIS ANCESTORS. A LOKI WRITES HIS OWN STORY.
AND SINCE YOU'VE BEEN DEAD FOR SO VERY LONG, FATHER, I'LL FORGIVE YOU FOR NOT KNOWING...
...BUT MY STORY HAS BEEN RATHER FAN-%#&#$-TASTICALLY GOOD FOR QUITE A LONG DAMN WHILE NOW.
I'M NOT THE SAME FRIGHTENED CHILD YOU USED TO SWAT ASIDE LIKE A FLY.
I AM THE LOKI WHO JUST SLAUGHTERED YOUR GREATEST WARRIORS WITH NOTHING BUT WORDS.
SO TELL ME, FATHER...ARE YOU GOING TO CONTINUE WASTING BOTH OUR TIME WITH YOUR TRIVIAL LITTLE TESTS...
...OR WOULD YOU LIKE TO SEE WHAT A LOKI CAN DO TO A THOR?

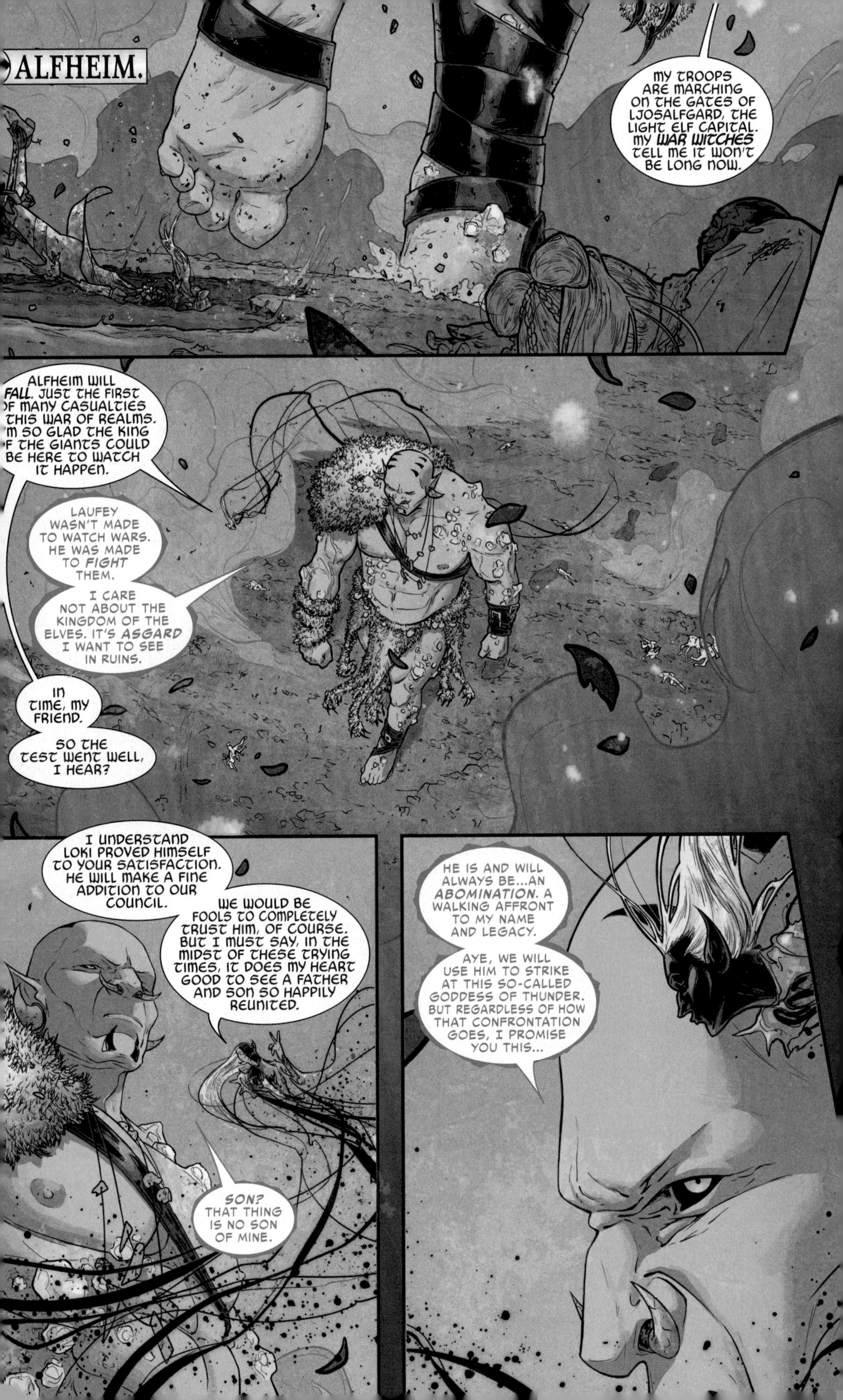
ALFHEIM.
MY TROOPS ARE MARCHING ON THE GATES OF LJOSALFGARD, THE LIGHT ELF CAPITAL. MY WAR WITCHES TELL ME IT WON'T BE LONG NOW.
ALFHEIM WILL FALL. JUST THE FIRST OF MANY CASUALTIES THIS WAR OF REALMS. I'M SO GLAD THE KING OF THE GIANTS COULD BE HERE TO WATCH IT HAPPEN.
LAUFEY WASN'T MADE TO WATCH WARS. HE WAS MADE TO FIGHT THEM.
I CARE NOT ABOUT THE KINGDOM OF THE ELVES. IT'S ASGARD I WANT TO SEE IN RUINS.
IN TIME, MY FRIEND.
SO THE TEST WENT WELL, I HEAR?
I UNDERSTAND LOKI PROVED HIMSELF TO YOUR SATISFACTION. HE WILL MAKE A FINE ADDITION TO OUR COUNCIL.
WE WOULD BE FOOLS TO COMPLETELY TRUST HIM, OF COURSE. BUT I MUST SAY, IN THE MIDST OF THESE TRYING TIMES, IT DOES MY HEART GOOD TO SEE A FATHER AND SON SO HAPPILY REUNITED.
SON? THAT THING IS NO SON OF MINE.
HE IS AND WILL ALWAYS BE...AN ABOMINATION. A WALKING AFFRONT TO MY NAME AND LEGACY.
AYE, WE WILL USE HIM TO STRIKE AT THIS SO-CALLED GODDESS OF THUNDER. BUT REGARDLESS OF HOW THAT CONFRONTATION GOES, I PROMISE YOU THIS...

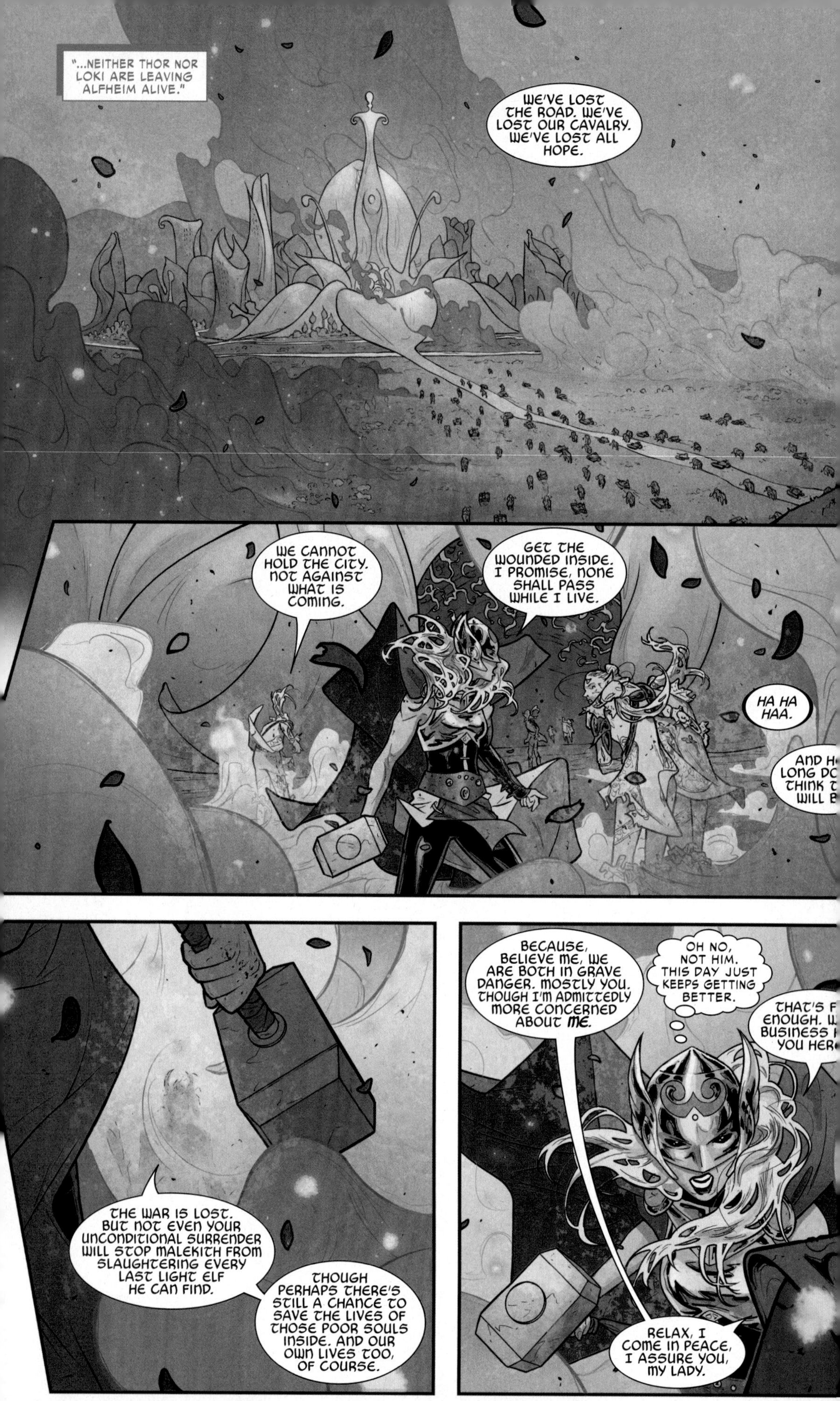
"...NEITHER THOR NOR LOKI ARE LEAVING ALFHEIM ALIVE."
WE'VE LOST THE ROAD. WE'VE LOST OUR CAVALRY. WE'VE LOST ALL HOPE.
WE CANNOT HOLD THE CITY. NOT AGAINST WHAT IS COMING.
GET THE WOUNDED INSIDE. I PROMISE, NONE SHALL PASS WHILE I LIVE.
HA HA HAA.
AND H
LONG DO
THINK T
WILL B
THE WAR IS LOST. BUT NOT EVEN YOUR UNCONDITIONAL SURRENDER WILL STOP MALEKITH FROM SLAUGHTERING EVERY LAST LIGHT ELF HE CAN FIND.
THOUGH PERHAPS THERE'S STILL A CHANCE TO SAVE THE LIVES OF THOSE POOR SOULS INSIDE. AND OUR OWN LIVES TOO, OF COURSE.
BECAUSE, BELIEVE ME, WE ARE BOTH IN GRAVE DANGER. MOSTLY YOU. THOUGH I'M ADMITTEDLY MORE CONCERNED ABOUT *ME*.
OH NO, NOT HIM. THIS DAY JUST KEEPS GETTING BETTER.
THAT'S F
ENOUGH. W
BUSINESS
YOU HER
RELAX, I COME IN PEACE, I ASSURE YOU, MY LADY.

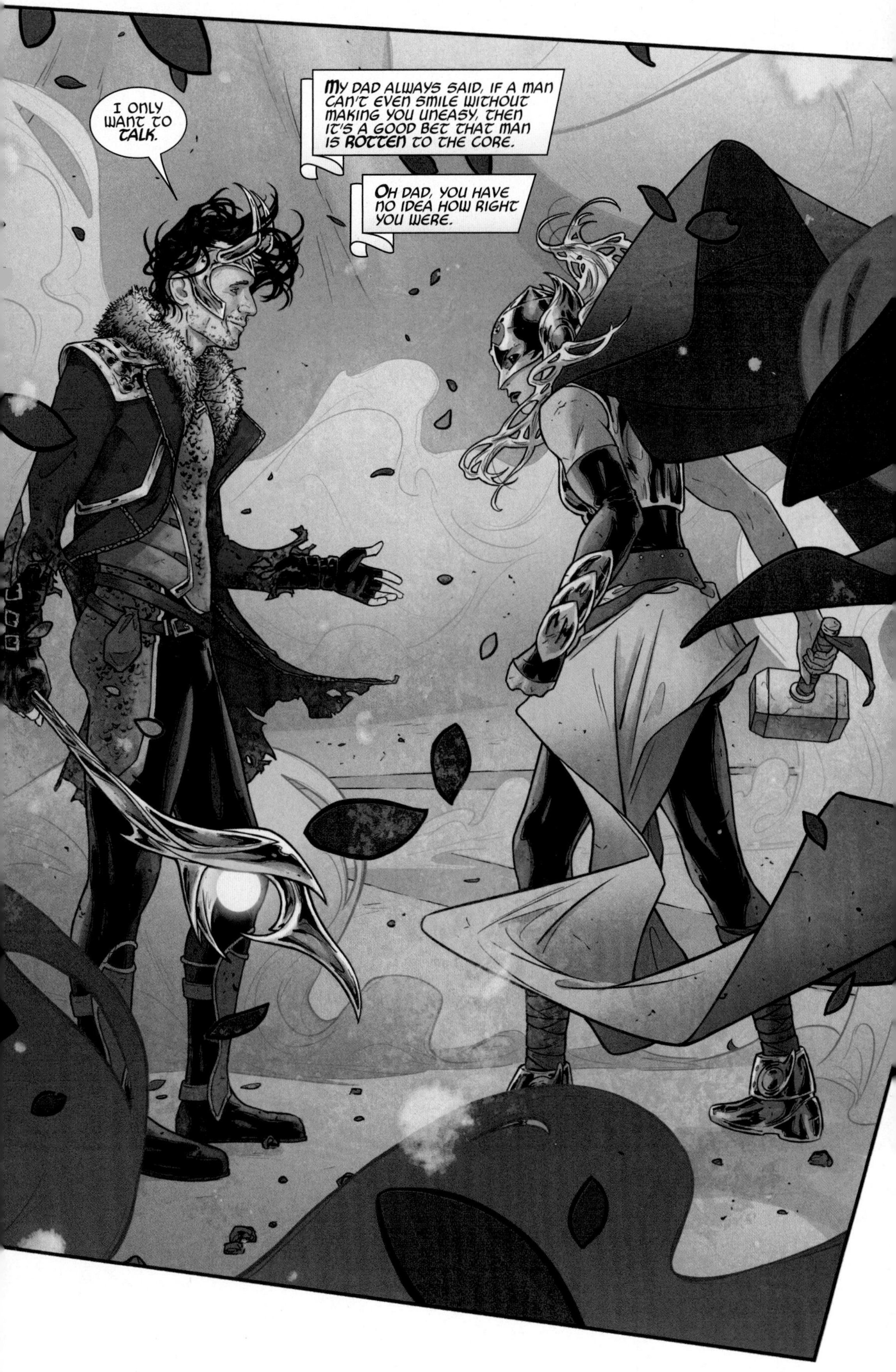
I ONLY WANT TO TALK.
MY DAD ALWAYS SAID, IF A MAN CAN'T EVEN SMILE WITHOUT MAKING YOU UNEASY, THEN IT'S A GOOD BET THAT MAN IS ROTTEN TO THE CORE.
OH DAD, YOU HAVE NO IDEA HOW RIGHT YOU WERE.

3

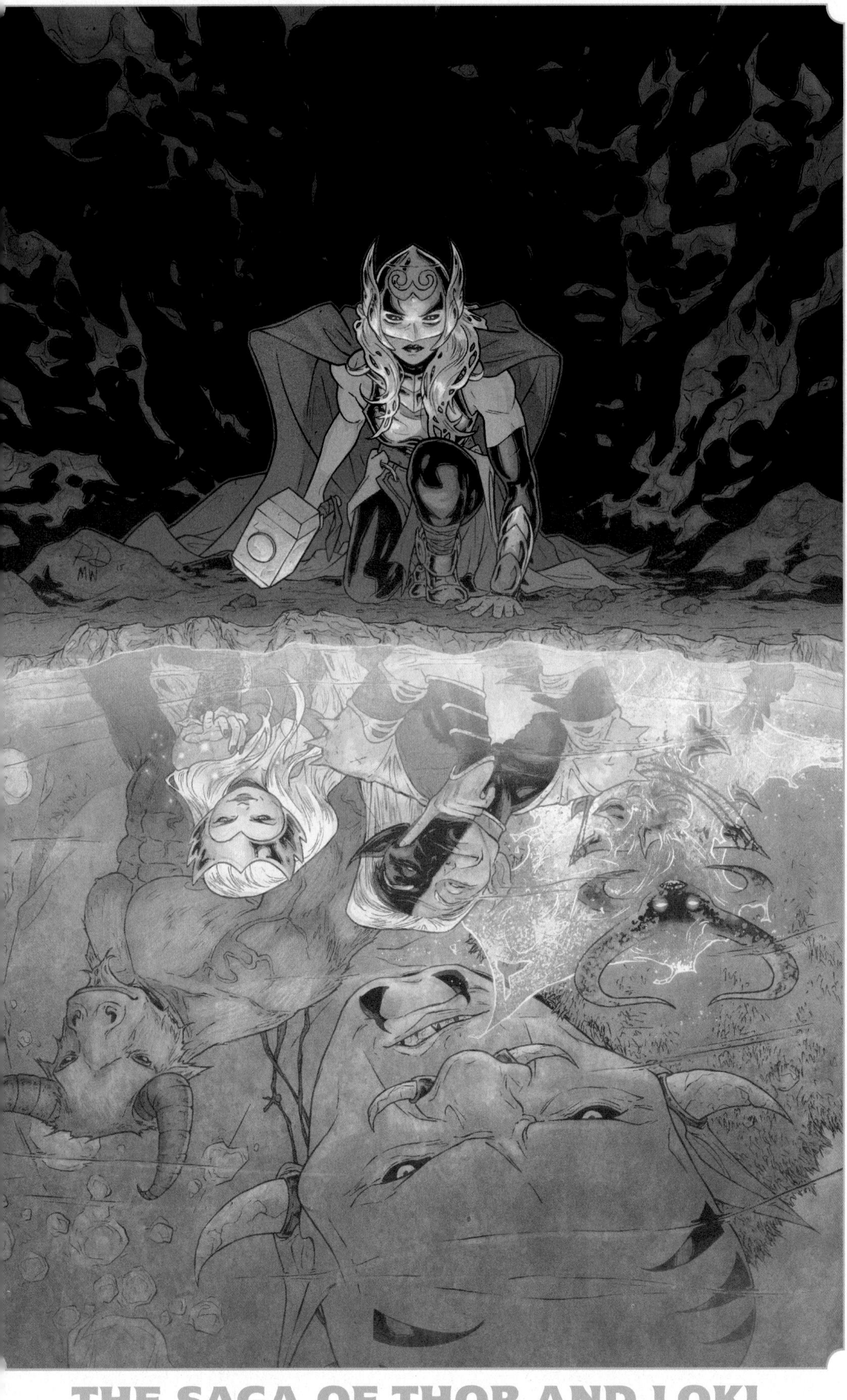

THE SAGA OF THOR AND LOKI

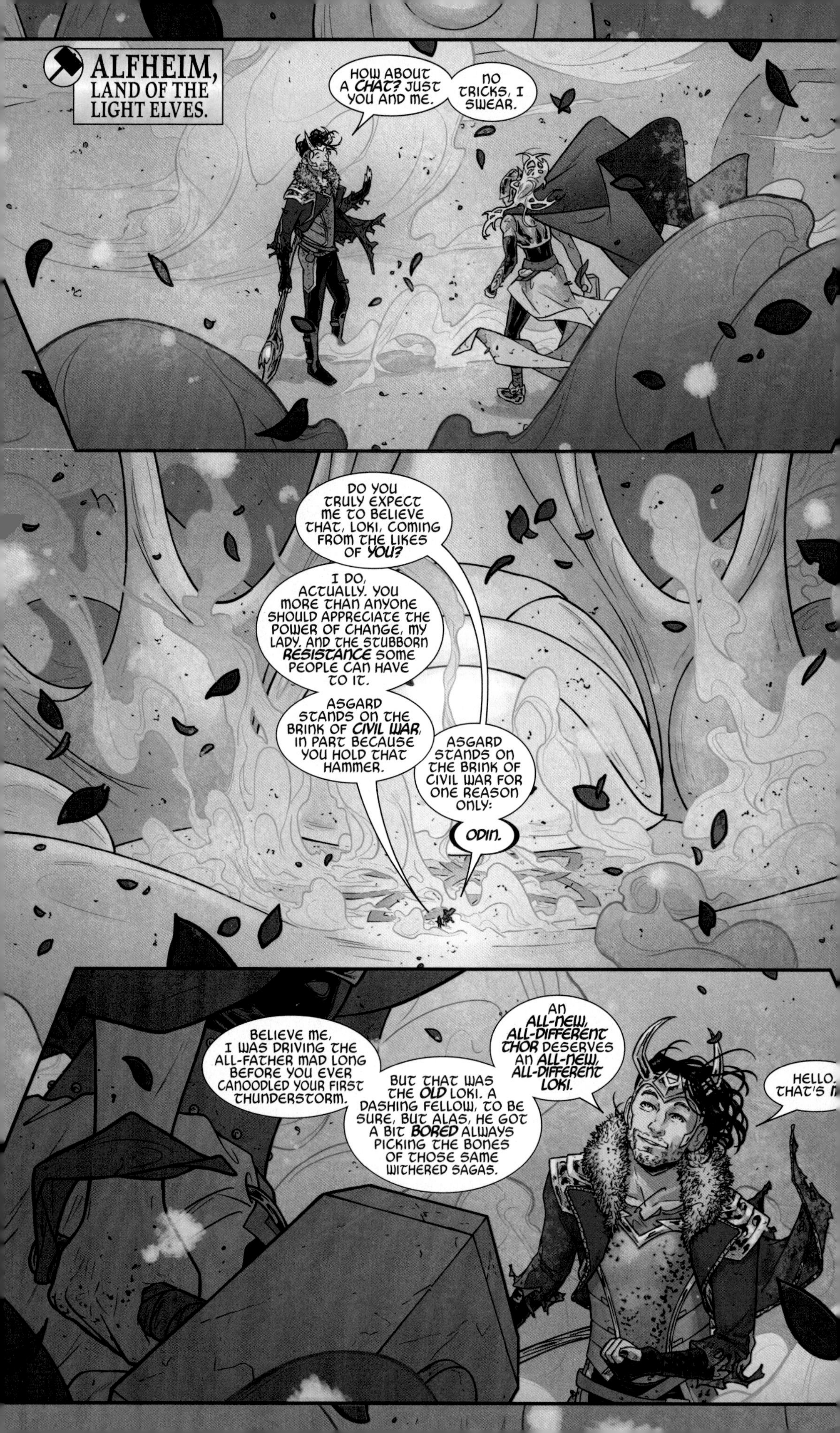
ALFHEIM, LAND OF THE LIGHT ELVES.
HOW ABOUT A CHAT? JUST YOU AND ME.
NO TRICKS, I SWEAR.
DO YOU TRULY EXPECT ME TO BELIEVE THAT, LOKI, COMING FROM THE LIKES OF YOU?
I DO, ACTUALLY. YOU MORE THAN ANYONE SHOULD APPRECIATE THE POWER OF CHANGE, MY LADY. AND THE STUBBORN RESISTANCE SOME PEOPLE CAN HAVE TO IT.
ASGARD STANDS ON THE BRINK OF CIVIL WAR, IN PART BECAUSE YOU HOLD THAT HAMMER.
ASGARD STANDS ON THE BRINK OF CIVIL WAR FOR ONE REASON ONLY:
ODIN.
BELIEVE ME, I WAS DRIVING THE ALL-FATHER MAD LONG BEFORE YOU EVER CANOODLED YOUR FIRST THUNDERSTORM.
BUT THAT WAS THE OLD LOKI. A DASHING FELLOW, TO BE SURE, BUT ALAS, HE GOT A BIT BORED ALWAYS PICKING THE BONES OF THOSE SAME WITHERED SAGAS.
AN ALL-NEW, ALL-DIFFERENT THOR DESERVES AN ALL-NEW, ALL-DIFFERENT LOKI.

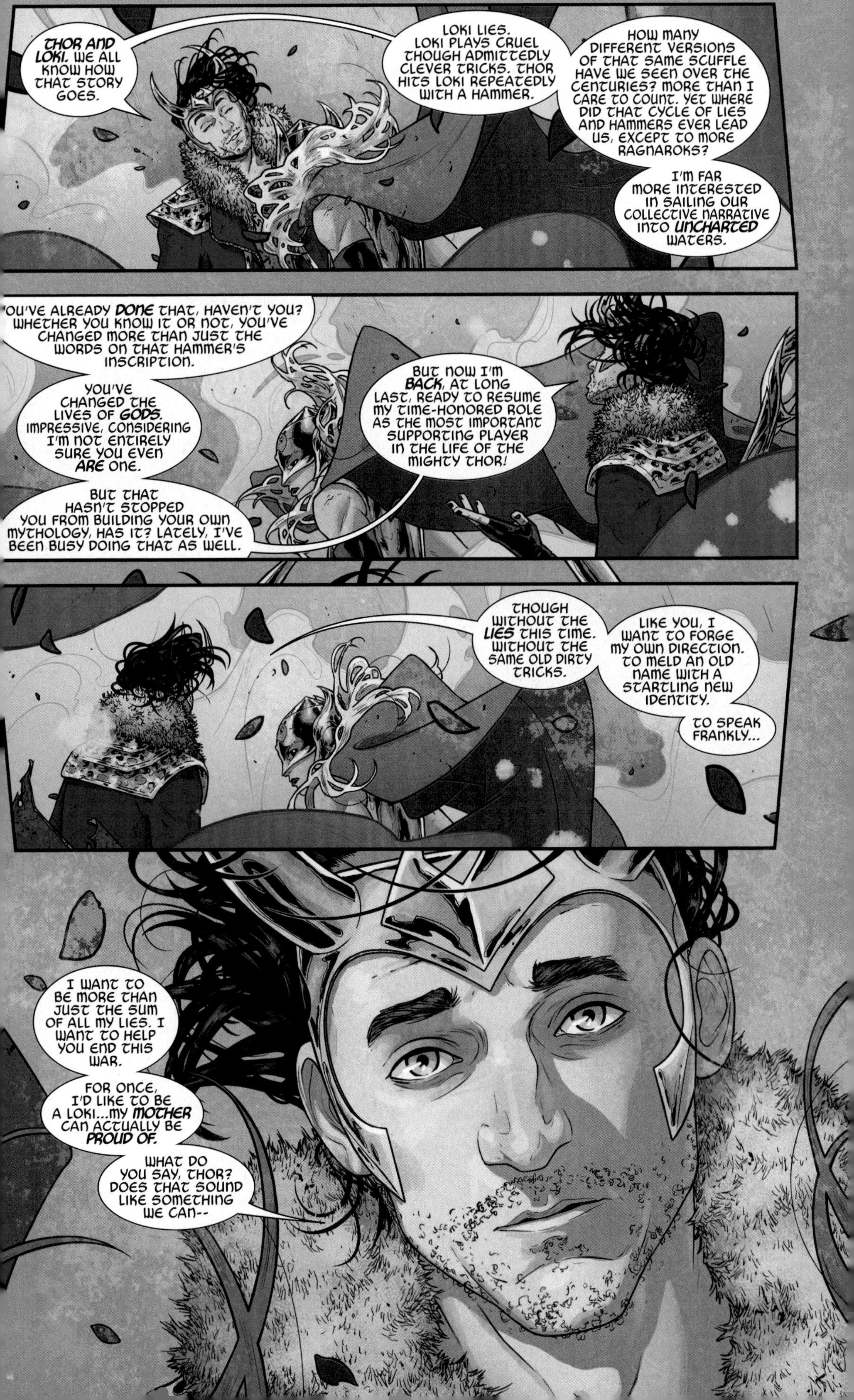
THOR AND LOKI. WE ALL KNOW HOW THAT STORY GOES.
LOKI LIES. LOKI PLAYS CRUEL THOUGH ADMITTEDLY CLEVER TRICKS. THOR HITS LOKI REPEATEDLY WITH A HAMMER.
HOW MANY DIFFERENT VERSIONS OF THAT SAME SCUFFLE HAVE WE SEEN OVER THE CENTURIES? MORE THAN I CARE TO COUNT. YET WHERE DID THAT CYCLE OF LIES AND HAMMERS EVER LEAD US, EXCEPT TO MORE RAGNAROKS?
I'M FAR MORE INTERESTED IN SAILING OUR COLLECTIVE NARRATIVE INTO UNCHARTED WATERS.
YOU'VE ALREADY DONE THAT, HAVEN'T YOU? WHETHER YOU KNOW IT OR NOT, YOU'VE CHANGED MORE THAN JUST THE WORDS ON THAT HAMMER'S INSCRIPTION.
YOU'VE CHANGED THE LIVES OF GODS. IMPRESSIVE, CONSIDERING I'M NOT ENTIRELY SURE YOU EVEN ARE ONE.
BUT THAT HASN'T STOPPED YOU FROM BUILDING YOUR OWN MYTHOLOGY, HAS IT? LATELY, I'VE BEEN BUSY DOING THAT AS WELL.
BUT NOW I'M BACK, AT LONG LAST, READY TO RESUME MY TIME-HONORED ROLE AS THE MOST IMPORTANT SUPPORTING PLAYER IN THE LIFE OF THE MIGHTY THOR!
THOUGH WITHOUT THE LIES THIS TIME. WITHOUT THE SAME OLD DIRTY TRICKS.
LIKE YOU, I WANT TO FORGE MY OWN DIRECTION. TO MELD AN OLD NAME WITH A STARTLING NEW IDENTITY.
TO SPEAK FRANKLY...
I WANT TO BE MORE THAN JUST THE SUM OF ALL MY LIES. I WANT TO HELP YOU END THIS WAR.
FOR ONCE, I'D LIKE TO BE A LOKI...MY MOTHER CAN ACTUALLY BE PROUD OF.
WHAT DO YOU SAY, THOR? DOES THAT SOUND LIKE SOMETHING WE CAN--

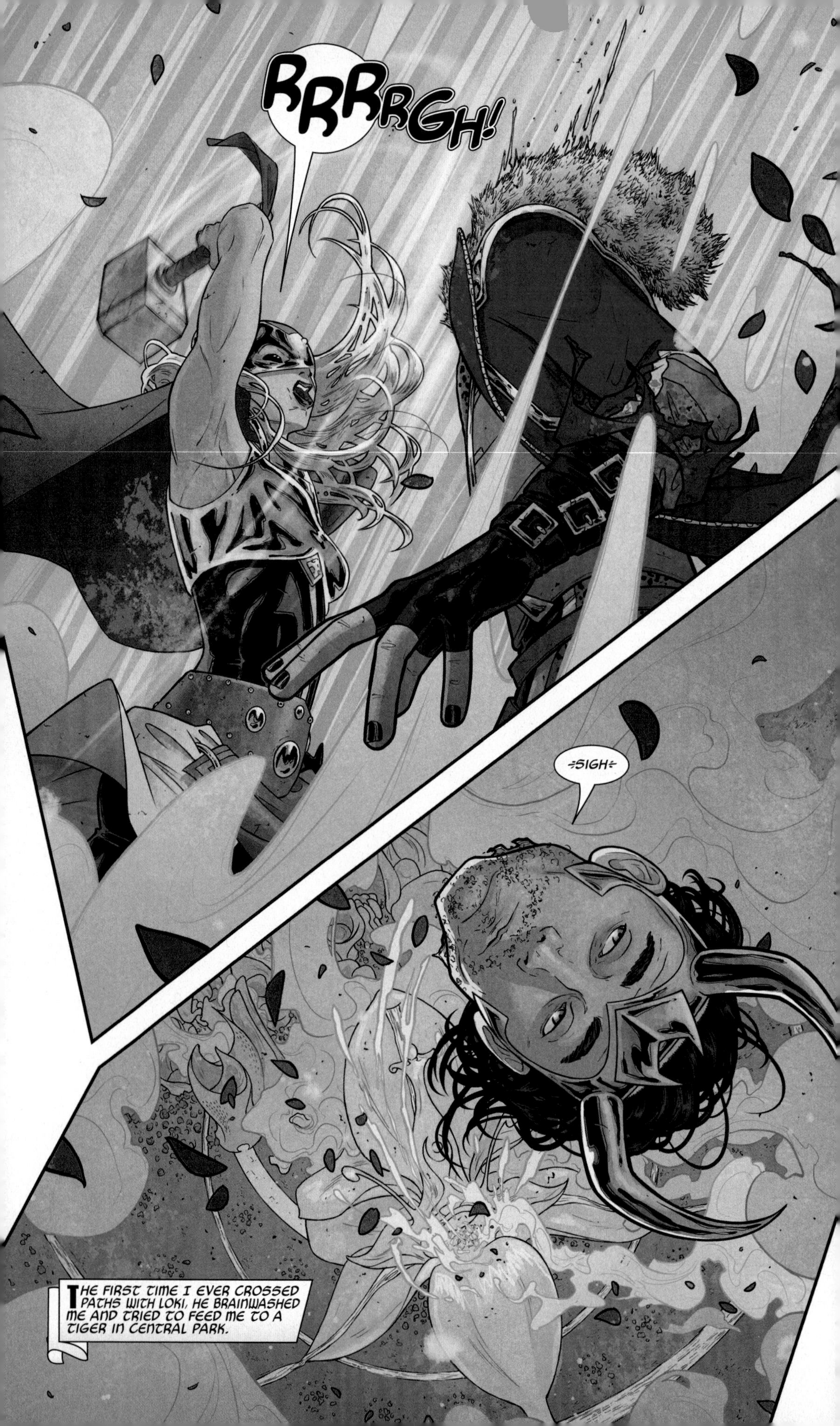
RRRRRGH!
=SIGH=
THE FIRST TIME I EVER CROSSED PATHS WITH LOKI, HE BRAINWASHED ME AND TRIED TO FEED ME TO A TIGER IN CENTRAL PARK.

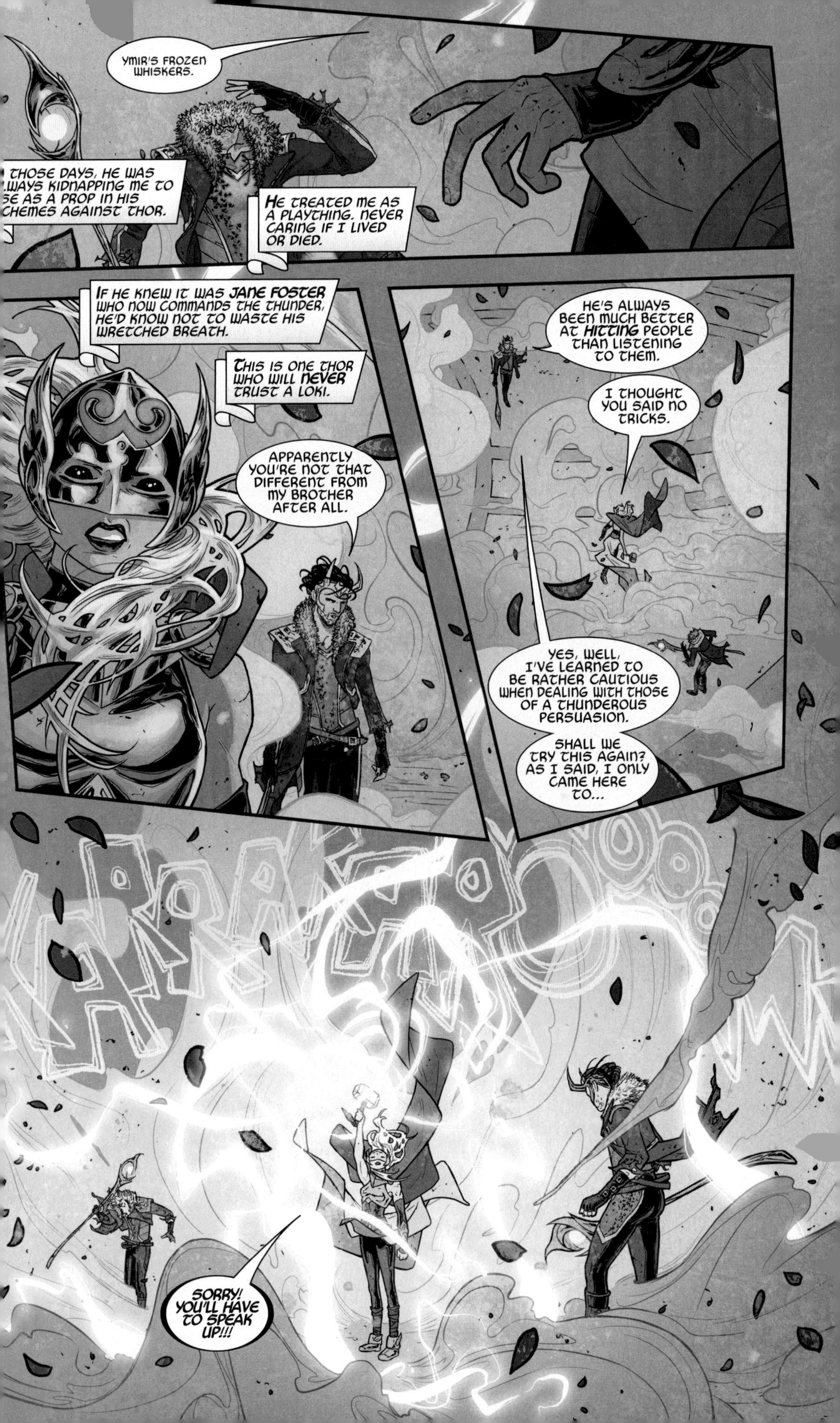

YMIR'S FROZEN WHISKERS.
IN THOSE DAYS, HE WAS ALWAYS KIDNAPPING ME TO USE AS A PROP IN HIS SCHEMES AGAINST THOR.
HE TREATED ME AS A PLAYTHING. NEVER CARING IF I LIVED OR DIED.
IF HE KNEW IT WAS JANE FOSTER WHO NOW COMMANDS THE THUNDER, HE'D KNOW NOT TO WASTE HIS WRETCHED BREATH.
THIS IS ONE THOR WHO WILL NEVER TRUST A LOKI.
APPARENTLY YOU'RE NOT THAT DIFFERENT FROM MY BROTHER AFTER ALL.
HE'S ALWAYS BEEN MUCH BETTER AT HITTING PEOPLE THAN LISTENING TO THEM.
I THOUGHT YOU SAID NO TRICKS.
YES, WELL, I'VE LEARNED TO BE RATHER CAUTIOUS WHEN DEALING WITH THOSE OF A THUNDEROUS PERSUASION.
SHALL WE TRY THIS AGAIN? AS I SAID, I ONLY CAME HERE TO...
SORRY! YOU'LL HAVE TO SPEAK UP!!!

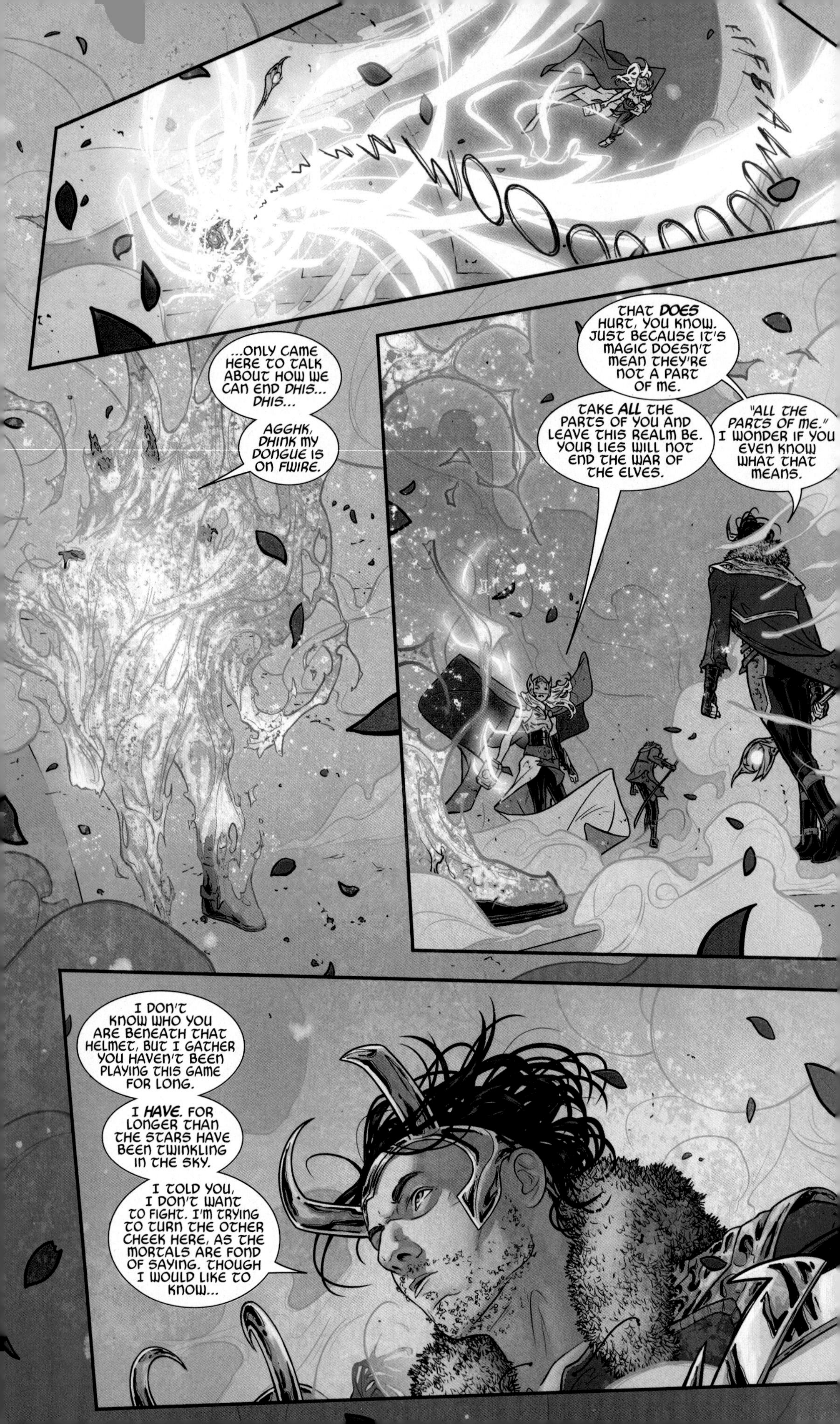
WWWWWOOOOOOOOOOOOOMMM
FFFEAAAAM
...ONLY CAME HERE TO TALK ABOUT HOW WE CAN END DHIS... DHIS...
AGGHK, DHINK MY DONGUE IS ON FWIRE.
THAT DOES HURT, YOU KNOW. JUST BECAUSE IT'S MAGIC DOESN'T MEAN THEY'RE NOT A PART OF ME.
TAKE ALL THE PARTS OF YOU AND LEAVE THIS REALM BE. YOUR LIES WILL NOT END THE WAR OF THE ELVES.
"ALL THE PARTS OF ME." I WONDER IF YOU EVEN KNOW WHAT THAT MEANS.
I DON'T KNOW WHO YOU ARE BENEATH THAT HELMET, BUT I GATHER YOU HAVEN'T BEEN PLAYING THIS GAME FOR LONG.
I HAVE. FOR LONGER THAN THE STARS HAVE BEEN TWINKLING IN THE SKY.
I TOLD YOU, I DON'T WANT TO FIGHT. I'M TRYING TO TURN THE OTHER CHEEK HERE, AS THE MORTALS ARE FOND OF SAYING. THOUGH I WOULD LIKE TO KNOW...

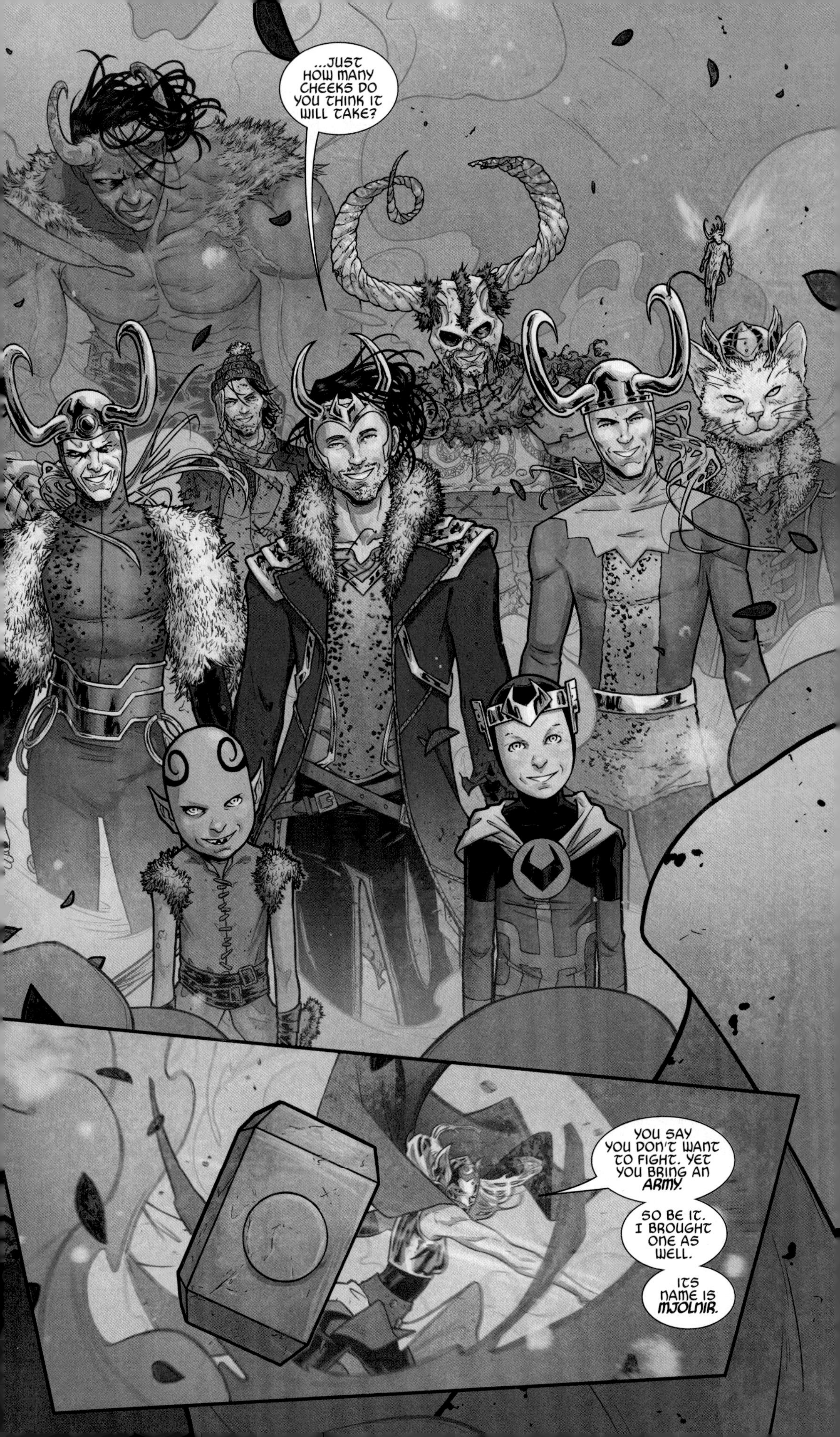
...JUST HOW MANY CHEEKS DO YOU THINK IT WILL TAKE?
YOU SAY YOU DON'T WANT TO FIGHT. YET YOU BRING AN ARMY.
SO BE IT. I BROUGHT ONE AS WELL.
ITS NAME IS MJOLNIR.

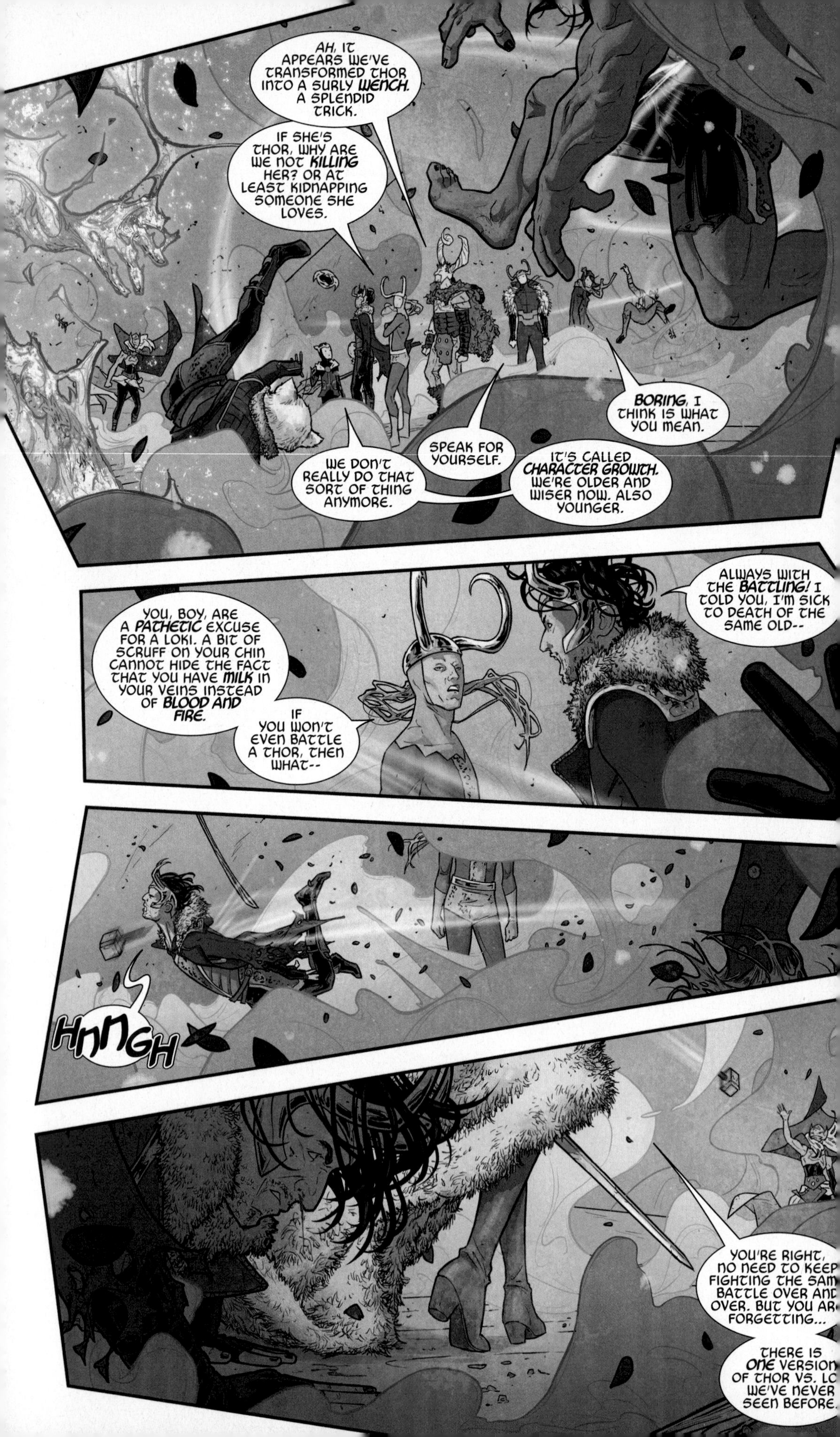

AH, IT APPEARS WE'VE TRANSFORMED THOR INTO A SURLY WENCH. A SPLENDID TRICK.
IF SHE'S THOR, WHY ARE WE NOT KILLING HER? OR AT LEAST KIDNAPPING SOMEONE SHE LOVES.
WE DON'T REALLY DO THAT SORT OF THING ANYMORE.
SPEAK FOR YOURSELF.
BORING, I THINK IS WHAT YOU MEAN.
IT'S CALLED CHARACTER GROWTH. WE'RE OLDER AND WISER NOW. ALSO YOUNGER.
YOU, BOY, ARE A PATHETIC EXCUSE FOR A LOKI. A BIT OF SCRUFF ON YOUR CHIN CANNOT HIDE THE FACT THAT YOU HAVE MILK IN YOUR VEINS INSTEAD OF BLOOD AND FIRE.
IF YOU WON'T EVEN BATTLE A THOR, THEN WHAT--
ALWAYS WITH THE BATTLING! I TOLD YOU, I'M SICK TO DEATH OF THE SAME OLD--
HNNGH
YOU'RE RIGHT, NO NEED TO KEEP FIGHTING THE SAM BATTLE OVER AND OVER. BUT YOU AR FORGETTING...
THERE IS ONE VERSION OF THOR VS. LO WE'VE NEVER SEEN BEFORE.

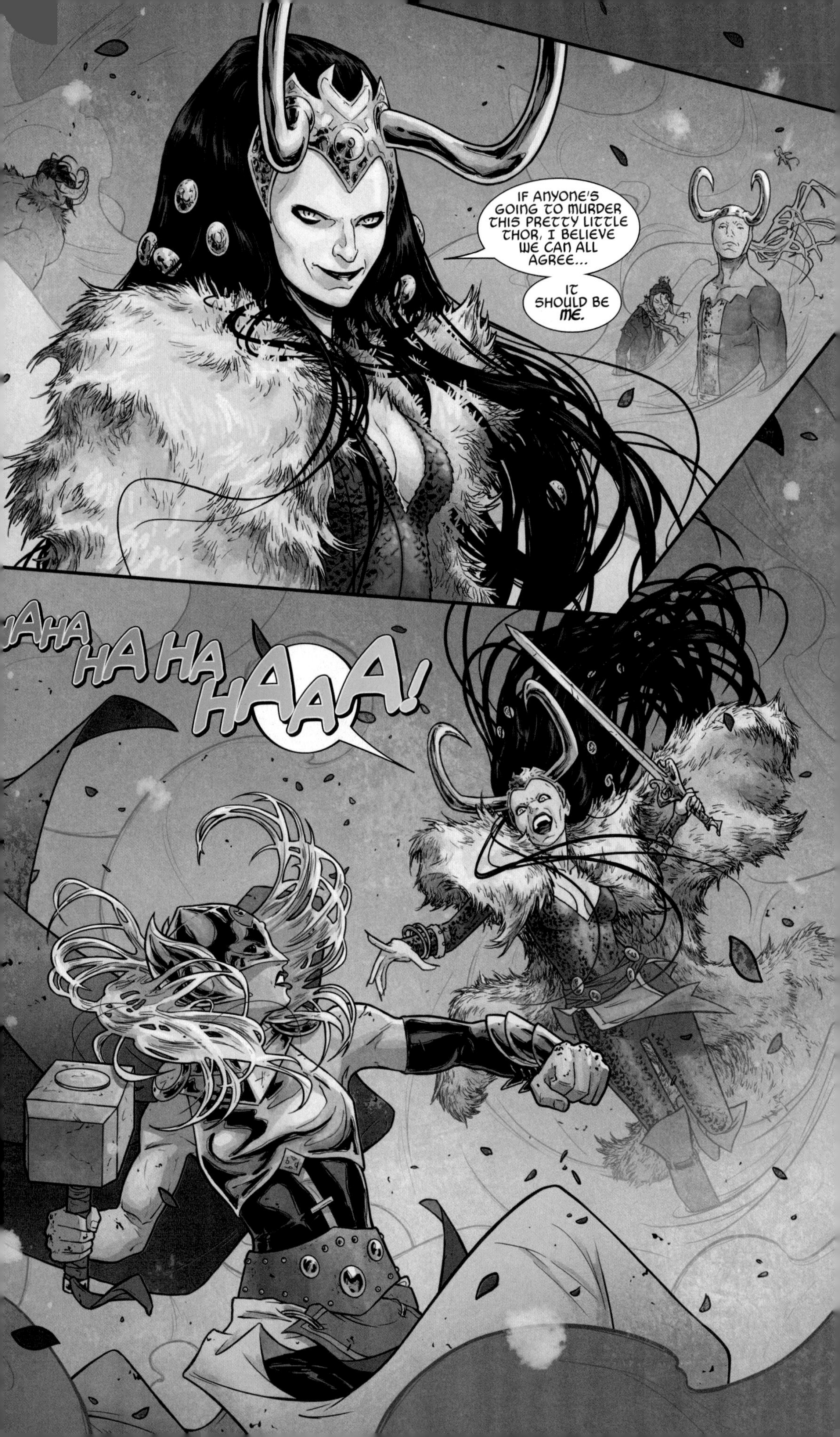
IF ANYONE'S GOING TO MURDER THIS PRETTY LITTLE THOR, I BELIEVE WE CAN ALL AGREE...
IT SHOULD BE ME.
AHA HA HA HAAAA!

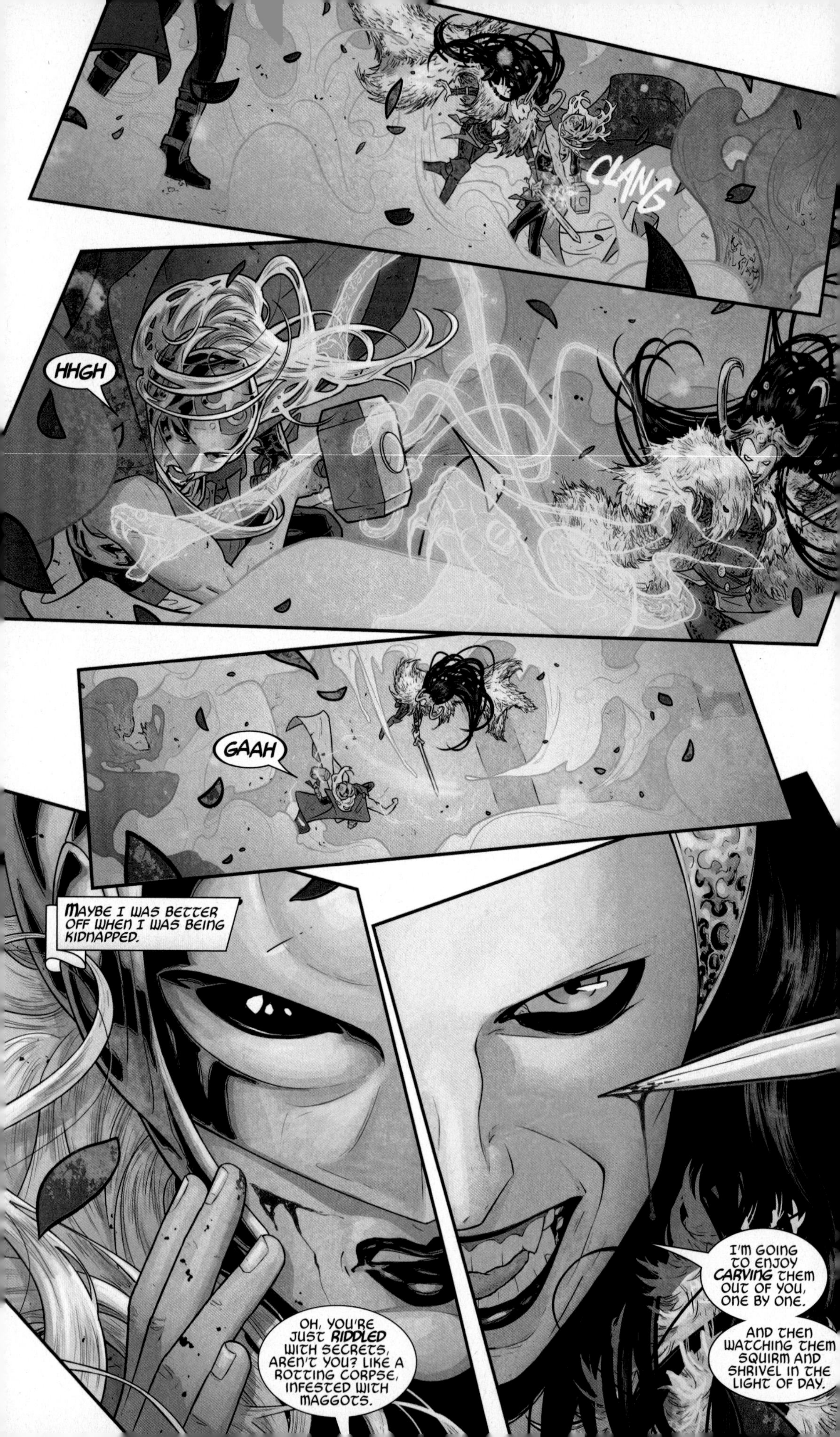
CLANG
HHGH
GAAH
MAYBE I WAS BETTER OFF WHEN I WAS BEING KIDNAPPED.
OH, YOU'RE JUST RIDDLED WITH SECRETS, AREN'T YOU? LIKE A ROTTING CORPSE, INFESTED WITH MAGGOTS.
I'M GOING TO ENJOY CARVING THEM OUT OF YOU, ONE BY ONE.
AND THEN WATCHING THEM SQUIRM AND SHRIVEL IN THE LIGHT OF DAY.

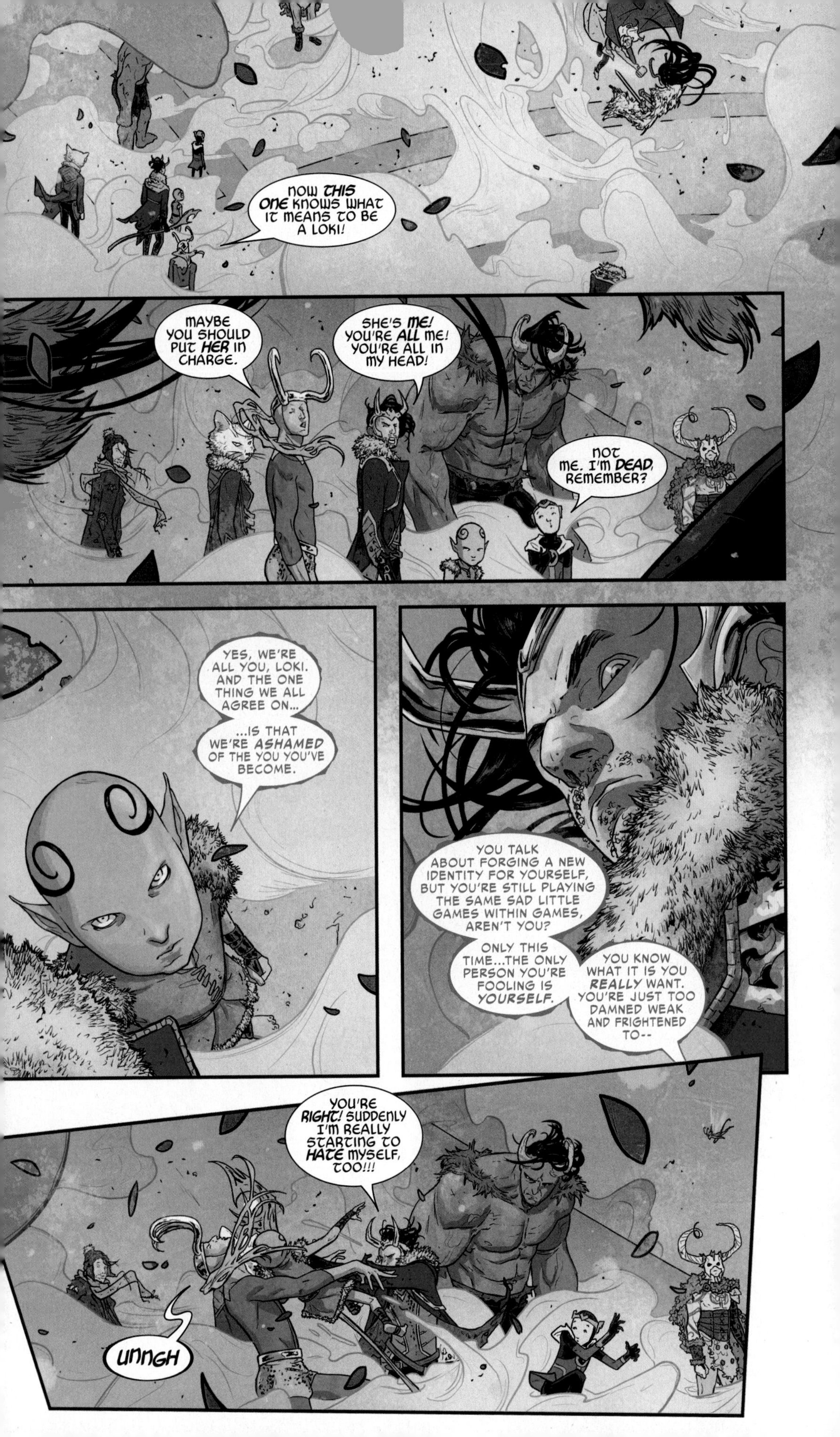
NOW THIS ONE KNOWS WHAT IT MEANS TO BE A LOKI!
MAYBE YOU SHOULD PUT HER IN CHARGE.
SHE'S ME! YOU'RE ALL ME! YOU'RE ALL IN MY HEAD!
NOT ME. I'M DEAD, REMEMBER?
YES, WE'RE ALL YOU, LOKI. AND THE ONE THING WE ALL AGREE ON...
...IS THAT WE'RE ASHAMED OF THE YOU YOU'VE BECOME.
YOU TALK ABOUT FORGING A NEW IDENTITY FOR YOURSELF, BUT YOU'RE STILL PLAYING THE SAME SAD LITTLE GAMES WITHIN GAMES, AREN'T YOU?
ONLY THIS TIME...THE ONLY PERSON YOU'RE FOOLING IS YOURSELF.
YOU KNOW WHAT IT IS YOU REALLY WANT. YOU'RE JUST TOO DAMNED WEAK AND FRIGHTENED TO--
YOU'RE RIGHT! SUDDENLY I'M REALLY STARTING TO HATE MYSELF, TOO!!!
UNNGH

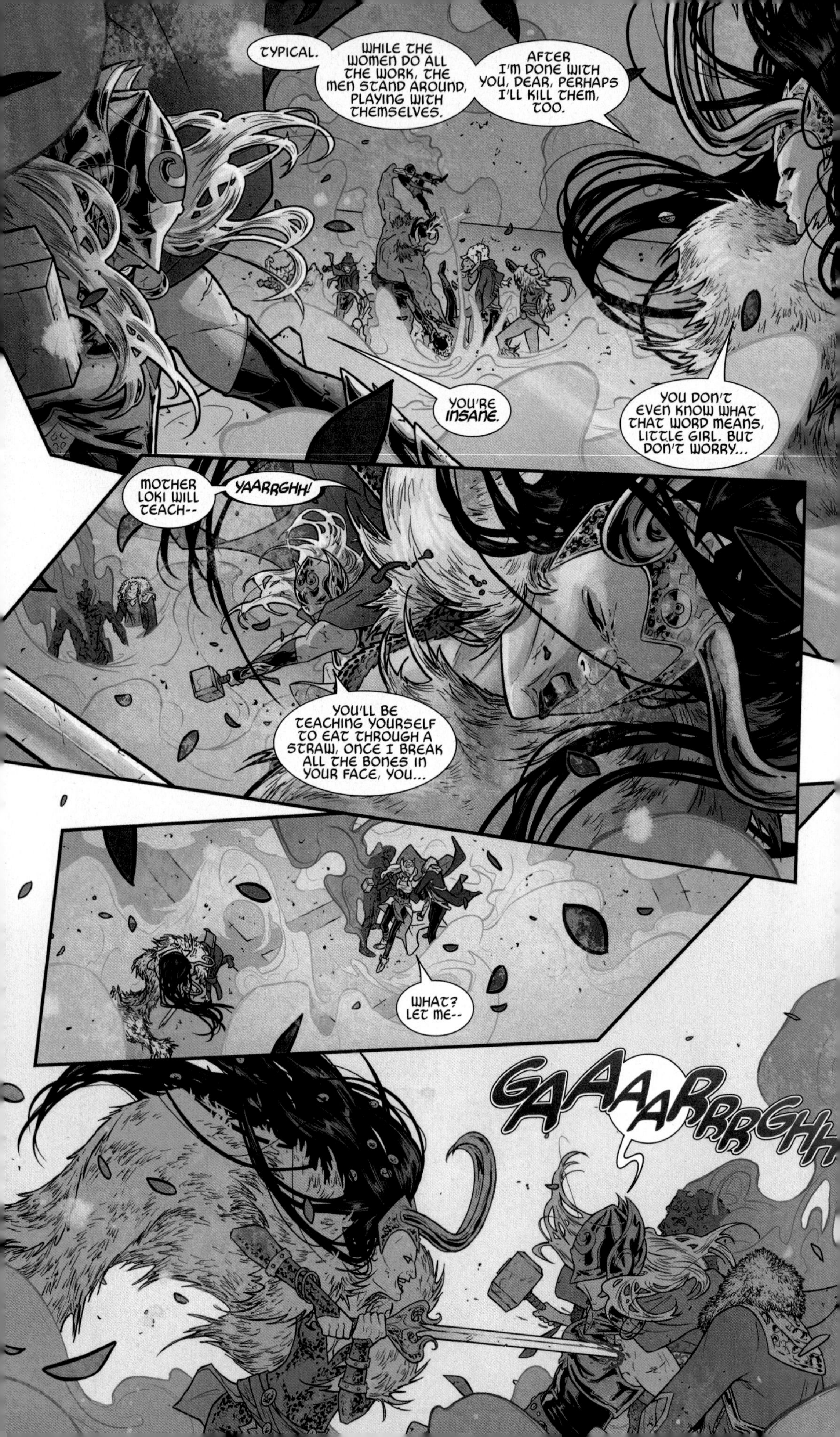
TYPICAL.
WHILE THE WOMEN DO ALL THE WORK, THE MEN STAND AROUND, PLAYING WITH THEMSELVES.
AFTER I'M DONE WITH YOU, DEAR, PERHAPS I'LL KILL THEM, TOO.
YOU'RE INSANE.
YOU DON'T EVEN KNOW WHAT THAT WORD MEANS, LITTLE GIRL. BUT DON'T WORRY...
MOTHER LOKI WILL TEACH--
YAARRGHH!
YOU'LL BE TEACHING YOURSELF TO EAT THROUGH A STRAW, ONCE I BREAK ALL THE BONES IN YOUR FACE, YOU...
WHAT? LET ME--
GAAAARRRGHH

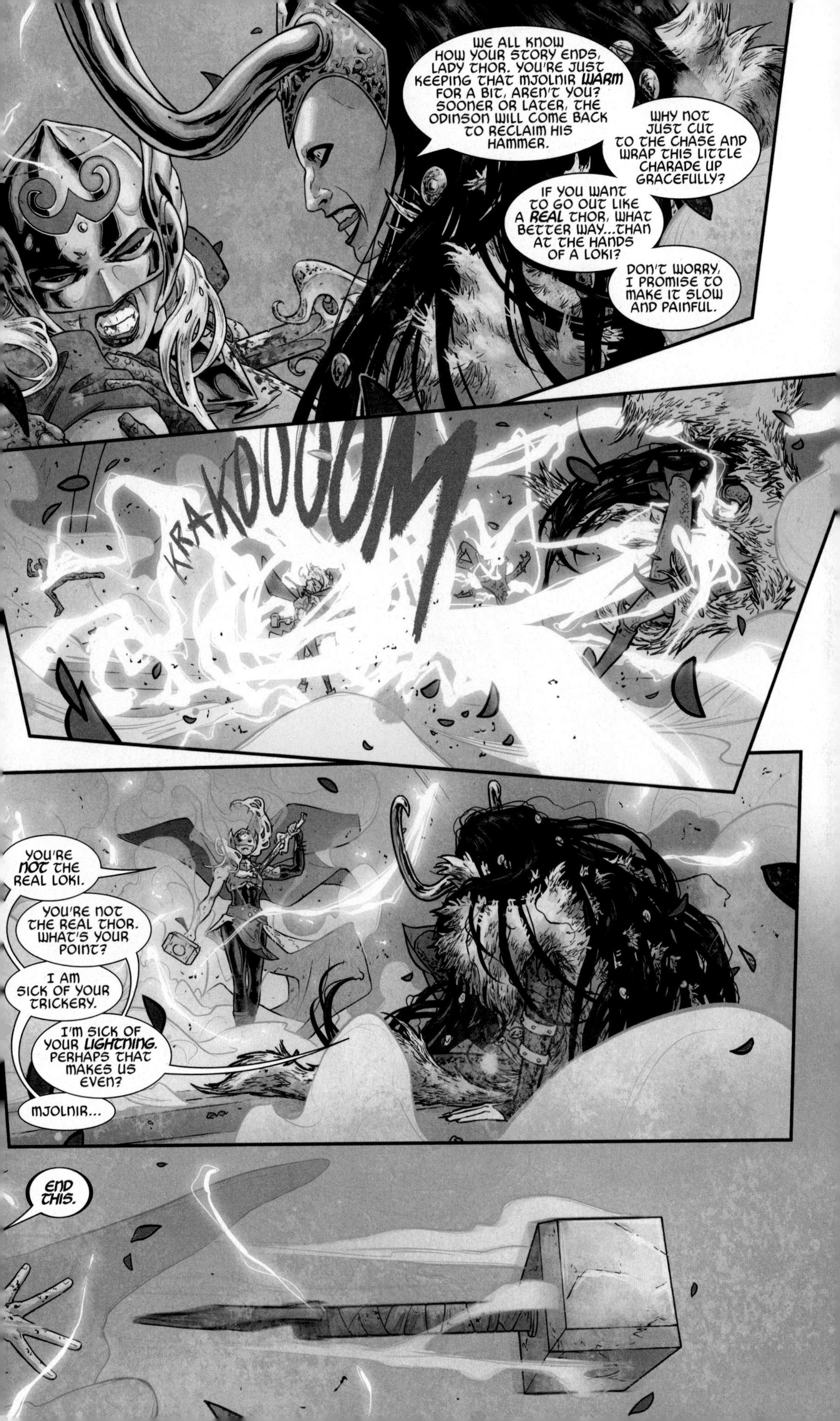
WE ALL KNOW HOW YOUR STORY ENDS, LADY THOR. YOU'RE JUST KEEPING THAT MJOLNIR WARM FOR A BIT, AREN'T YOU? SOONER OR LATER, THE ODINSON WILL COME BACK TO RECLAIM HIS HAMMER.
WHY NOT JUST CUT TO THE CHASE AND WRAP THIS LITTLE CHARADE UP GRACEFULLY?
IF YOU WANT TO GO OUT LIKE A REAL THOR, WHAT BETTER WAY...THAN AT THE HANDS OF A LOKI?
DON'T WORRY, I PROMISE TO MAKE IT SLOW AND PAINFUL.
KRAKOOOOM
YOU'RE NOT THE REAL LOKI.
YOU'RE NOT THE REAL THOR. WHAT'S YOUR POINT?
I AM SICK OF YOUR TRICKERY.
I'M SICK OF YOUR LIGHTNING. PERHAPS THAT MAKES US EVEN?
MJOLNIR...
END THIS.

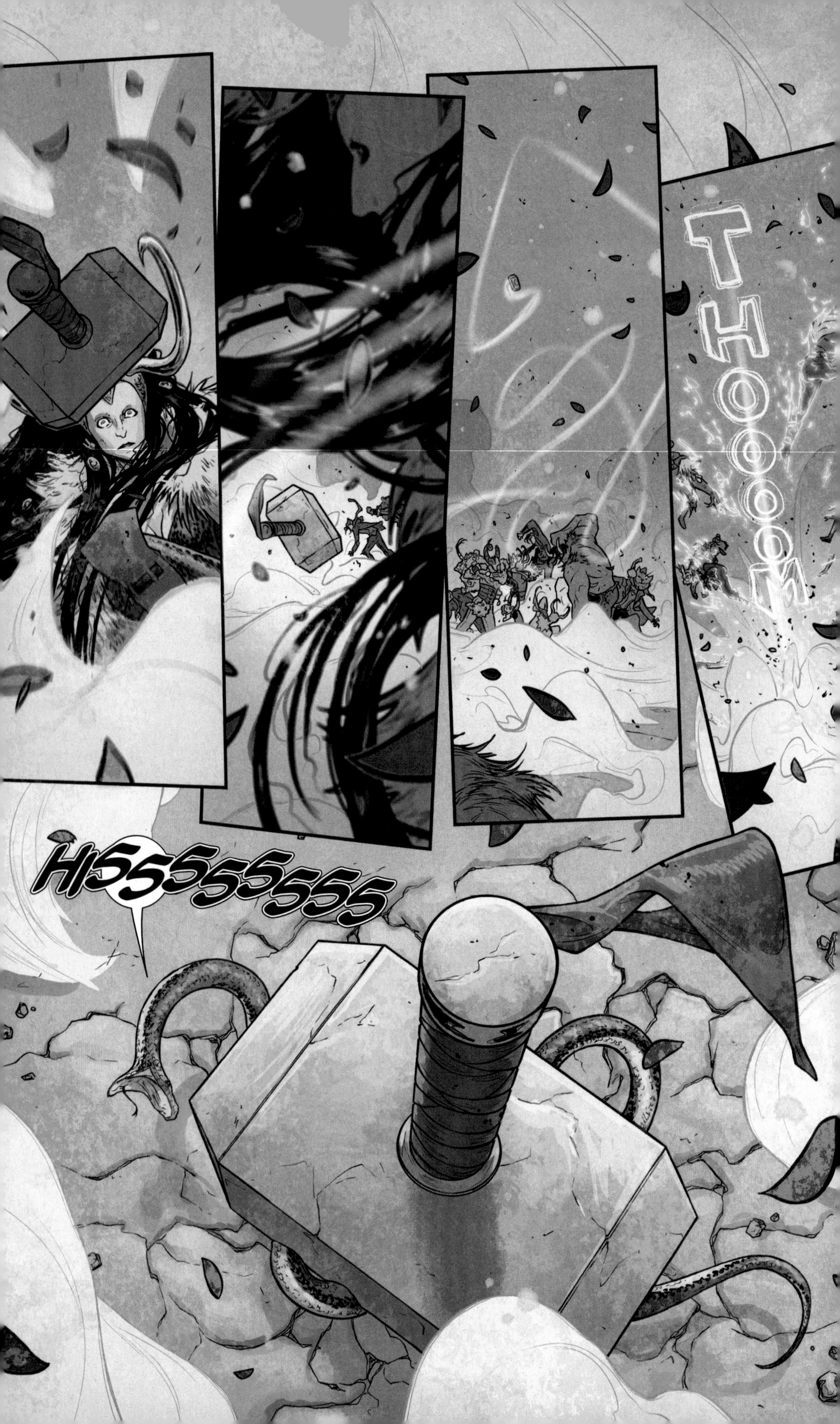
THOOOOM
HISSSSSSSS

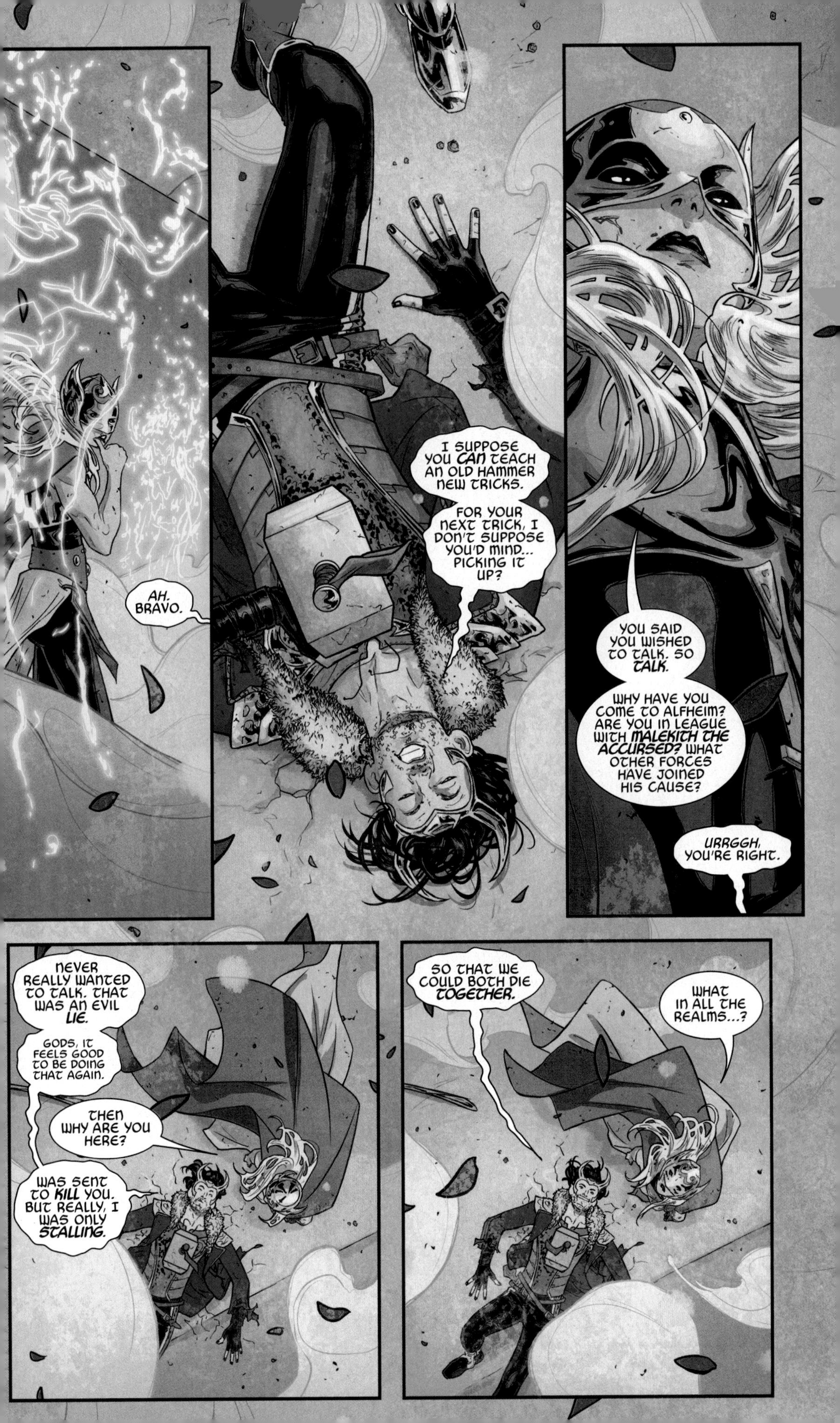
AH. BRAVO.
I SUPPOSE YOU CAN TEACH AN OLD HAMMER NEW TRICKS.
FOR YOUR NEXT TRICK, I DON'T SUPPOSE YOU'D MIND... PICKING IT UP?
YOU SAID YOU WISHED TO TALK. SO TALK.
WHY HAVE YOU COME TO ALFHEIM? ARE YOU IN LEAGUE WITH MALEKITH THE ACCURSED? WHAT OTHER FORCES HAVE JOINED HIS CAUSE?
URRGGH, YOU'RE RIGHT.
NEVER REALLY WANTED TO TALK. THAT WAS AN EVIL LIE.
GODS, IT FEELS GOOD TO BE DOING THAT AGAIN.
THEN WHY ARE YOU HERE?
WAS SENT TO KILL YOU. BUT REALLY, I WAS ONLY STALLING.
SO THAT WE COULD BOTH DIE TOGETHER.
WHAT IN ALL THE REALMS...?

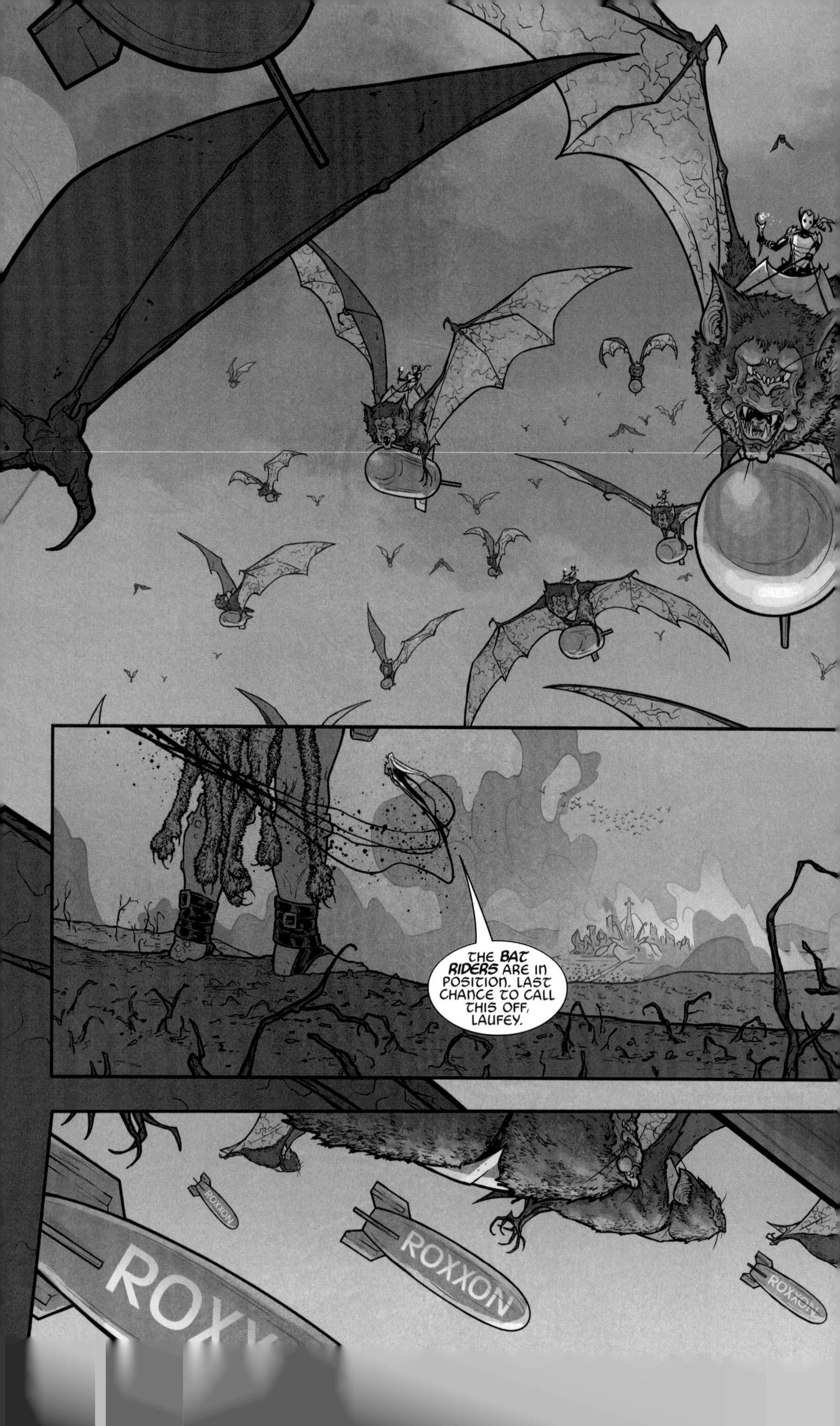
THE BAT RIDERS ARE IN POSITION. LAST CHANCE TO CALL THIS OFF, LAUFEY.
ROXXON
ROXXON
ROXXON
ROXXON

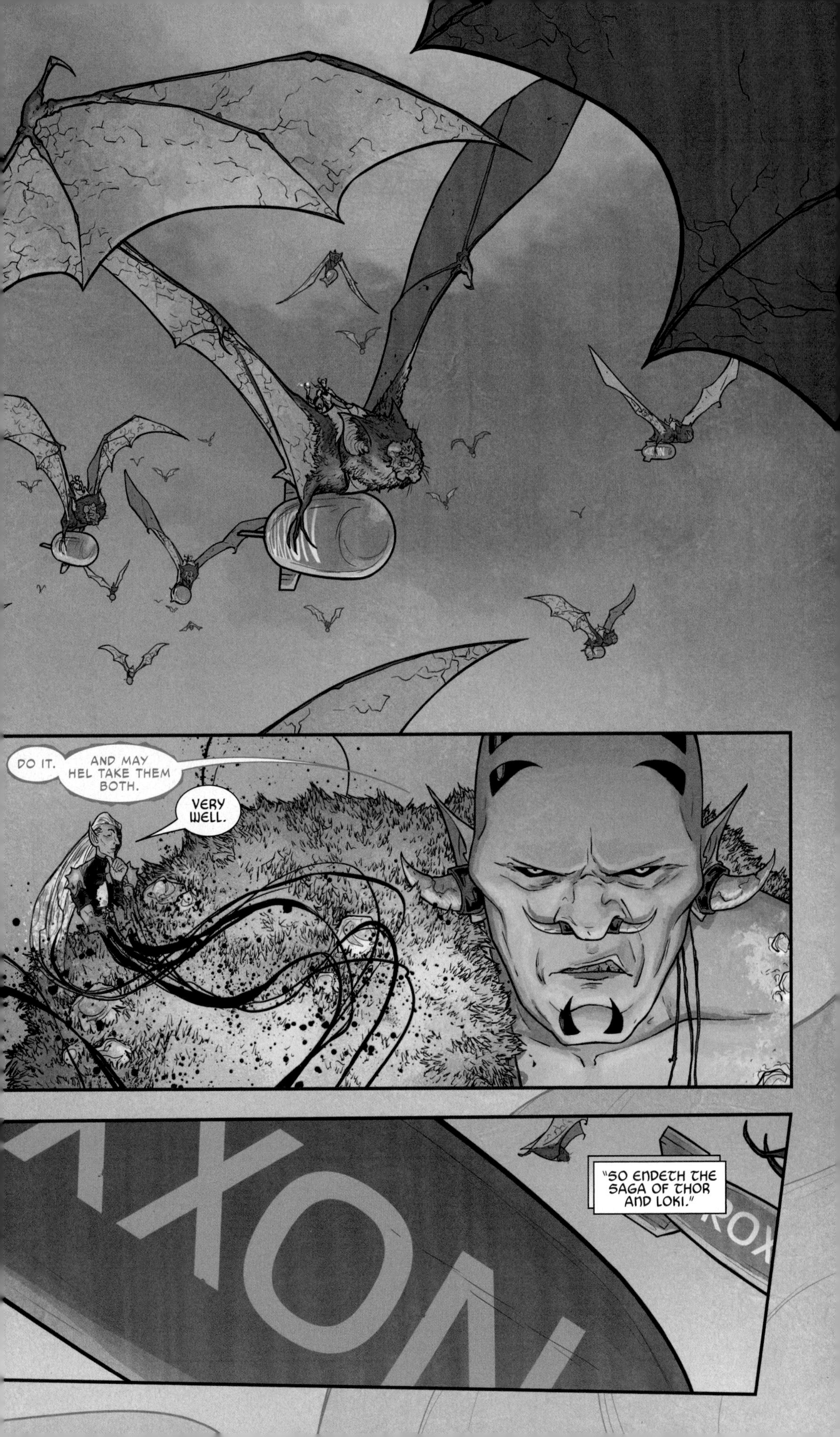
DO IT.
AND MAY HEL TAKE THEM BOTH.
VERY WELL.
"SO ENDETH THE SAGA OF THOR AND LOKI."

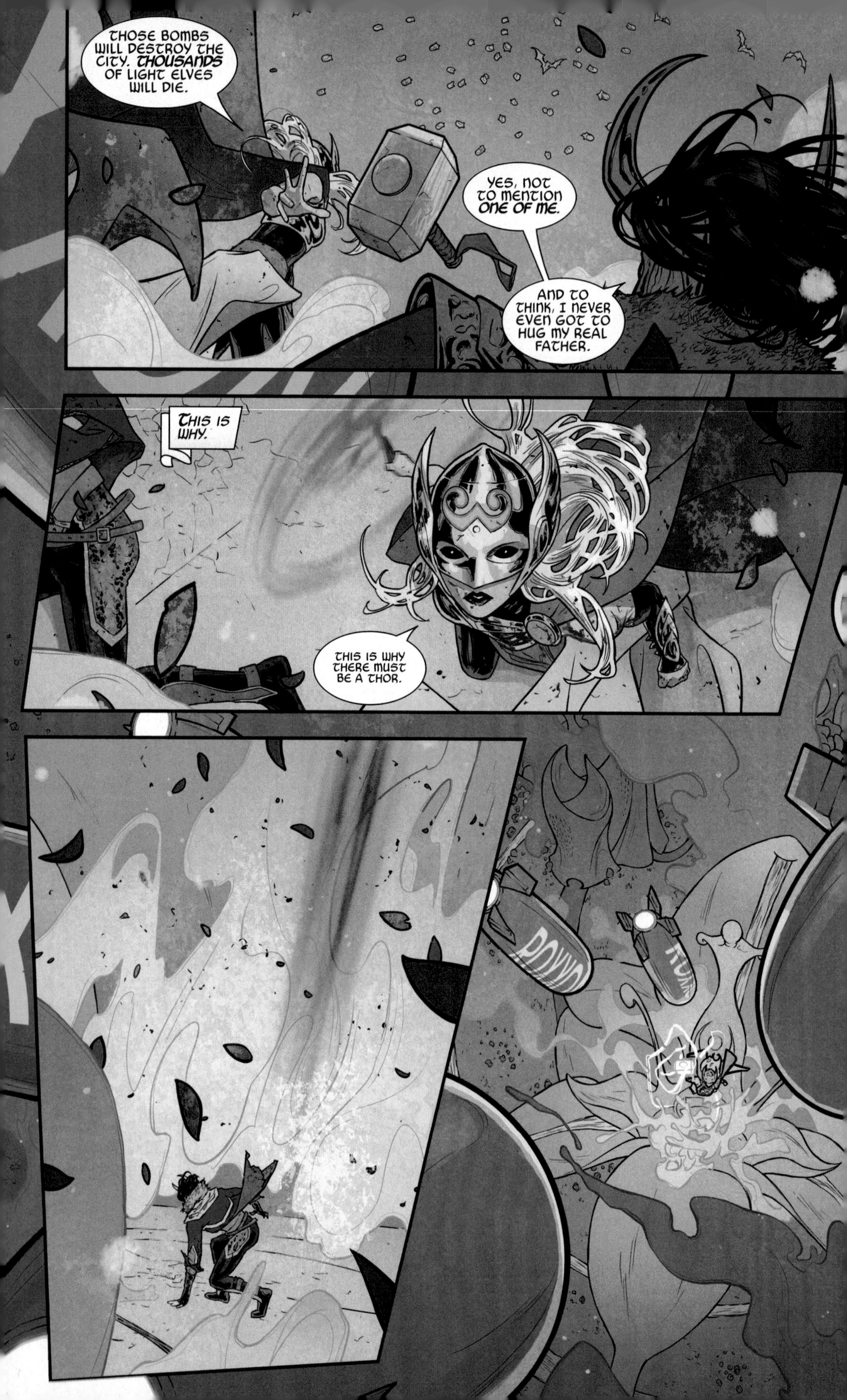
THOSE BOMBS WILL DESTROY THE CITY. THOUSANDS OF LIGHT ELVES WILL DIE.
YES, NOT TO MENTION ONE OF ME.
AND TO THINK, I NEVER EVEN GOT TO HUG MY REAL FATHER.
THIS IS WHY.
THIS IS WHY THERE MUST BE A THOR.

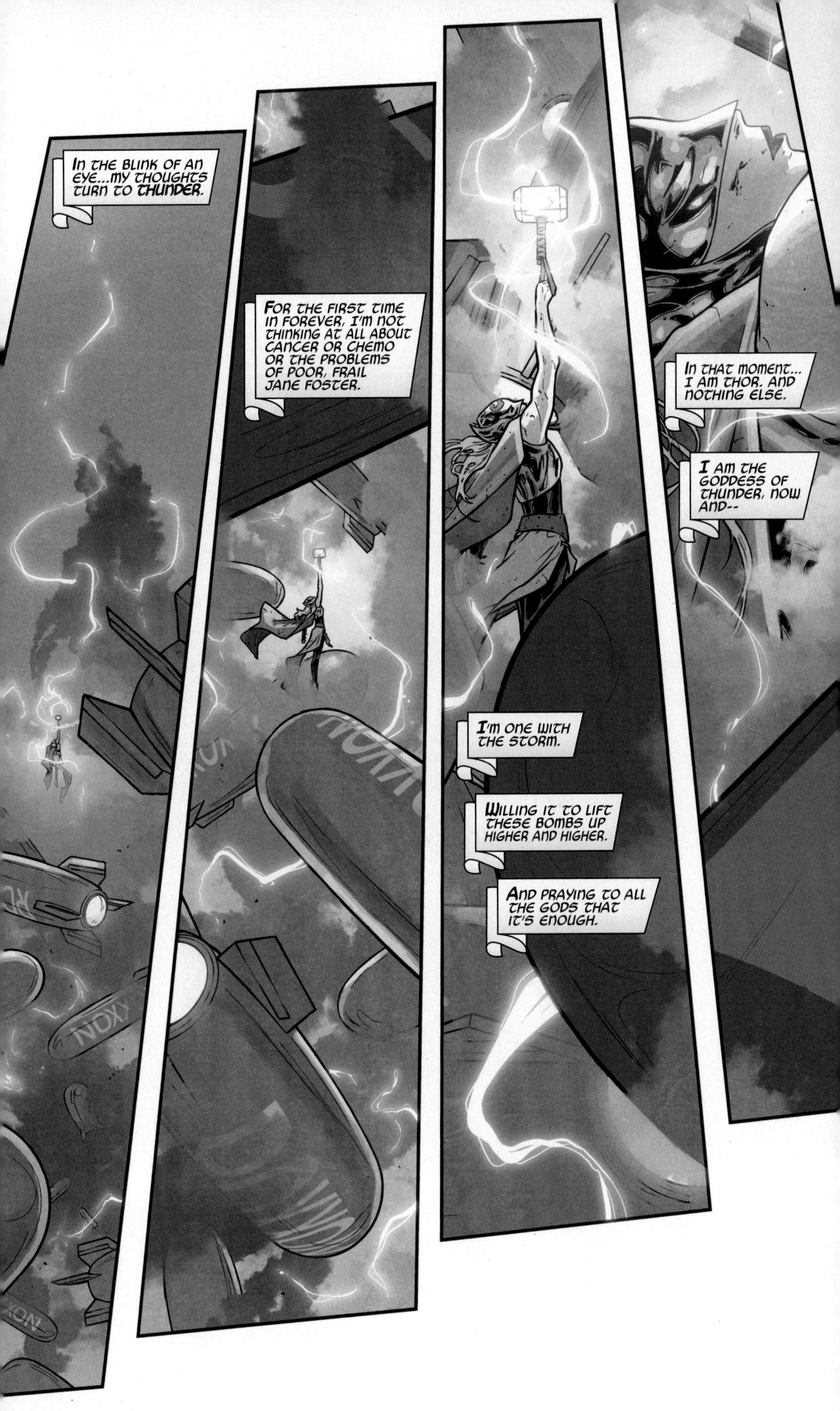

IN THE BLINK OF AN EYE...MY THOUGHTS TURN TO THUNDER.
FOR THE FIRST TIME IN FOREVER, I'M NOT THINKING AT ALL ABOUT CANCER OR CHEMO OR THE PROBLEMS OF POOR, FRAIL JANE FOSTER.
I'M ONE WITH THE STORM.
WILLING IT TO LIFT THESE BOMBS UP HIGHER AND HIGHER.
AND PRAYING TO ALL THE GODS THAT IT'S ENOUGH.
IN THAT MOMENT... I AM THOR. AND NOTHING ELSE.
I AM THE GODDESS OF THUNDER, NOW AND--

I CAN'T BELIEVE I'M SAYING THIS...
BUT I DO HOPE I DIDN'T JUST WITNESS THE LAST ACT OF THOR.
YOU AND I HAVE A LOT OF WORK TO DO, *MS. THUNDER.* AND BELIEVE ME...
"...THIS LITTLE WAR IN ALFHEIM IS *NOTHING* COMPARED TO THE ONE THAT'S JUST ABOUT TO EXPLODE...

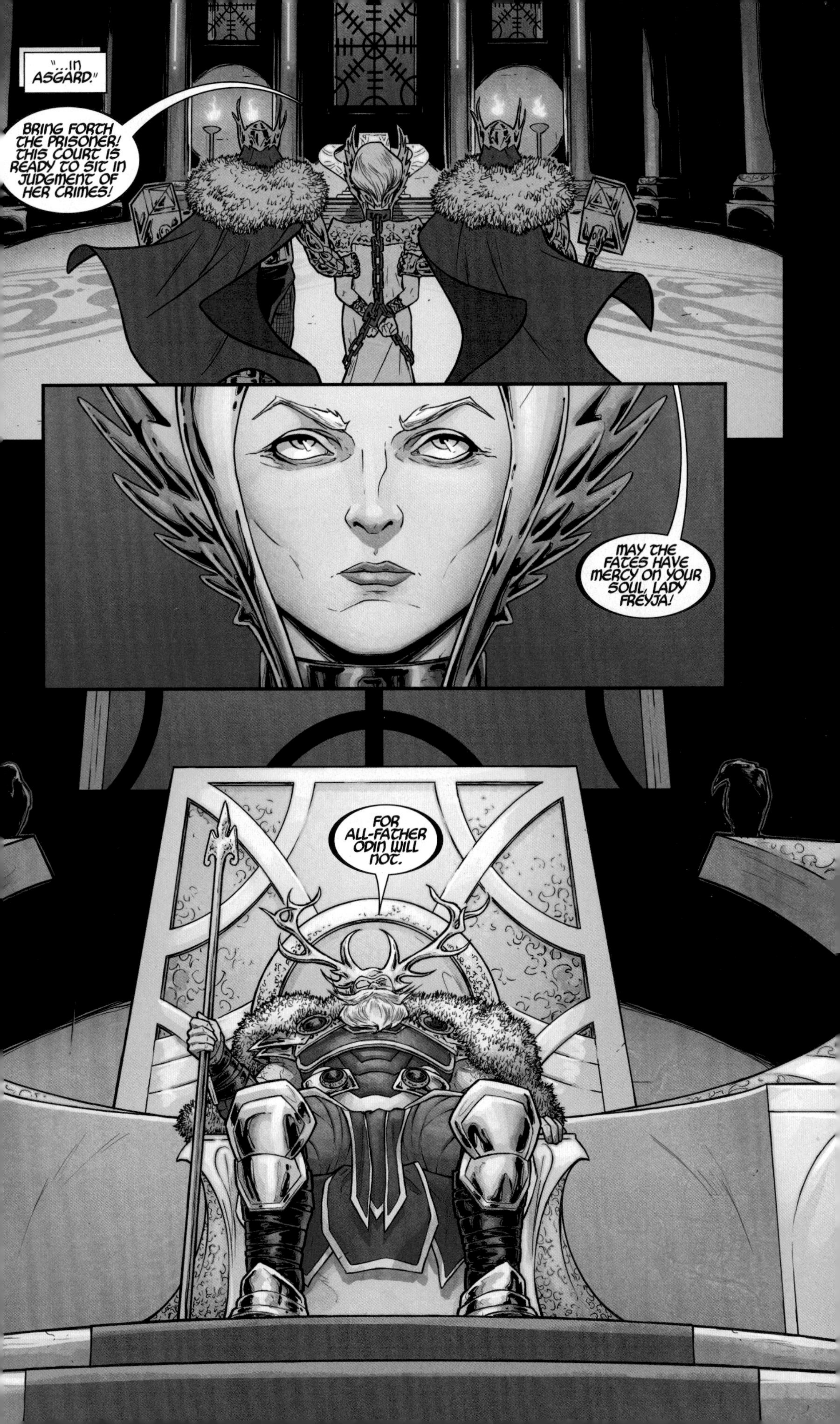
"...IN ASGARD."
BRING FORTH THE PRISONER! THIS COURT IS READY TO SIT IN JUDGMENT OF HER CRIMES!
MAY THE FATES HAVE MERCY ON YOUR SOUL, LADY FREYJA!
FOR ALL-FATHER ODIN WILL NOT.

— 4 —

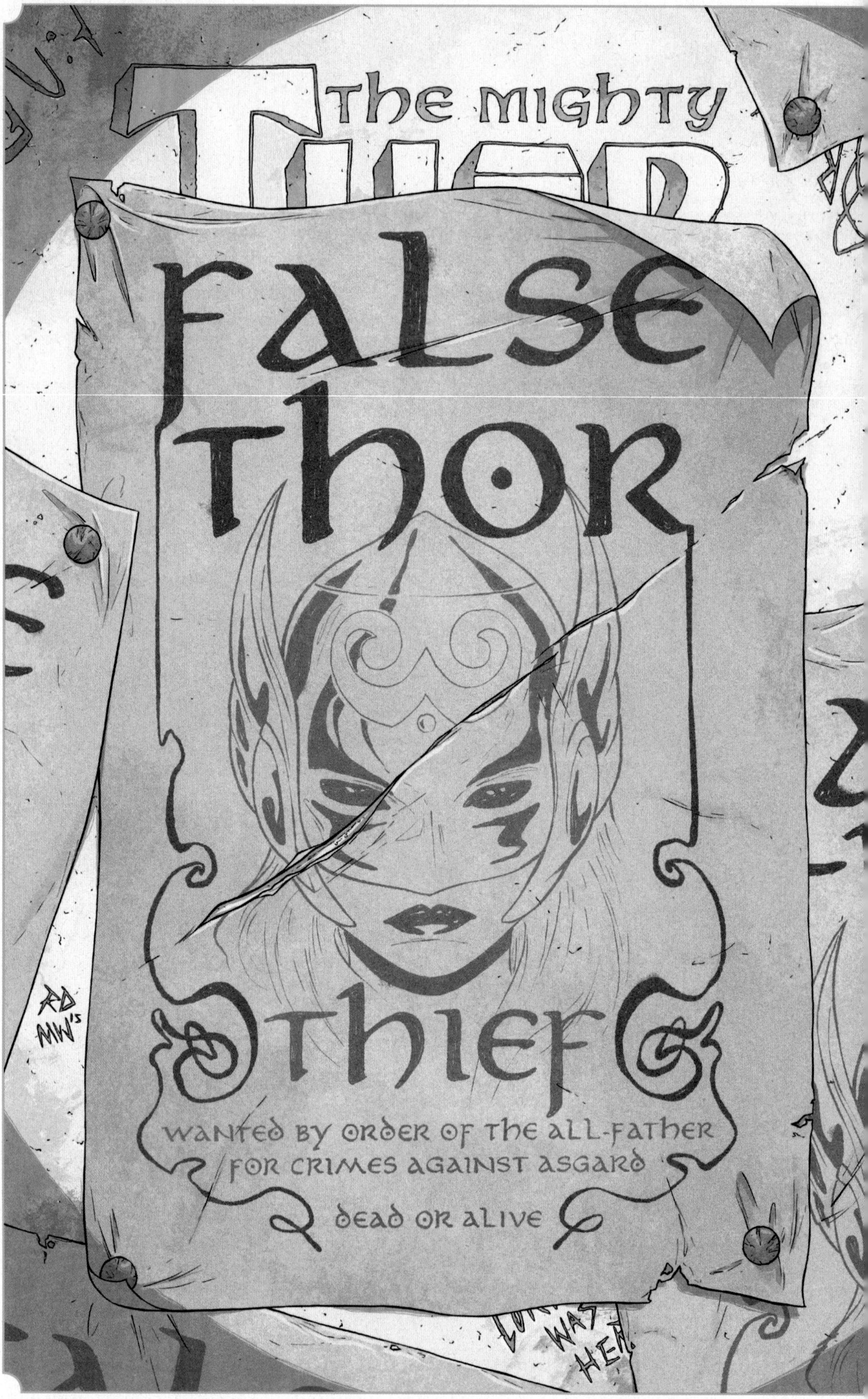
THE MIGHTY
FALSE THOR
THIEF
WANTED BY ORDER OF THE ALL-FATHER
FOR CRIMES AGAINST ASGARD
DEAD OR ALIVE

THE TRIAL OF THE ALL-MOTHER

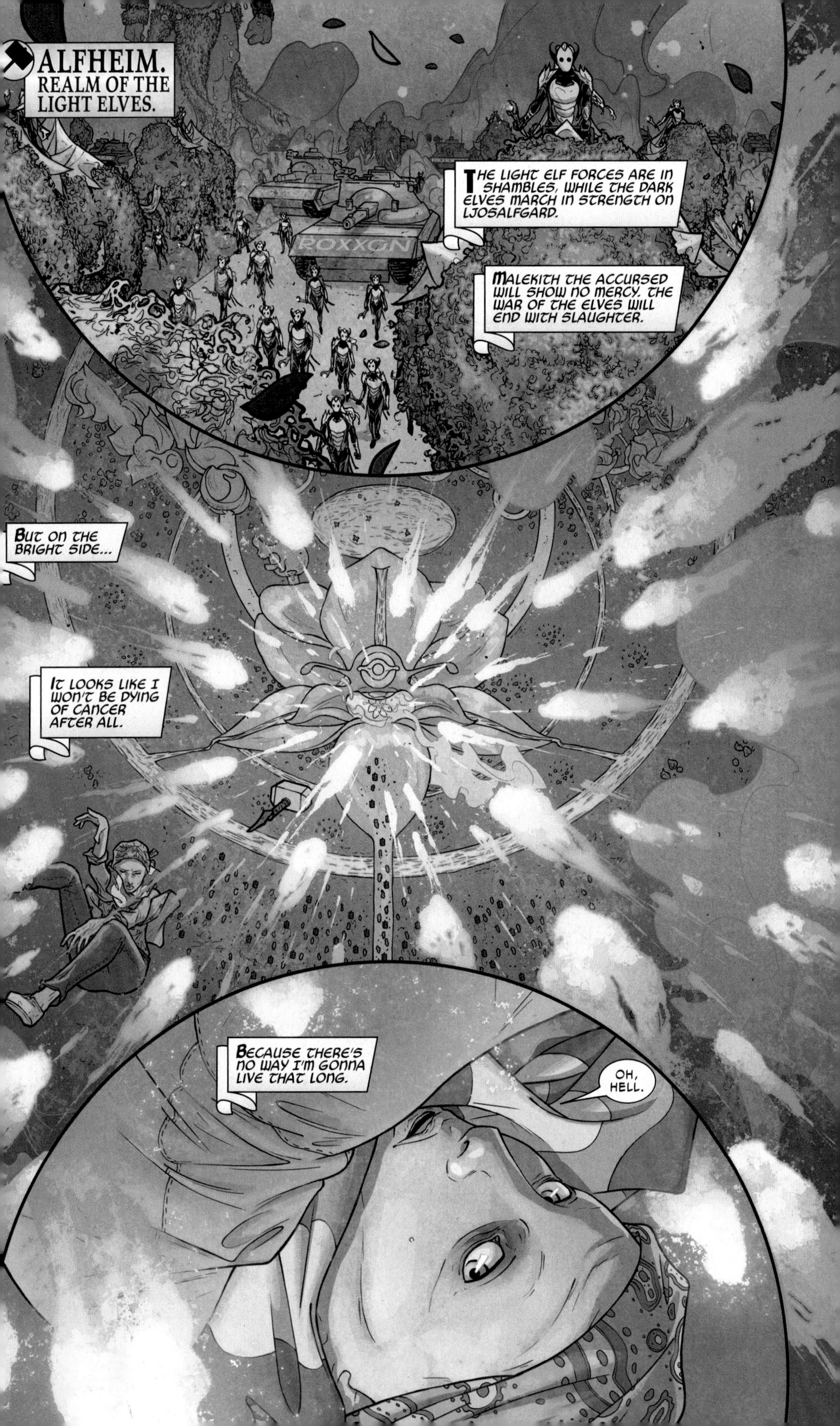
ALFHEIM. REALM OF THE LIGHT ELVES.
ROXXON
THE LIGHT ELF FORCES ARE IN SHAMBLES, WHILE THE DARK ELVES MARCH IN STRENGTH ON LJOSALFGARD.
MALEKITH THE ACCURSED WILL SHOW NO MERCY. THE WAR OF THE ELVES WILL END WITH SLAUGHTER.
BUT ON THE BRIGHT SIDE...
IT LOOKS LIKE I WON'T BE DYING OF CANCER AFTER ALL.
BECAUSE THERE'S NO WAY I'M GONNA LIVE THAT LONG.
OH, HELL.

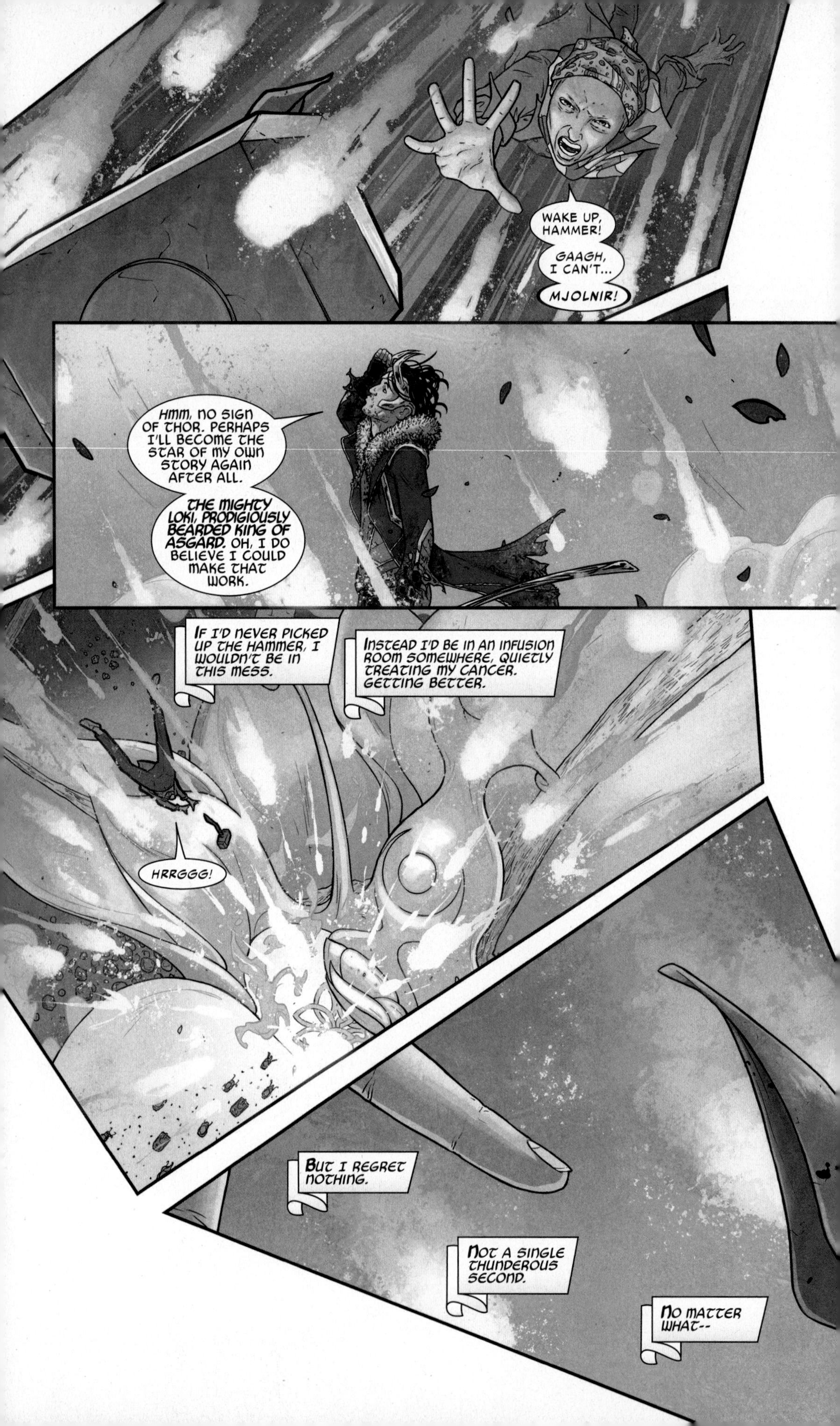

WAKE UP, HAMMER!
GAAGH, I CAN'T...
MJOLNIR!
HMM, NO SIGN OF THOR. PERHAPS I'LL BECOME THE STAR OF MY OWN STORY AGAIN AFTER ALL.
THE MIGHTY LOKI, PRODIGIOUSLY BEARDED KING OF ASGARD. OH, I DO BELIEVE I COULD MAKE THAT WORK.
IF I'D NEVER PICKED UP THE HAMMER, I WOULDN'T BE IN THIS MESS.
INSTEAD I'D BE IN AN INFUSION ROOM SOMEWHERE, QUIETLY TREATING MY CANCER. GETTING BETTER.
HRRGGG!
BUT I REGRET NOTHING.
NOT A SINGLE THUNDEROUS SECOND.
NO MATTER WHAT--

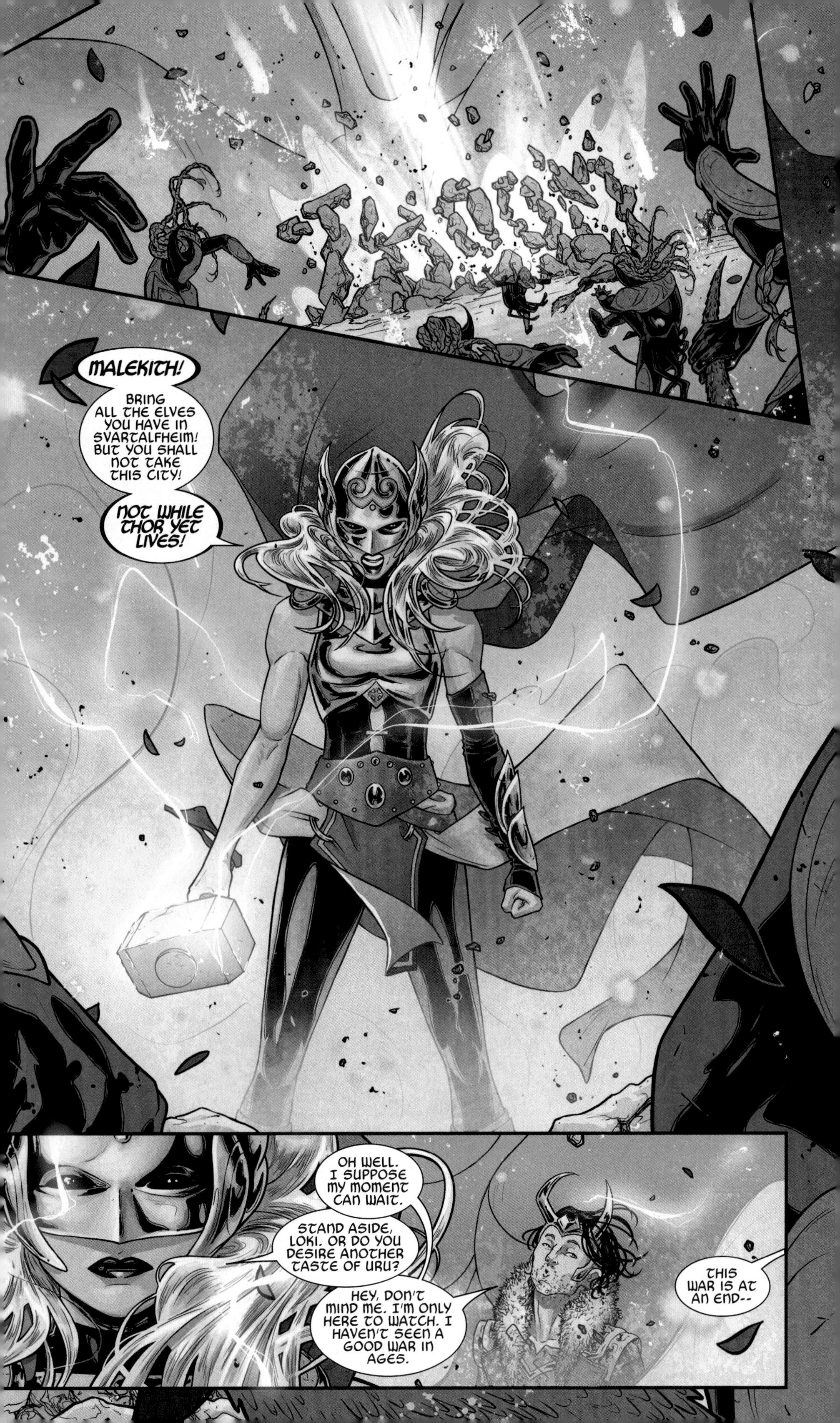

MALEKITH!
BRING ALL THE ELVES YOU HAVE IN SVARTALFHEIM! BUT YOU SHALL NOT TAKE THIS CITY!
NOT WHILE THOR YET LIVES!
OH WELL. I SUPPOSE MY MOMENT CAN WAIT.
STAND ASIDE, LOKI. OR DO YOU DESIRE ANOTHER TASTE OF URU?
HEY, DON'T MIND ME. I'M ONLY HERE TO WATCH. I HAVEN'T SEEN A GOOD WAR IN AGES.
THIS WAR IS AT AN END--

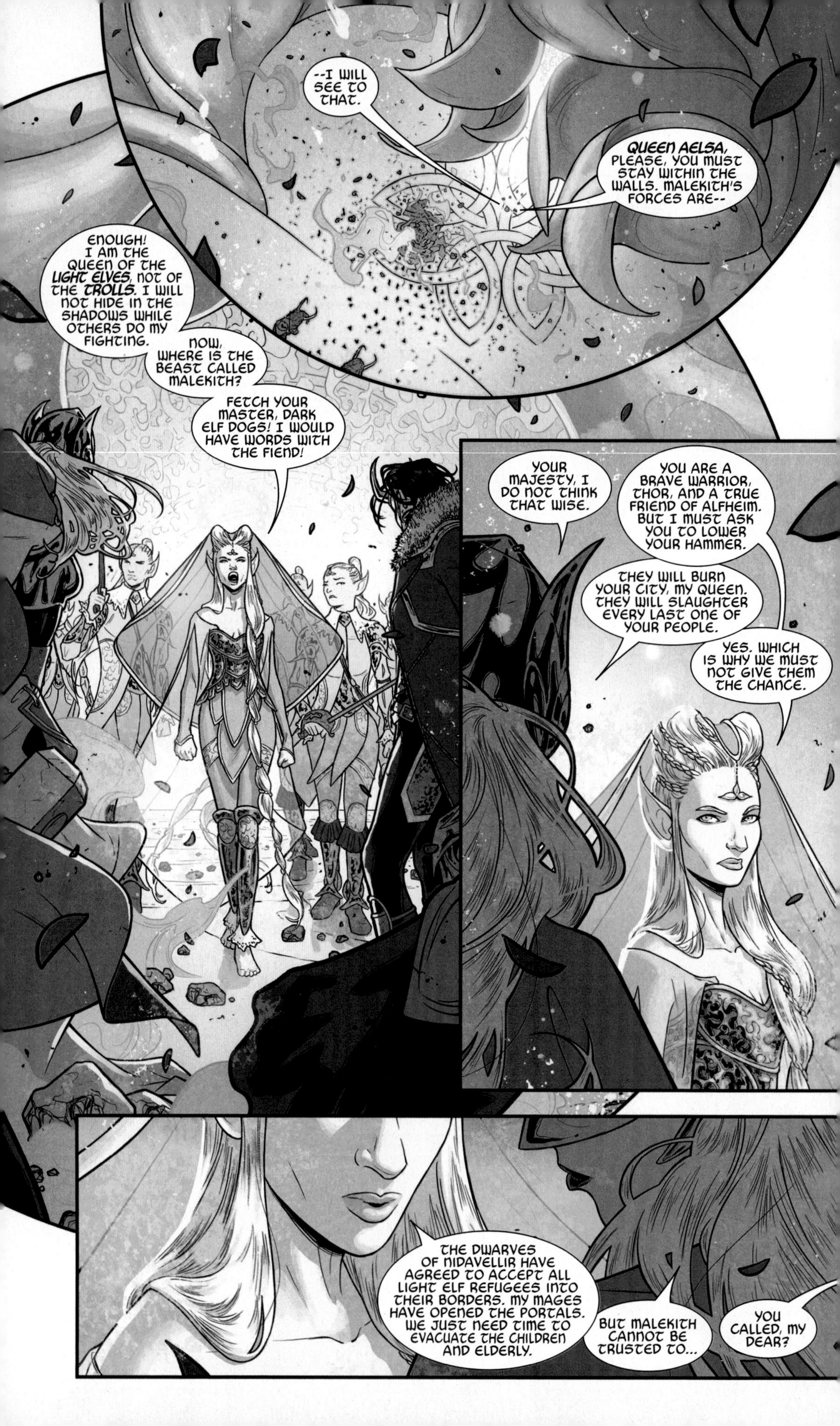

--I WILL SEE TO THAT.
QUEEN AELSA, PLEASE, YOU MUST STAY WITHIN THE WALLS. MALEKITH'S FORCES ARE--
ENOUGH! I AM THE QUEEN OF THE LIGHT ELVES, NOT OF THE TROLLS. I WILL NOT HIDE IN THE SHADOWS WHILE OTHERS DO MY FIGHTING.
NOW, WHERE IS THE BEAST CALLED MALEKITH?
FETCH YOUR MASTER, DARK ELF DOGS! I WOULD HAVE WORDS WITH THE FIEND!
YOUR MAJESTY, I DO NOT THINK THAT WISE.
YOU ARE A BRAVE WARRIOR, THOR, AND A TRUE FRIEND OF ALFHEIM. BUT I MUST ASK YOU TO LOWER YOUR HAMMER.
THEY WILL BURN YOUR CITY, MY QUEEN. THEY WILL SLAUGHTER EVERY LAST ONE OF YOUR PEOPLE.
YES. WHICH IS WHY WE MUST NOT GIVE THEM THE CHANCE.
THE DWARVES OF NIDAVELLIR HAVE AGREED TO ACCEPT ALL LIGHT ELF REFUGEES INTO THEIR BORDERS. MY MAGES HAVE OPENED THE PORTALS. WE JUST NEED TIME TO EVACUATE THE CHILDREN AND ELDERLY.
BUT MALEKITH CANNOT BE TRUSTED TO...
YOU CALLED, MY DEAR?

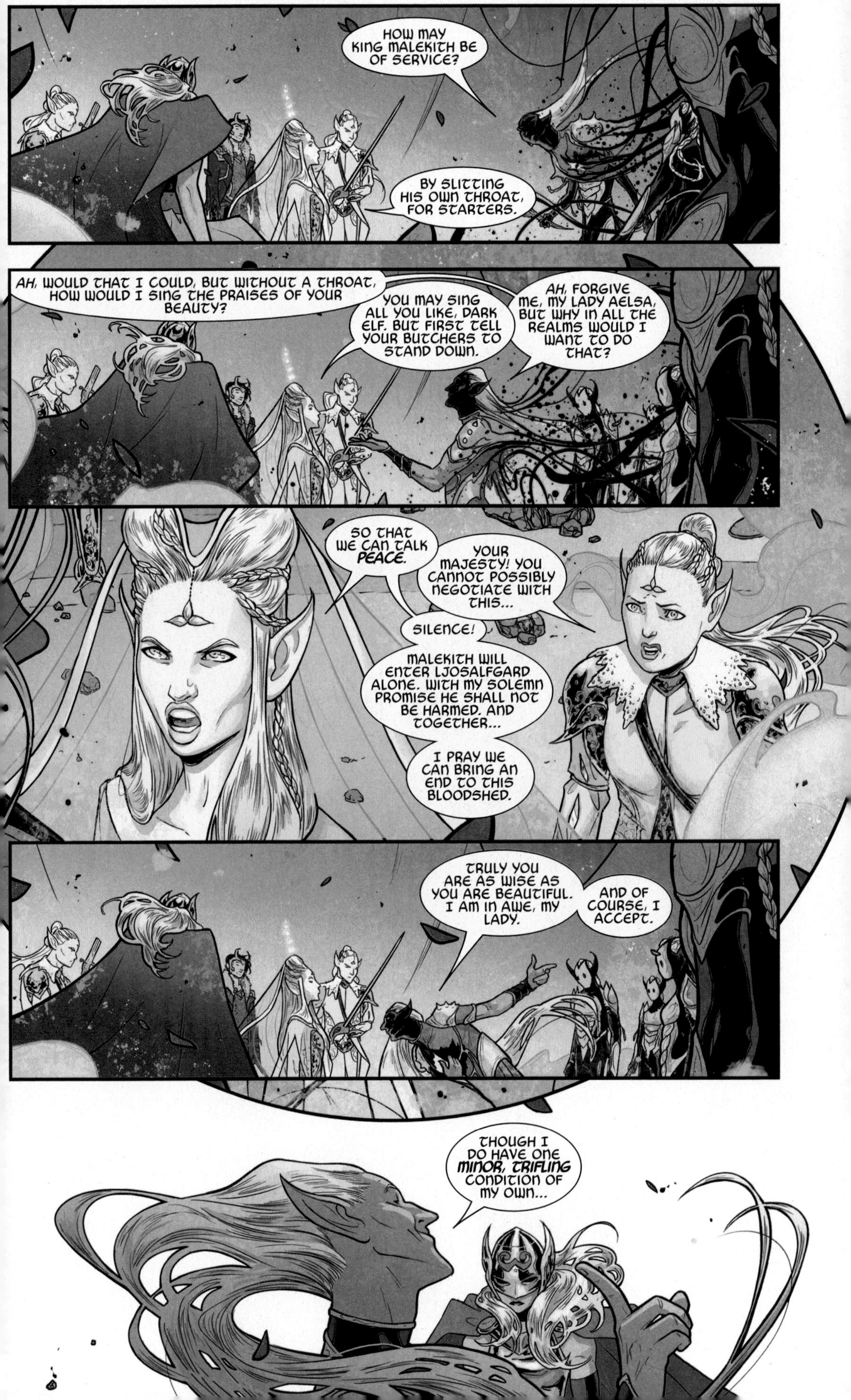
HOW MAY KING MALEKITH BE OF SERVICE?
BY SLITTING HIS OWN THROAT, FOR STARTERS.
AH, WOULD THAT I COULD, BUT WITHOUT A THROAT, HOW WOULD I SING THE PRAISES OF YOUR BEAUTY?
YOU MAY SING ALL YOU LIKE, DARK ELF. BUT FIRST TELL YOUR BUTCHERS TO STAND DOWN.
AH, FORGIVE ME, MY LADY AELSA, BUT WHY IN ALL THE REALMS WOULD I WANT TO DO THAT?
SO THAT WE CAN TALK PEACE.
YOUR MAJESTY! YOU CANNOT POSSIBLY NEGOTIATE WITH THIS...
SILENCE!
MALEKITH WILL ENTER LJOSALFGARD ALONE. WITH MY SOLEMN PROMISE HE SHALL NOT BE HARMED. AND TOGETHER...
I PRAY WE CAN BRING AN END TO THIS BLOODSHED.
TRULY YOU ARE AS WISE AS YOU ARE BEAUTIFUL. I AM IN AWE, MY LADY.
AND OF COURSE, I ACCEPT.
THOUGH I DO HAVE ONE MINOR, TRIFLING CONDITION OF MY OWN...

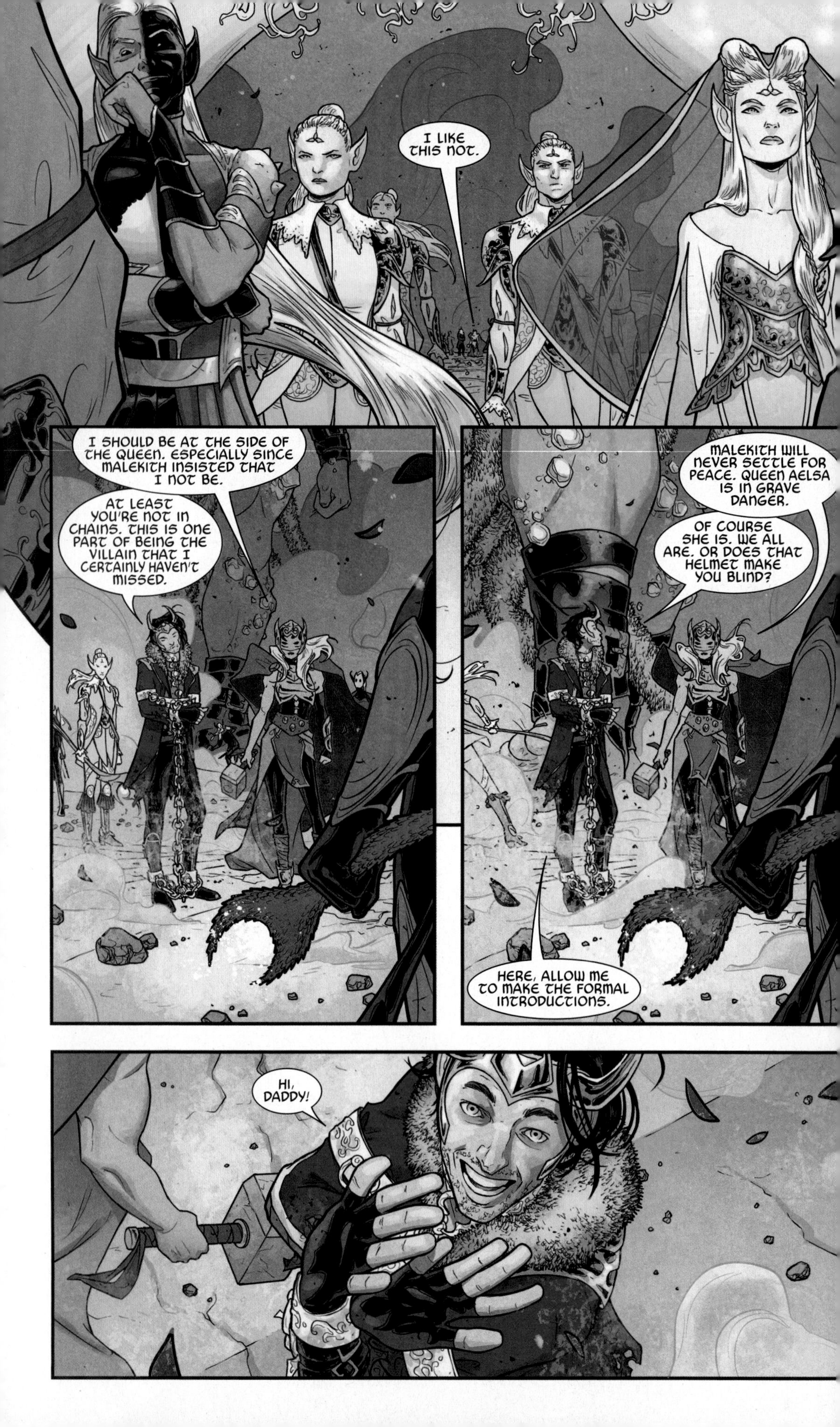
I LIKE THIS NOT.
I SHOULD BE AT THE SIDE OF THE QUEEN. ESPECIALLY SINCE MALEKITH INSISTED THAT I NOT BE.
AT LEAST YOU'RE NOT IN CHAINS. THIS IS ONE PART OF BEING THE VILLAIN THAT I CERTAINLY HAVEN'T MISSED.
MALEKITH WILL NEVER SETTLE FOR PEACE. QUEEN AELSA IS IN GRAVE DANGER.
OF COURSE SHE IS. WE ALL ARE. OR DOES THAT HELMET MAKE YOU BLIND?
HERE, ALLOW ME TO MAKE THE FORMAL INTRODUCTIONS.
HI, DADDY!

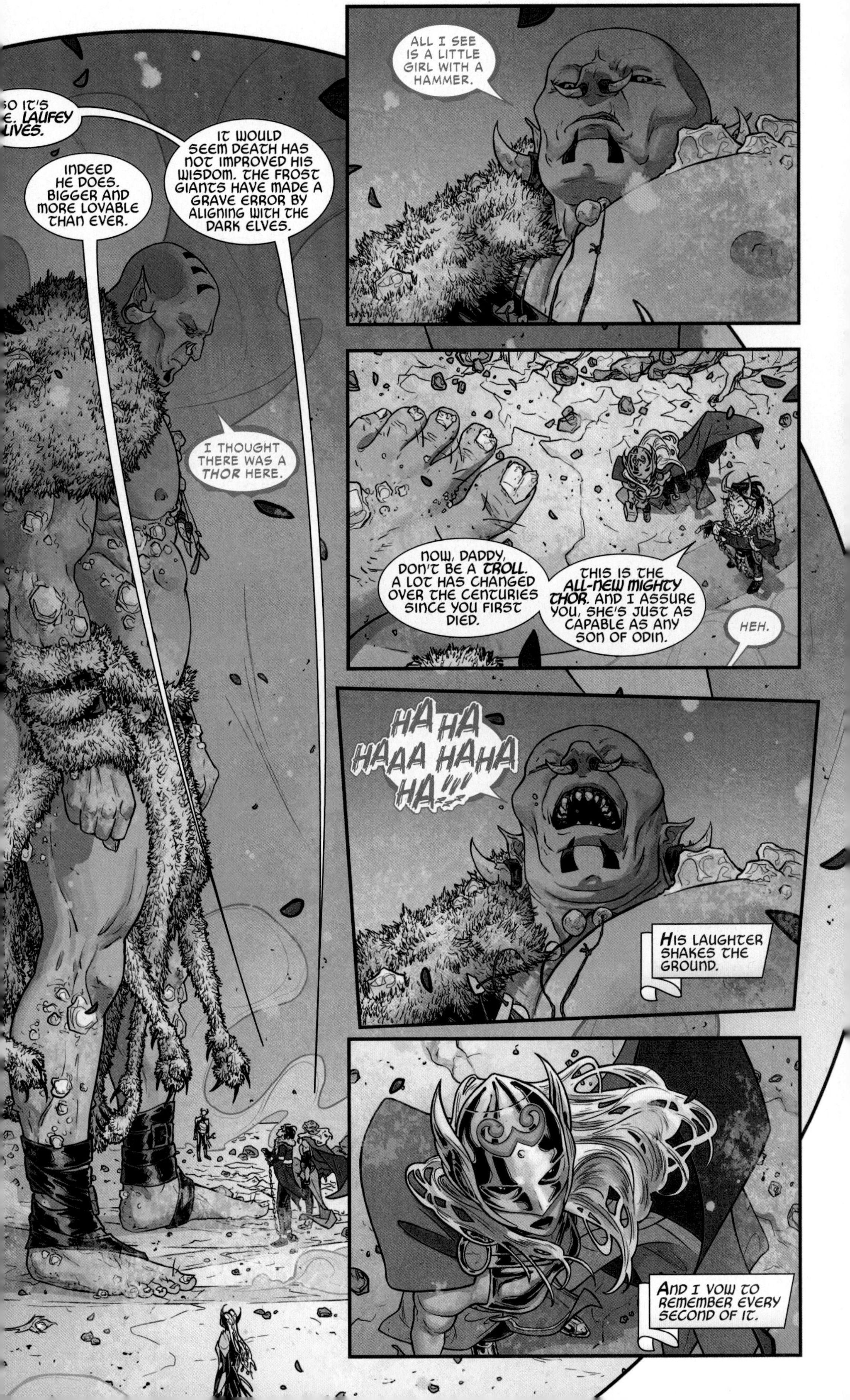

SO IT'S
E. LAUFEY
LIVES.
INDEED HE DOES. BIGGER AND MORE LOVABLE THAN EVER.
IT WOULD SEEM DEATH HAS NOT IMPROVED HIS WISDOM. THE FROST GIANTS HAVE MADE A GRAVE ERROR BY ALIGNING WITH THE DARK ELVES.
I THOUGHT THERE WAS A THOR HERE.
ALL I SEE IS A LITTLE GIRL WITH A HAMMER.
NOW, DADDY, DON'T BE A TROLL. A LOT HAS CHANGED OVER THE CENTURIES SINCE YOU FIRST DIED.
THIS IS THE ALL-NEW MIGHTY THOR. AND I ASSURE YOU, SHE'S JUST AS CAPABLE AS ANY SON OF ODIN.
HEH.
HA HA HAAA HAHA HA!!!
HIS LAUGHTER SHAKES THE GROUND.
AND I VOW TO REMEMBER EVERY SECOND OF IT.

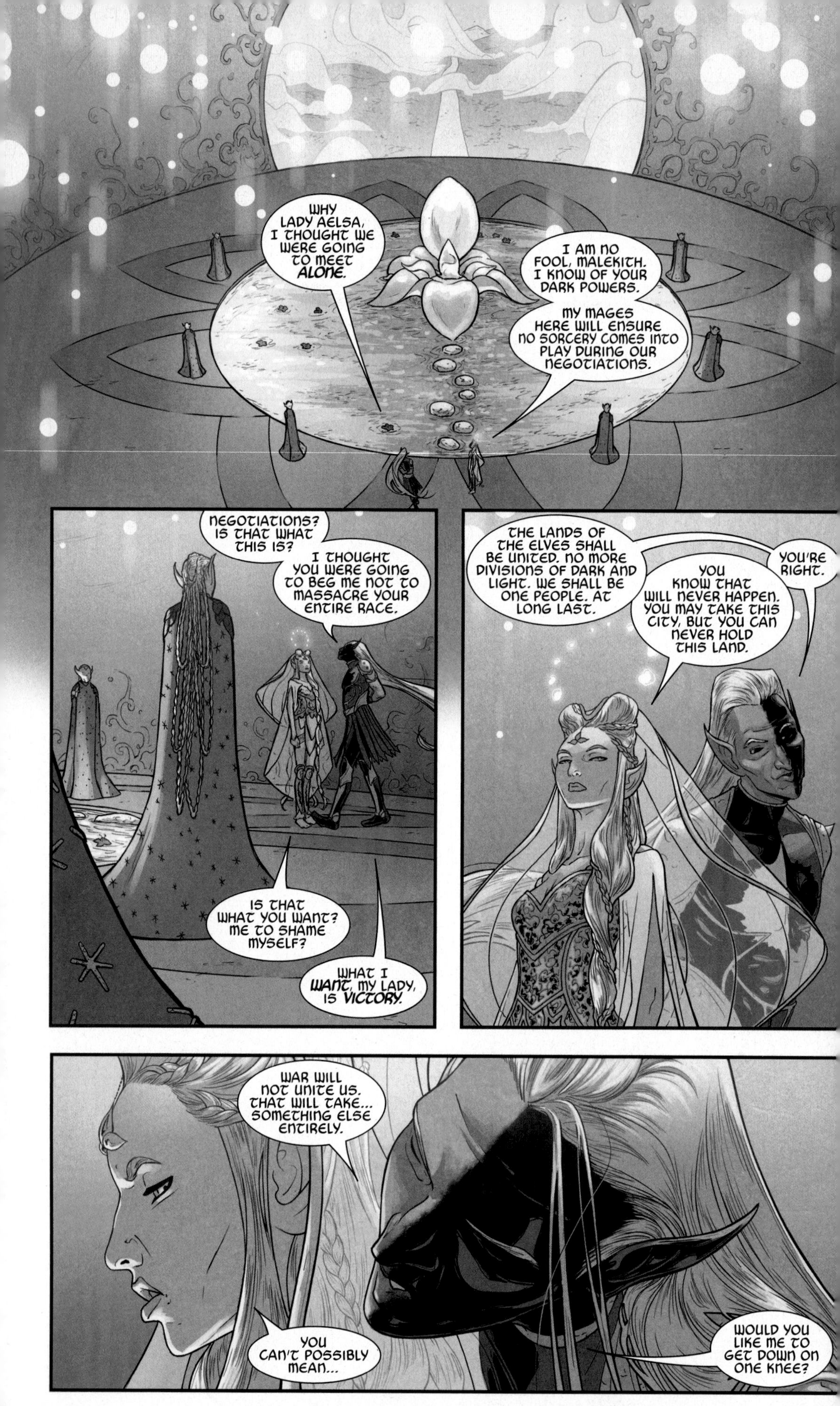
WHY LADY AELSA, I THOUGHT WE WERE GOING TO MEET ALONE.
I AM NO FOOL, MALEKITH. I KNOW OF YOUR DARK POWERS.
MY MAGES HERE WILL ENSURE NO SORCERY COMES INTO PLAY DURING OUR NEGOTIATIONS.
NEGOTIATIONS? IS THAT WHAT THIS IS?
I THOUGHT YOU WERE GOING TO BEG ME NOT TO MASSACRE YOUR ENTIRE RACE.
IS THAT WHAT YOU WANT? ME TO SHAME MYSELF?
WHAT I WANT, MY LADY, IS VICTORY.
THE LANDS OF THE ELVES SHALL BE UNITED. NO MORE DIVISIONS OF DARK AND LIGHT. WE SHALL BE ONE PEOPLE. AT LONG LAST.
YOU KNOW THAT WILL NEVER HAPPEN. YOU MAY TAKE THIS CITY, BUT YOU CAN NEVER HOLD THIS LAND.
YOU'RE RIGHT.
WAR WILL NOT UNITE US. THAT WILL TAKE... SOMETHING ELSE ENTIRELY.
YOU CAN'T POSSIBLY MEAN...
WOULD YOU LIKE ME TO GET DOWN ON ONE KNEE?

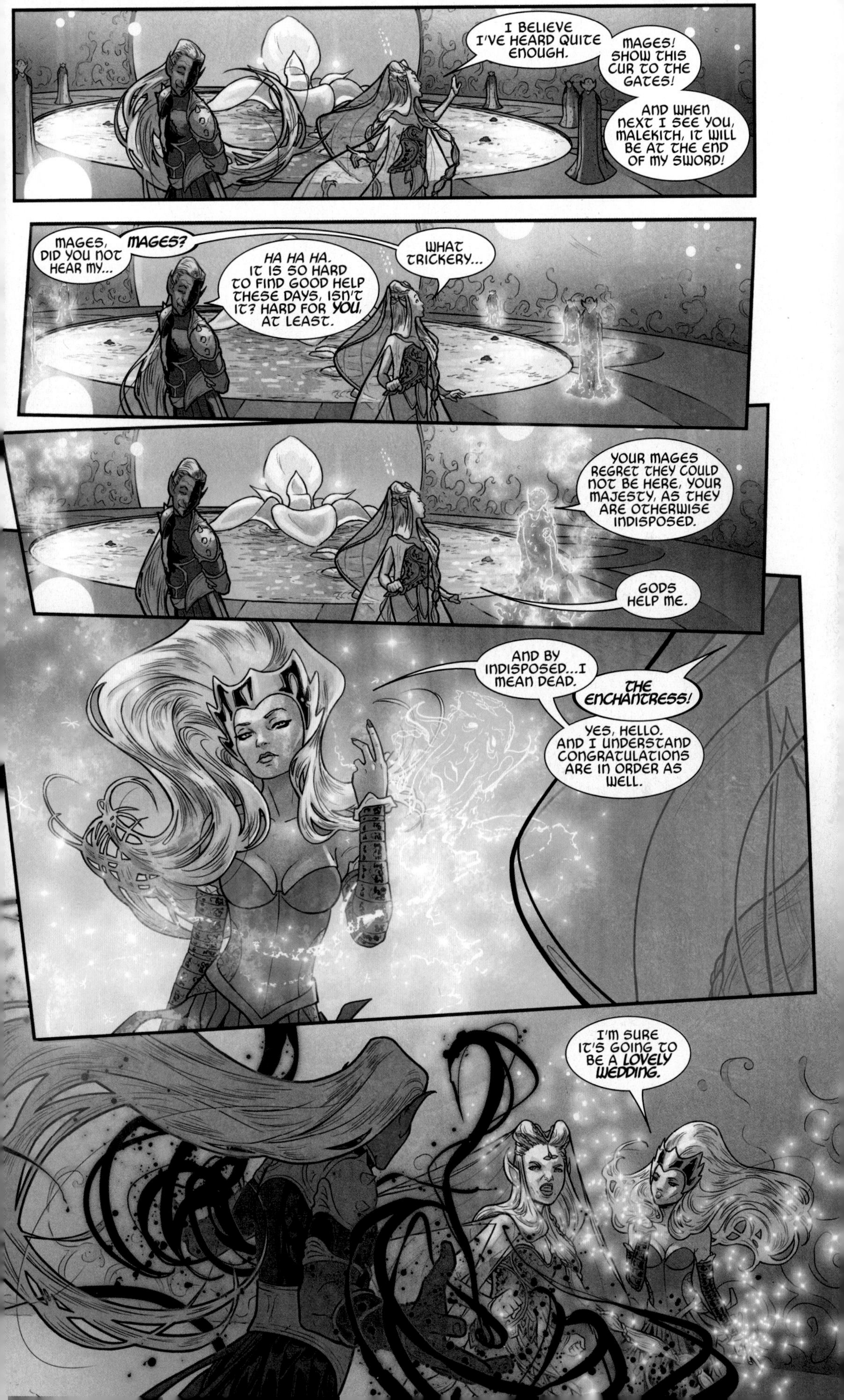
I BELIEVE I'VE HEARD QUITE ENOUGH.
MAGES! SHOW THIS CUR TO THE GATES!
AND WHEN NEXT I SEE YOU, MALEKITH, IT WILL BE AT THE END OF MY SWORD!
MAGES, DID YOU NOT HEAR MY...
MAGES?
HA HA HA. IT IS SO HARD TO FIND GOOD HELP THESE DAYS, ISN'T IT? HARD FOR YOU, AT LEAST.
WHAT TRICKERY...
YOUR MAGES REGRET THEY COULD NOT BE HERE, YOUR MAJESTY, AS THEY ARE OTHERWISE INDISPOSED.
GODS HELP ME.
AND BY INDISPOSED...I MEAN DEAD.
THE ENCHANTRESS!
YES, HELLO. AND I UNDERSTAND CONGRATULATIONS ARE IN ORDER AS WELL.
I'M SURE IT'S GOING TO BE A LOVELY WEDDING.

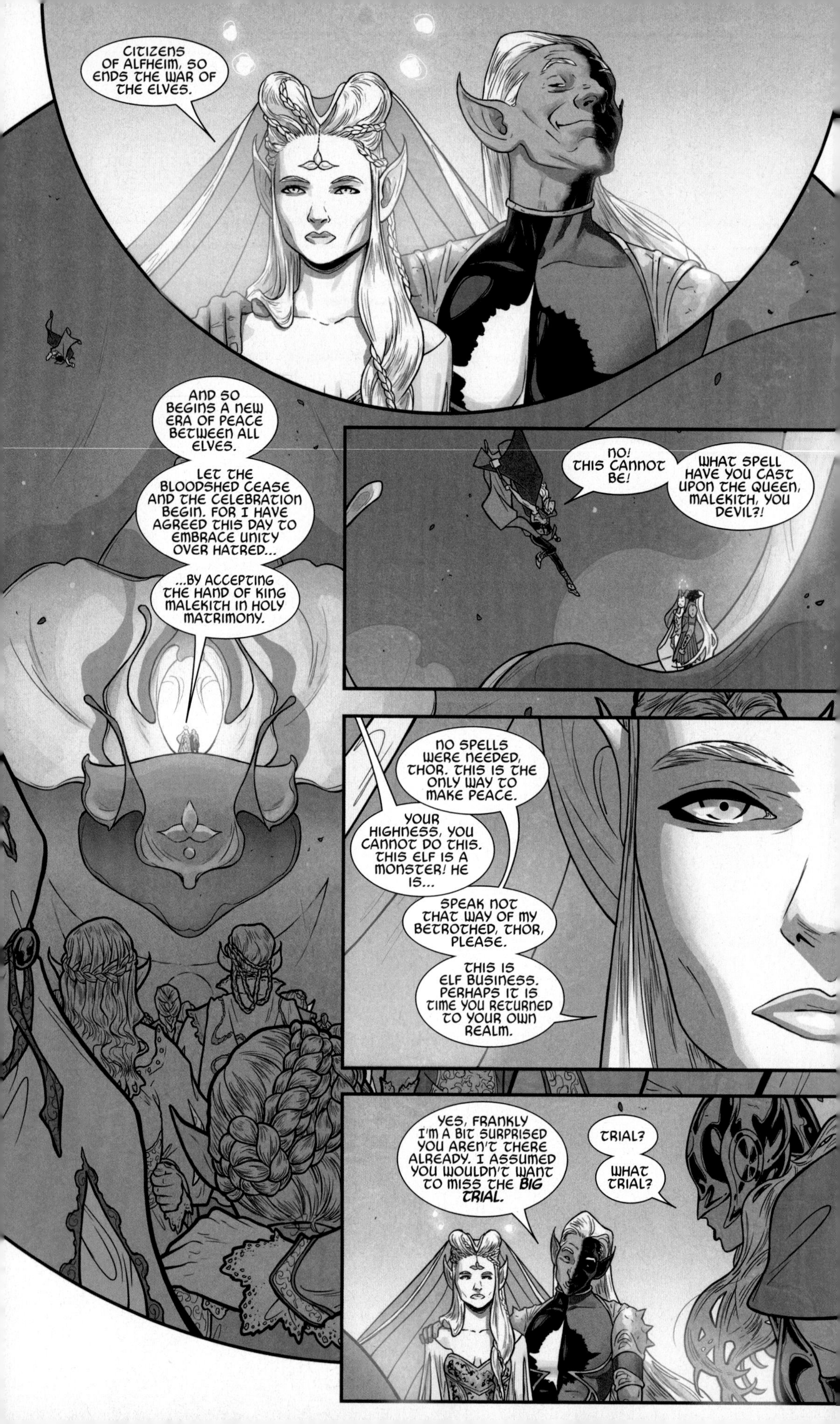
CITIZENS OF ALFHEIM, SO ENDS THE WAR OF THE ELVES.
AND SO BEGINS A NEW ERA OF PEACE BETWEEN ALL ELVES.
LET THE BLOODSHED CEASE AND THE CELEBRATION BEGIN. FOR I HAVE AGREED THIS DAY TO EMBRACE UNITY OVER HATRED...
...BY ACCEPTING THE HAND OF KING MALEKITH IN HOLY MATRIMONY.
NO! THIS CANNOT BE!
WHAT SPELL HAVE YOU CAST UPON THE QUEEN, MALEKITH, YOU DEVIL?!
NO SPELLS WERE NEEDED, THOR. THIS IS THE ONLY WAY TO MAKE PEACE.
YOUR HIGHNESS, YOU CANNOT DO THIS. THIS ELF IS A MONSTER! HE IS...
SPEAK NOT THAT WAY OF MY BETROTHED, THOR, PLEASE.
THIS IS ELF BUSINESS. PERHAPS IT IS TIME YOU RETURNED TO YOUR OWN REALM.
YES, FRANKLY I'M A BIT SURPRISED YOU AREN'T THERE ALREADY. I ASSUMED YOU WOULDN'T WANT TO MISS THE **BIG TRIAL.**
TRIAL?
WHAT TRIAL?

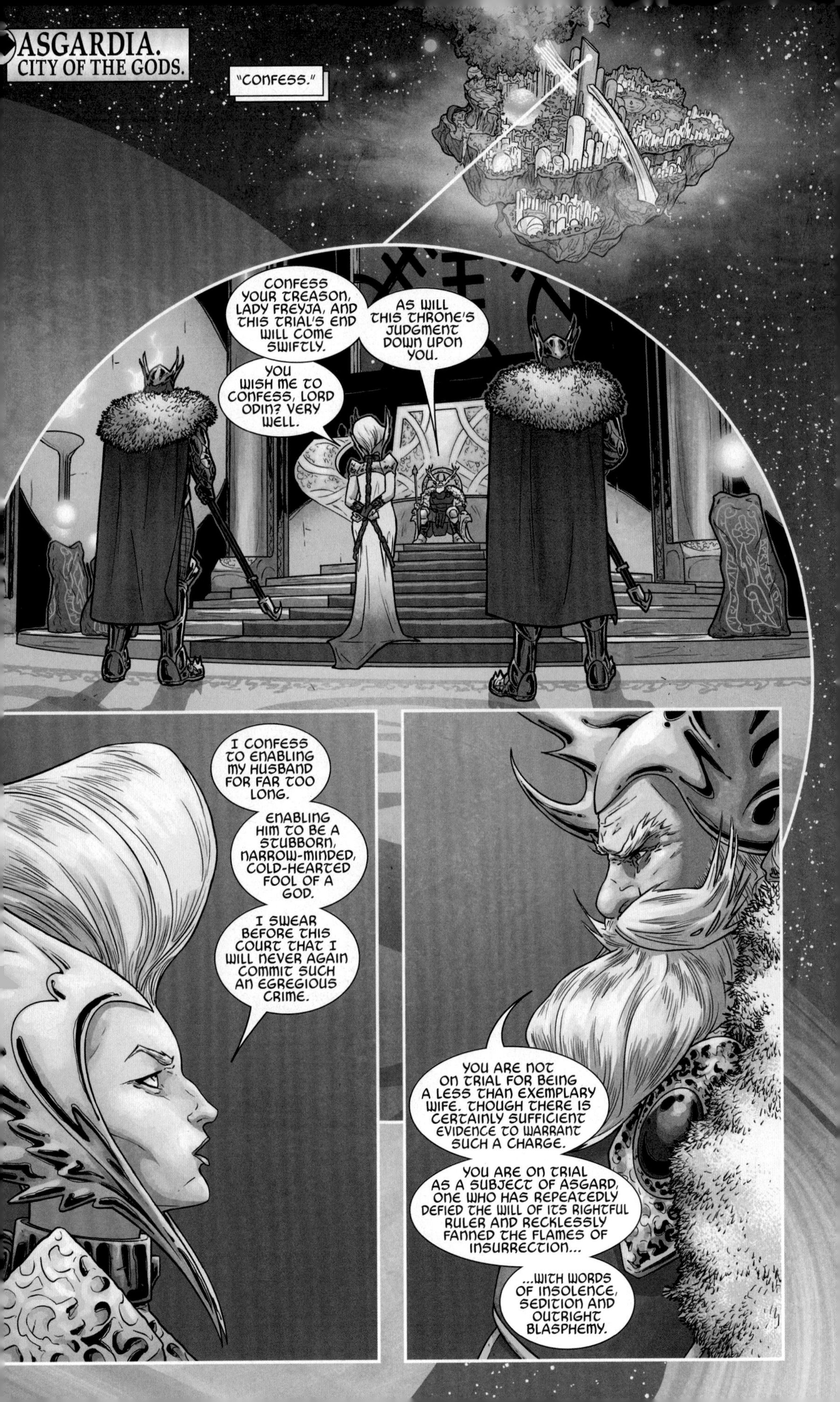
ASGARDIA. CITY OF THE GODS.
"CONFESS."
CONFESS YOUR TREASON, LADY FREYJA, AND THIS TRIAL'S END WILL COME SWIFTLY.
AS WILL THIS THRONE'S JUDGMENT DOWN UPON YOU.
YOU WISH ME TO CONFESS, LORD ODIN? VERY WELL.
I CONFESS TO ENABLING MY HUSBAND FOR FAR TOO LONG.
ENABLING HIM TO BE A STUBBORN, NARROW-MINDED, COLD-HEARTED FOOL OF A GOD.
I SWEAR BEFORE THIS COURT THAT I WILL NEVER AGAIN COMMIT SUCH AN EGREGIOUS CRIME.
YOU ARE NOT ON TRIAL FOR BEING A LESS THAN EXEMPLARY WIFE. THOUGH THERE IS CERTAINLY SUFFICIENT EVIDENCE TO WARRANT SUCH A CHARGE.
YOU ARE ON TRIAL AS A SUBJECT OF ASGARD, ONE WHO HAS REPEATEDLY DEFIED THE WILL OF ITS RIGHTFUL RULER AND RECKLESSLY FANNED THE FLAMES OF INSURRECTION...
...WITH WORDS OF INSOLENCE, SEDITION AND OUTRIGHT BLASPHEMY.

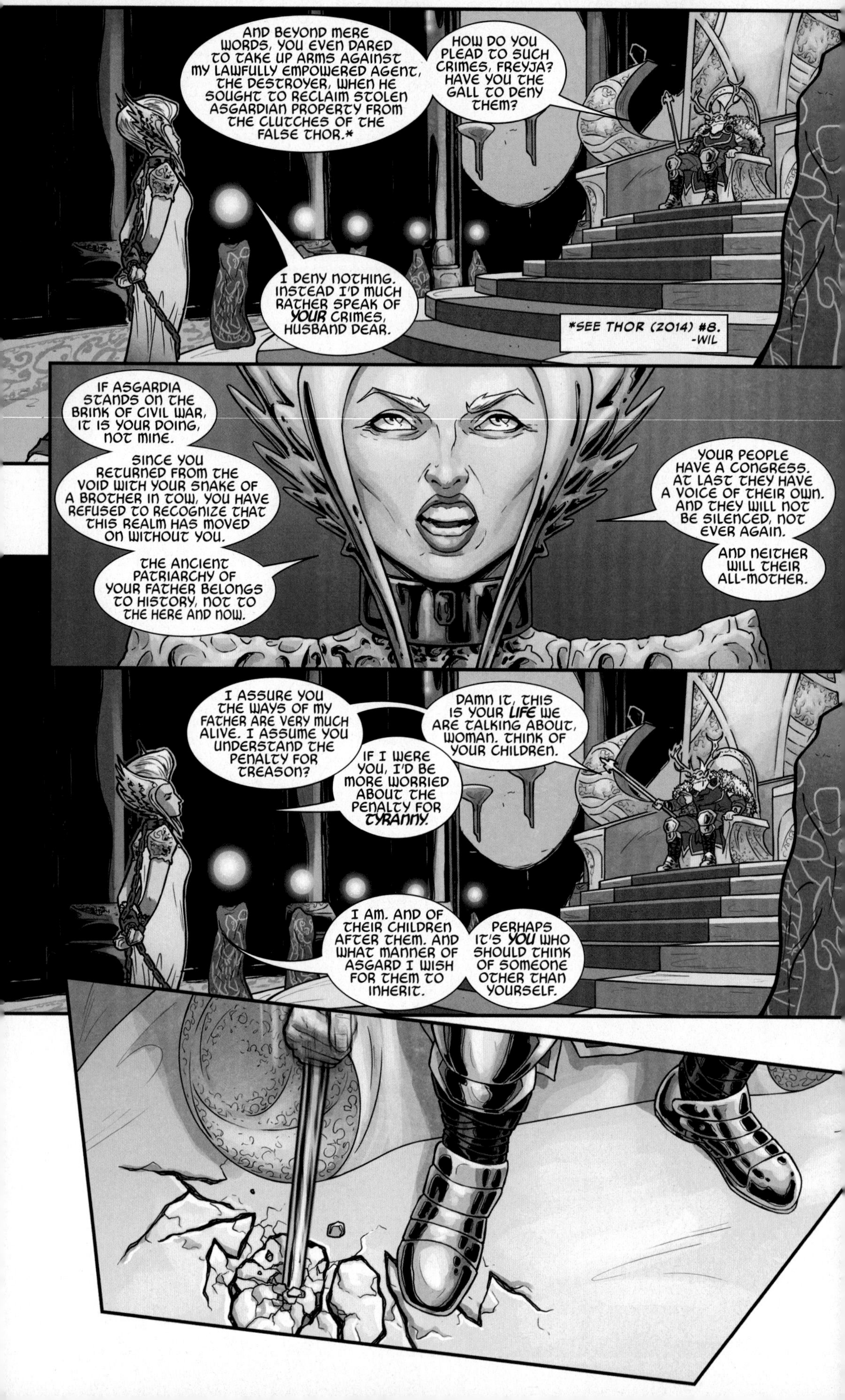
AND BEYOND MERE WORDS, YOU EVEN DARED TO TAKE UP ARMS AGAINST MY LAWFULLY EMPOWERED AGENT, THE DESTROYER, WHEN HE SOUGHT TO RECLAIM STOLEN ASGARDIAN PROPERTY FROM THE CLUTCHES OF THE FALSE THOR.*
HOW DO YOU PLEAD TO SUCH CRIMES, FREYJA? HAVE YOU THE GALL TO DENY THEM?
I DENY NOTHING. INSTEAD I'D MUCH RATHER SPEAK OF *YOUR* CRIMES, HUSBAND DEAR.
*SEE THOR (2014) #8. -WIL
IF ASGARDIA STANDS ON THE BRINK OF CIVIL WAR, IT IS YOUR DOING, NOT MINE.
SINCE YOU RETURNED FROM THE VOID WITH YOUR SNAKE OF A BROTHER IN TOW, YOU HAVE REFUSED TO RECOGNIZE THAT THIS REALM HAS MOVED ON WITHOUT YOU.
THE ANCIENT PATRIARCHY OF YOUR FATHER BELONGS TO HISTORY, NOT TO THE HERE AND NOW.
YOUR PEOPLE HAVE A CONGRESS. AT LAST THEY HAVE A VOICE OF THEIR OWN. AND THEY WILL NOT BE SILENCED, NOT EVER AGAIN.
AND NEITHER WILL THEIR ALL-MOTHER.
I ASSURE YOU THE WAYS OF MY FATHER ARE VERY MUCH ALIVE. I ASSUME YOU UNDERSTAND THE PENALTY FOR TREASON?
IF I WERE YOU, I'D BE MORE WORRIED ABOUT THE PENALTY FOR *TYRANNY*.
DAMN IT, THIS IS YOUR *LIFE* WE ARE TALKING ABOUT, WOMAN. THINK OF YOUR CHILDREN.
I AM. AND OF THEIR CHILDREN AFTER THEM. AND WHAT MANNER OF ASGARD I WISH FOR THEM TO INHERIT.
PERHAPS IT'S *YOU* WHO SHOULD THINK OF SOMEONE OTHER THAN YOURSELF.

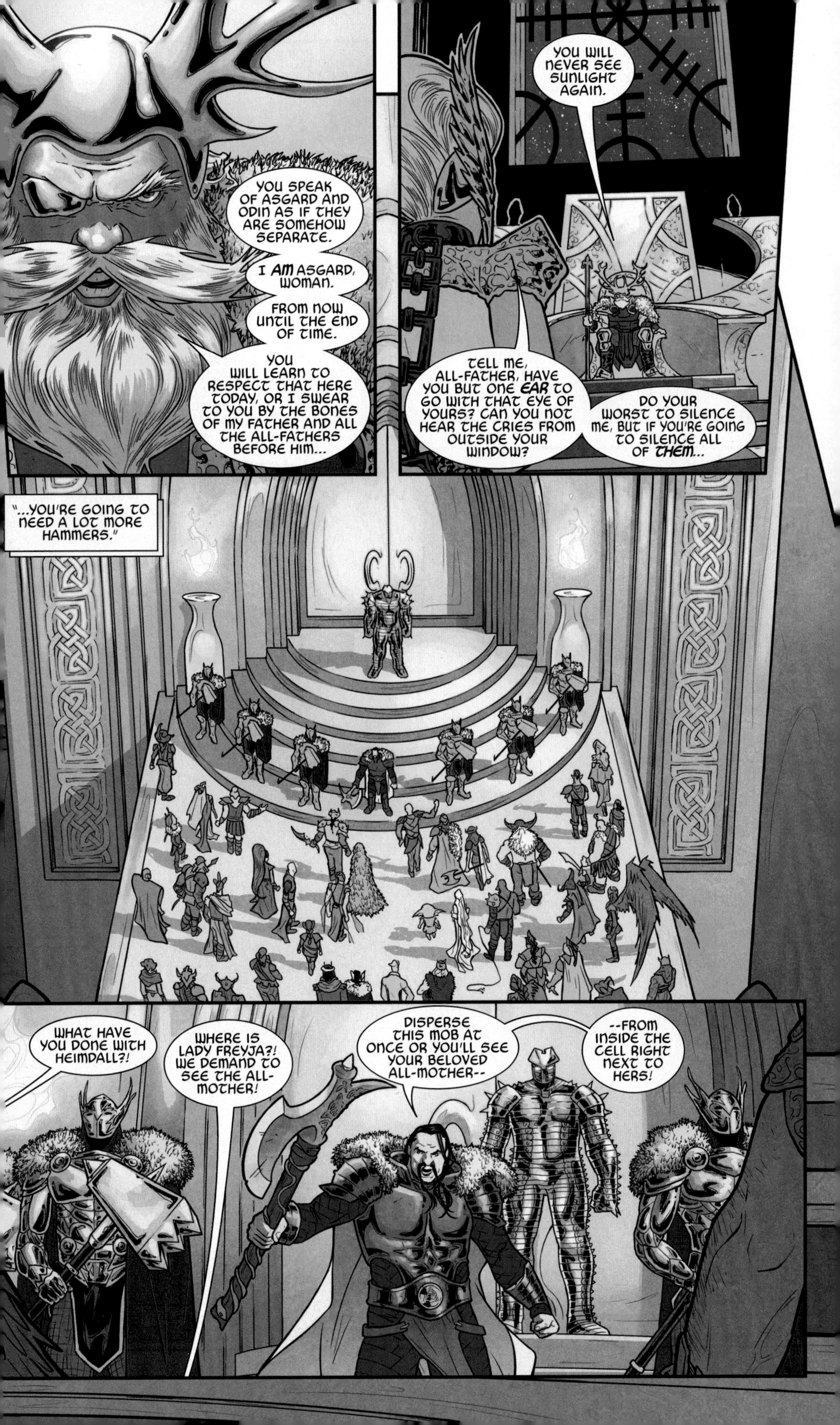
YOU SPEAK OF ASGARD AND ODIN AS IF THEY ARE SOMEHOW SEPARATE.
I AM ASGARD, WOMAN.
FROM NOW UNTIL THE END OF TIME.
YOU WILL LEARN TO RESPECT THAT HERE TODAY, OR I SWEAR TO YOU BY THE BONES OF MY FATHER AND ALL THE ALL-FATHERS BEFORE HIM...
YOU WILL NEVER SEE SUNLIGHT AGAIN.
TELL ME, ALL-FATHER, HAVE YOU BUT ONE EAR TO GO WITH THAT EYE OF YOURS? CAN YOU NOT HEAR THE CRIES FROM OUTSIDE YOUR WINDOW?
DO YOUR WORST TO SILENCE ME, BUT IF YOU'RE GOING TO SILENCE ALL OF THEM...
"...YOU'RE GOING TO NEED A LOT MORE HAMMERS."
WHAT HAVE YOU DONE WITH HEIMDALL?!
WHERE IS LADY FREYJA?! WE DEMAND TO SEE THE ALL-MOTHER!
DISPERSE THIS MOB AT ONCE OR YOU'LL SEE YOUR BELOVED ALL-MOTHER--
--FROM INSIDE THE CELL RIGHT NEXT TO HERS!

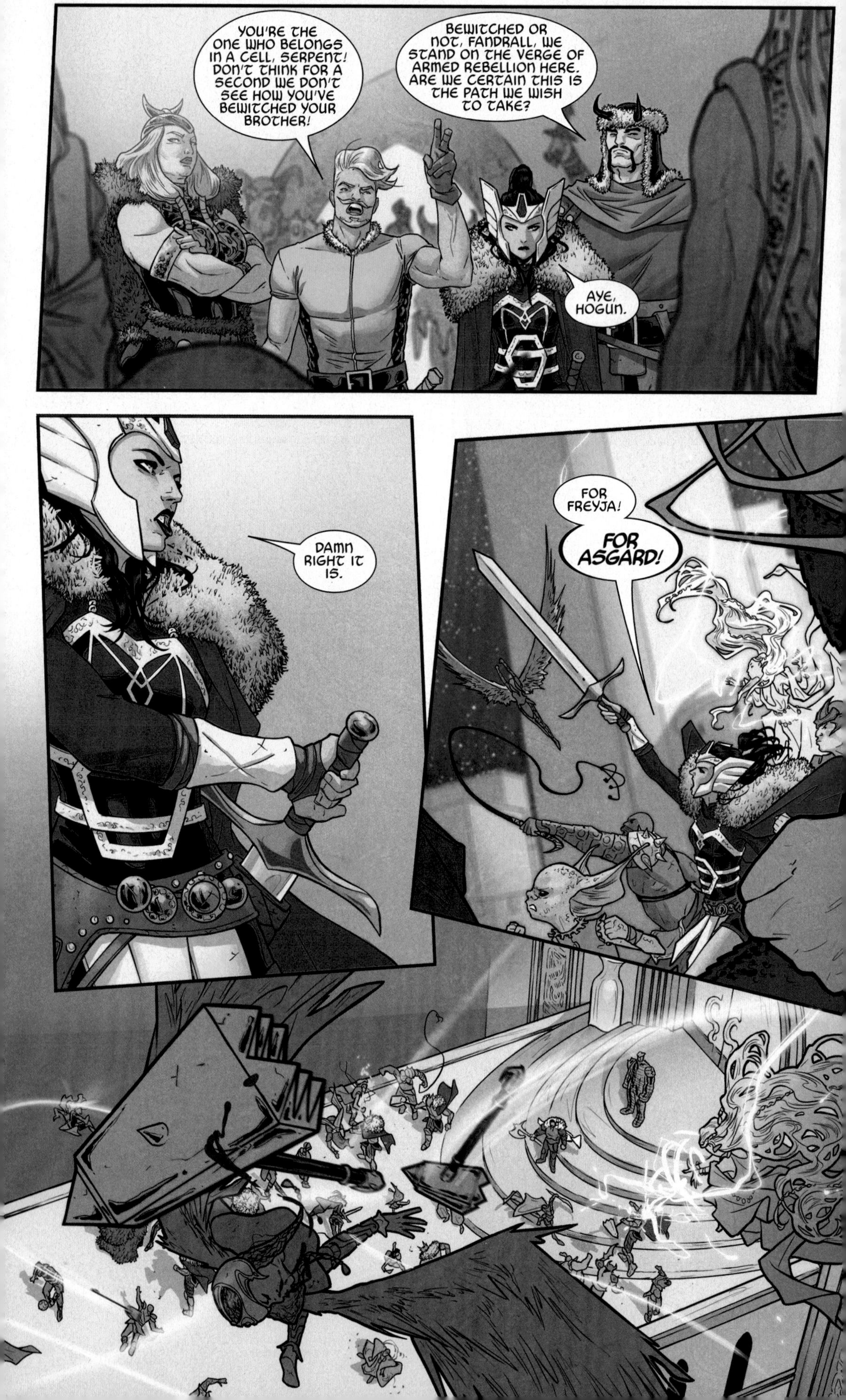
YOU'RE THE ONE WHO BELONGS IN A CELL, SERPENT! DON'T THINK FOR A SECOND WE DON'T SEE HOW YOU'VE BEWITCHED YOUR BROTHER!
BEWITCHED OR NOT, FANDRALL, WE STAND ON THE VERGE OF ARMED REBELLION HERE. ARE WE CERTAIN THIS IS THE PATH WE WISH TO TAKE?
AYE, HOGUN.
DAMN RIGHT IT IS.
FOR FREYJA!
FOR ASGARD!

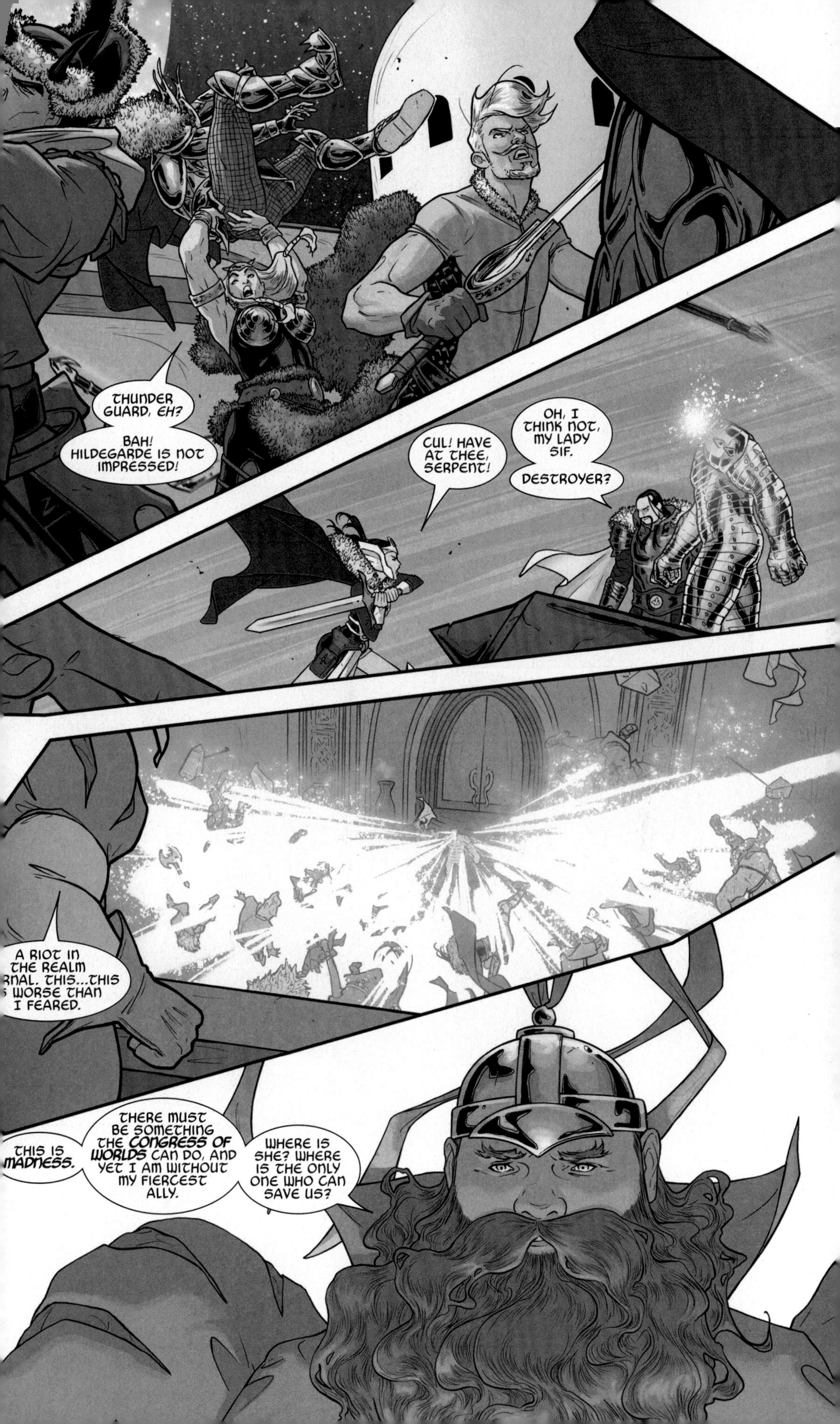
THUNDER GUARD, EH?
BAH! HILDEGARDE IS NOT IMPRESSED!
CUL! HAVE AT THEE, SERPENT!
OH, I THINK NOT, MY LADY SIF.
DESTROYER?
A RIOT IN THE REALM ...RNAL. THIS...THIS ...S WORSE THAN I FEARED.
THIS IS MADNESS.
THERE MUST BE SOMETHING THE CONGRESS OF WORLDS CAN DO, AND YET I AM WITHOUT MY FIERCEST ALLY.
WHERE IS SHE? WHERE IS THE ONLY ONE WHO CAN SAVE US?

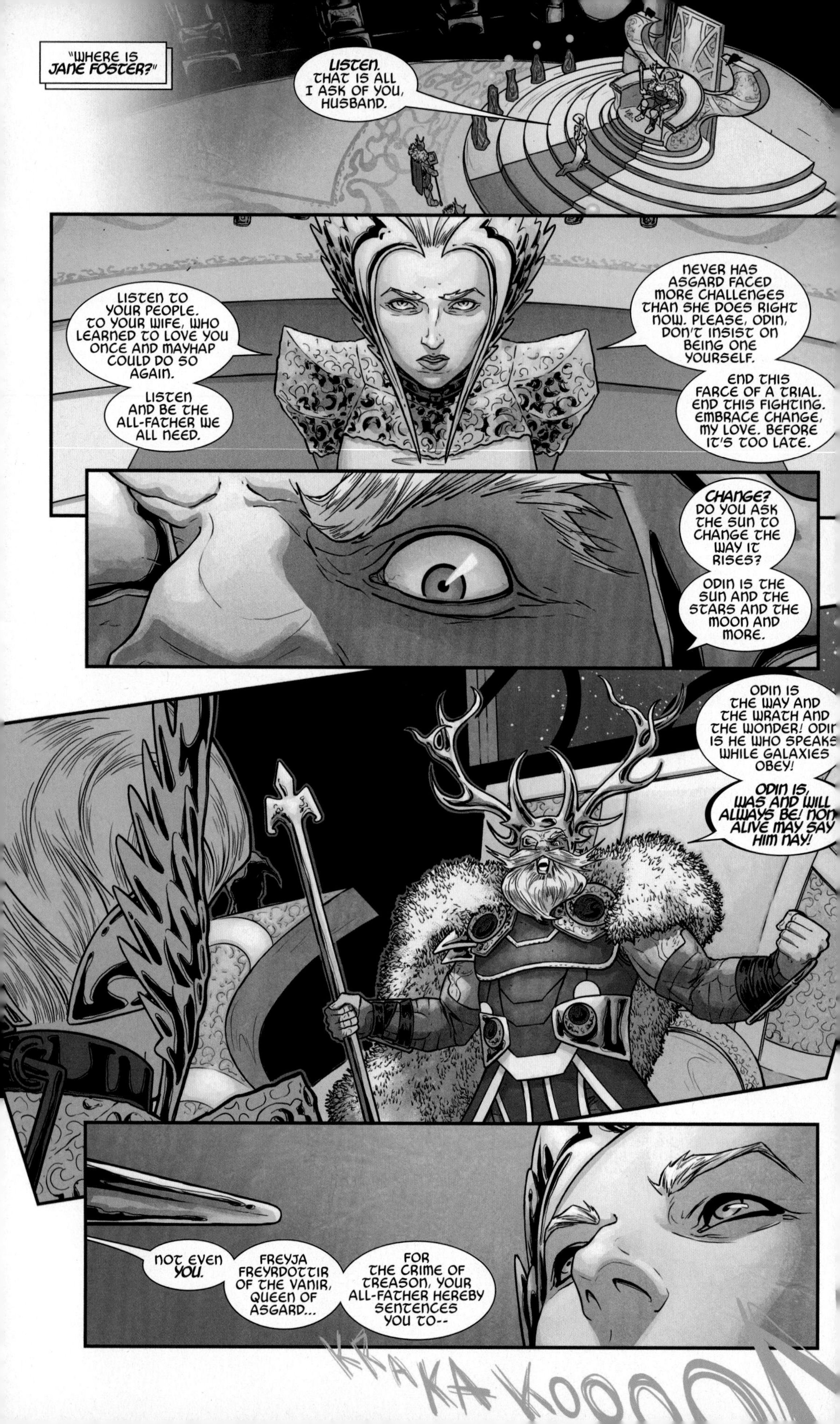
"WHERE IS JANE FOSTER?"
LISTEN. THAT IS ALL I ASK OF YOU, HUSBAND.
LISTEN TO YOUR PEOPLE. TO YOUR WIFE, WHO LEARNED TO LOVE YOU ONCE AND MAYHAP COULD DO SO AGAIN.
LISTEN AND BE THE ALL-FATHER WE ALL NEED.
NEVER HAS ASGARD FACED MORE CHALLENGES THAN SHE DOES RIGHT NOW. PLEASE, ODIN, DON'T INSIST ON BEING ONE YOURSELF.
END THIS FARCE OF A TRIAL. END THIS FIGHTING. EMBRACE CHANGE, MY LOVE. BEFORE IT'S TOO LATE.
CHANGE? DO YOU ASK THE SUN TO CHANGE THE WAY IT RISES?
ODIN IS THE SUN AND THE STARS AND THE MOON AND MORE.
ODIN IS THE WAY AND THE WRATH AND THE WONDER! ODIN IS HE WHO SPEAKS WHILE GALAXIES OBEY!
ODIN IS, WAS AND WILL ALWAYS BE! NON ALIVE MAY SAY HIM NAY!
NOT EVEN YOU.
FREYJA FREYRDOTTIR OF THE VANIR, QUEEN OF ASGARD...
FOR THE CRIME OF TREASON, YOUR ALL-FATHER HEREBY SENTENCES YOU TO--
KRAKAKOOOOM

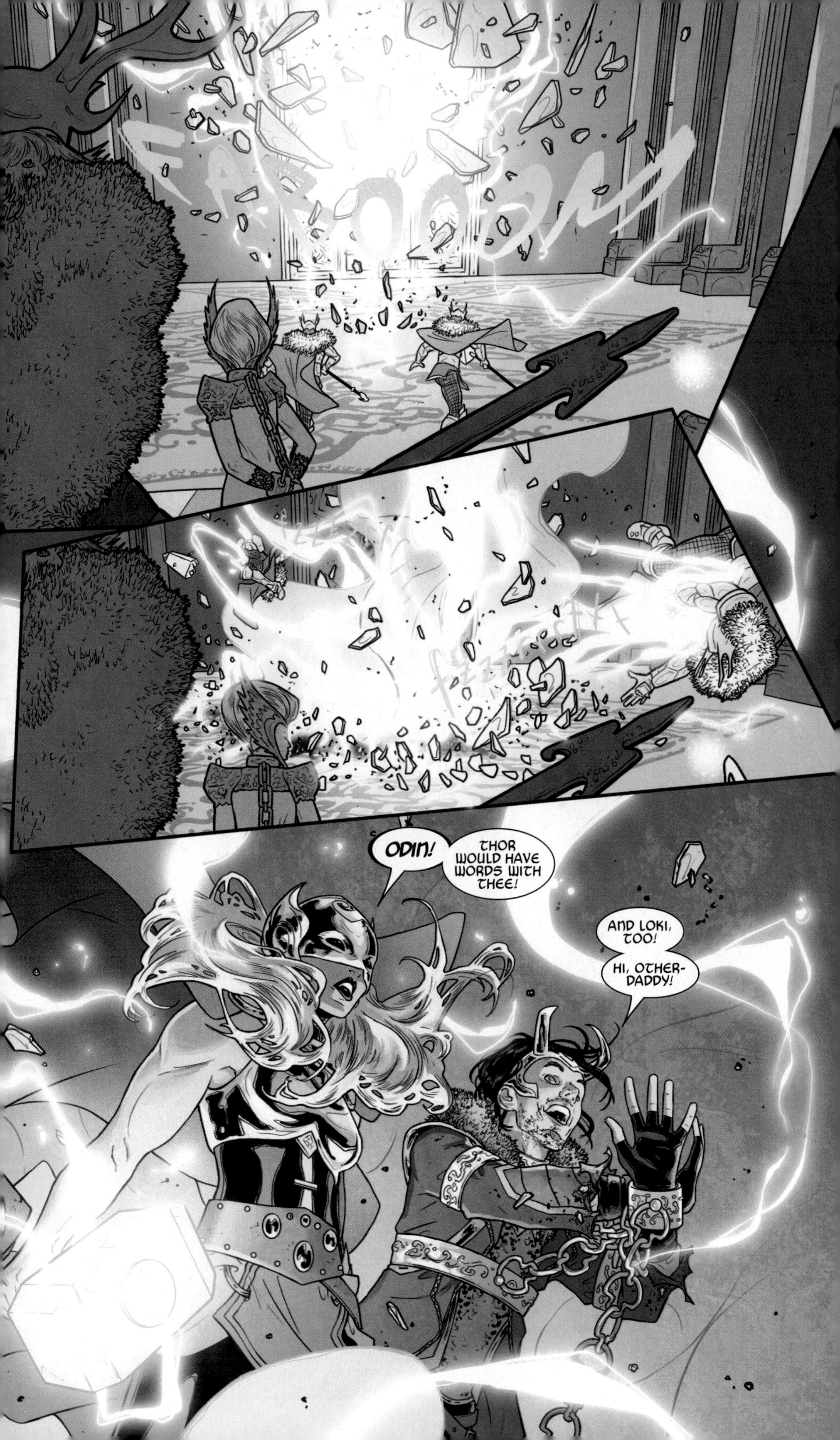
ODIN!
THOR WOULD HAVE WORDS WITH THEE!
AND LOKI, TOO!
HI, OTHER-DADDY!

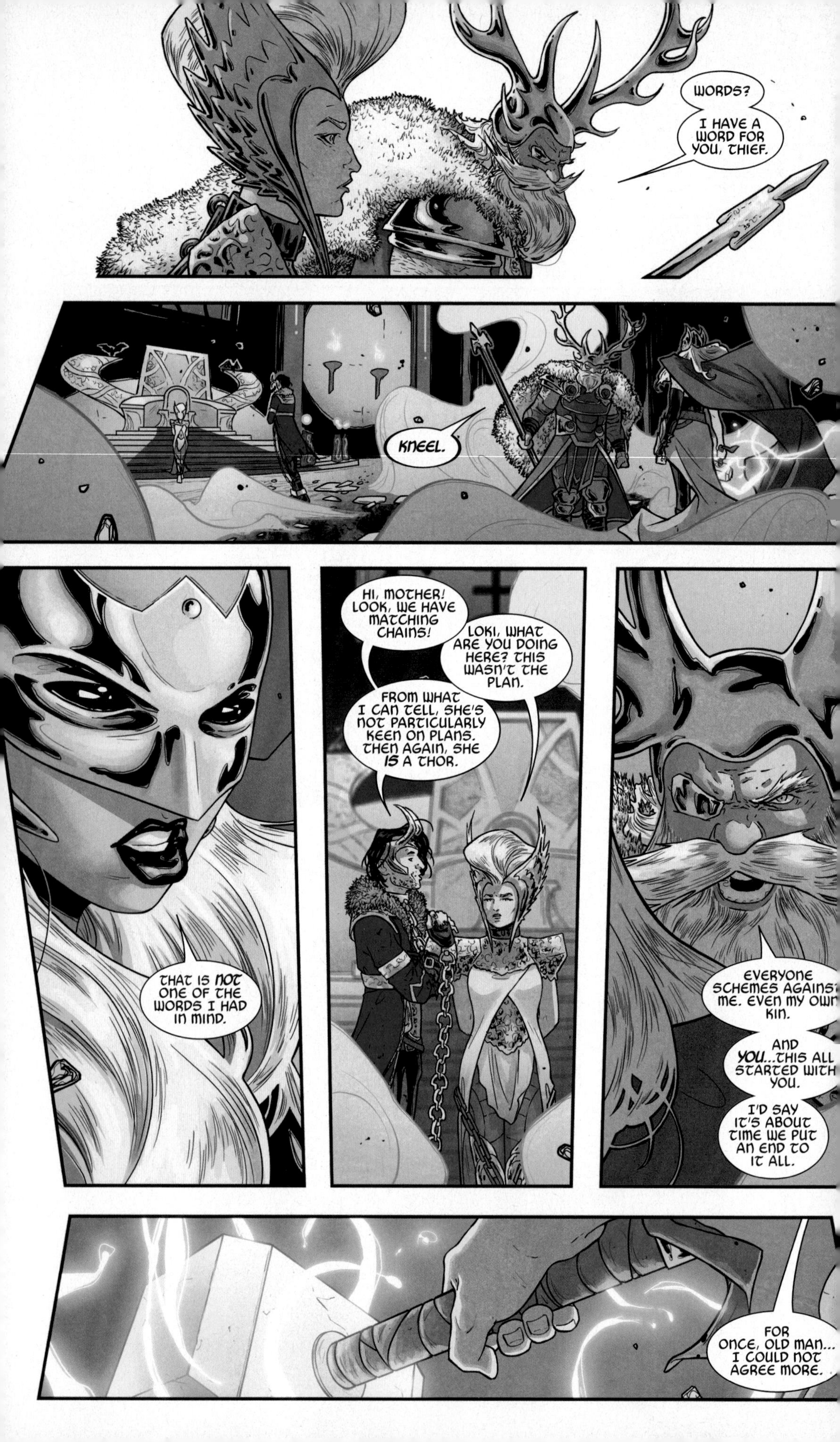
WORDS?
I HAVE A WORD FOR YOU, THIEF.
KNEEL.
THAT IS NOT ONE OF THE WORDS I HAD IN MIND.
HI, MOTHER! LOOK, WE HAVE MATCHING CHAINS!
LOKI, WHAT ARE YOU DOING HERE? THIS WASN'T THE PLAN.
FROM WHAT I CAN TELL, SHE'S NOT PARTICULARLY KEEN ON PLANS. THEN AGAIN, SHE IS A THOR.
EVERYONE SCHEMES AGAINST ME. EVEN MY OWN KIN.
AND YOU...THIS ALL STARTED WITH YOU.
I'D SAY IT'S ABOUT TIME WE PUT AN END TO IT ALL.
FOR ONCE, OLD MAN... I COULD NOT AGREE MORE.

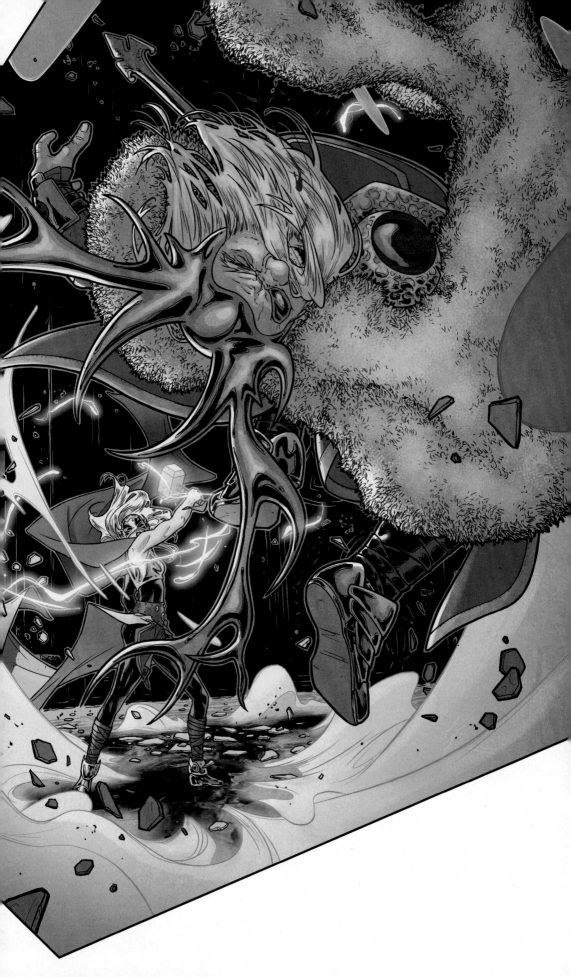

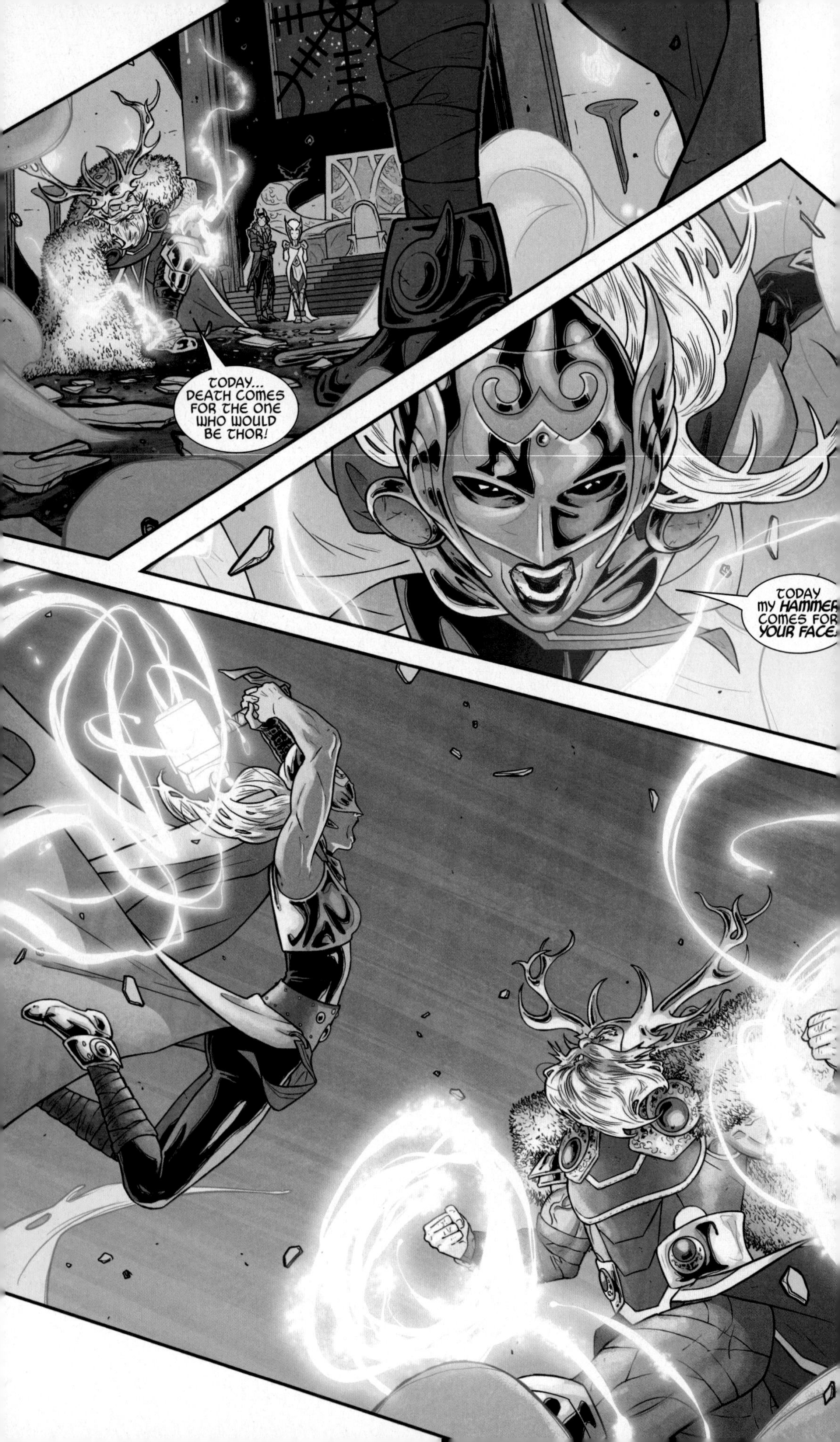
TODAY... DEATH COMES FOR THE ONE WHO WOULD BE THOR!
TODAY my HAMMER COMES FOR YOUR FACE!

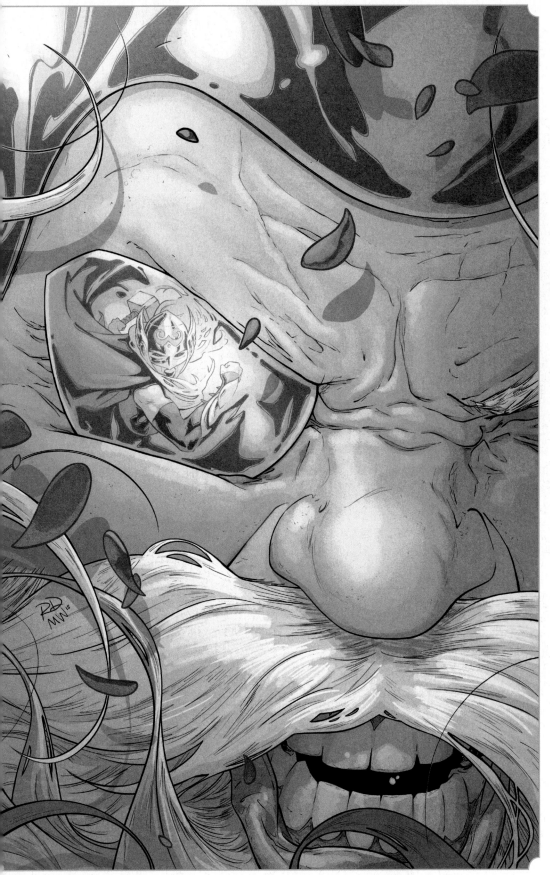

THE CIVIL WAR OF THE GODS

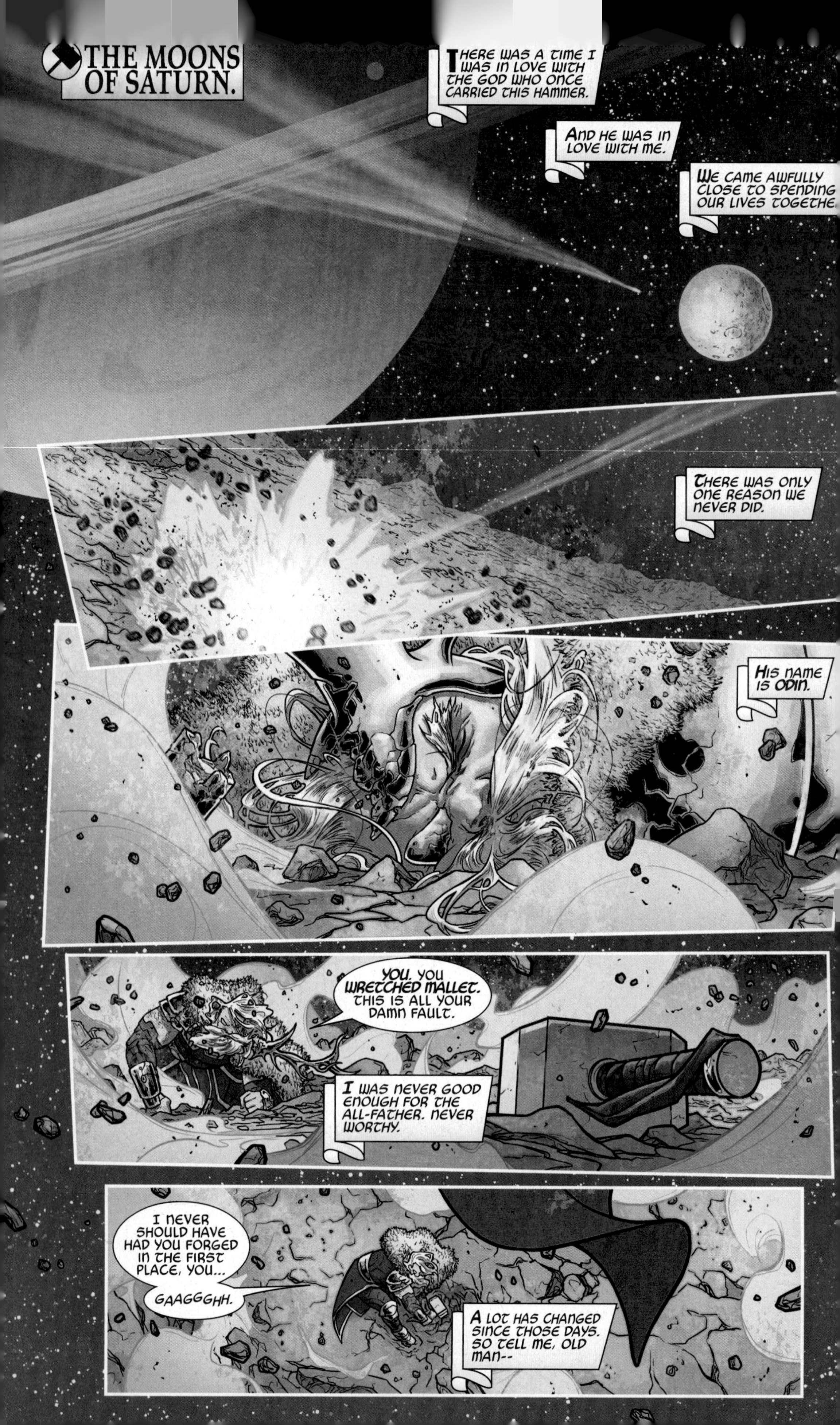

THE MOONS OF SATURN.
THERE WAS A TIME I WAS IN LOVE WITH THE GOD WHO ONCE CARRIED THIS HAMMER.
AND HE WAS IN LOVE WITH ME.
WE CAME AWFULLY CLOSE TO SPENDING OUR LIVES TOGETHE
THERE WAS ONLY ONE REASON WE NEVER DID.
HIS NAME IS ODIN.
YOU. YOU WRETCHED MALLET. THIS IS ALL YOUR DAMN FAULT.
I WAS NEVER GOOD ENOUGH FOR THE ALL-FATHER. NEVER WORTHY.
I NEVER SHOULD HAVE HAD YOU FORGED IN THE FIRST PLACE, YOU...
GAAGGGHH.
A LOT HAS CHANGED SINCE THOSE DAYS. SO TELL ME, OLD MAN--

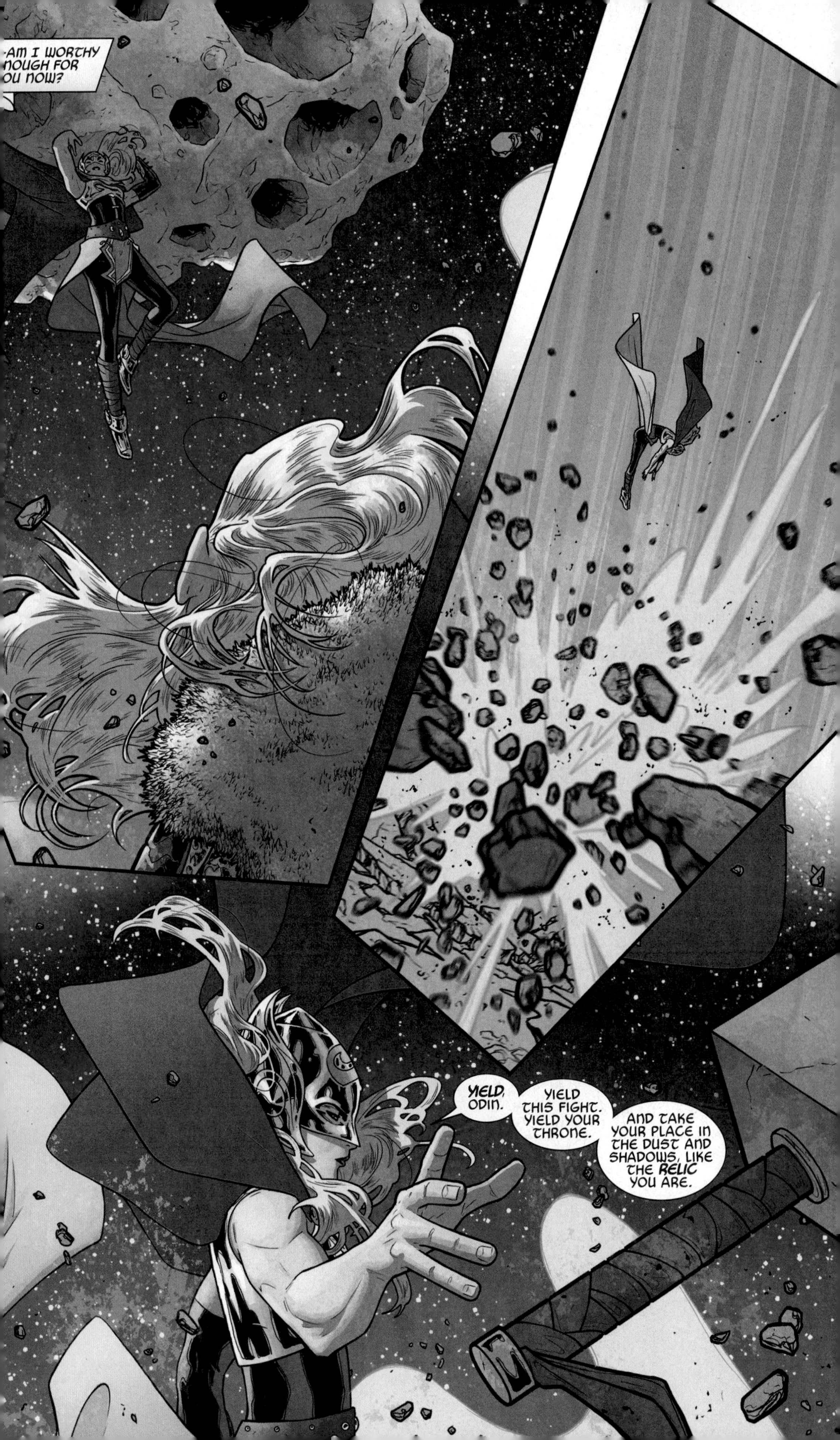
-AM I WORTHY
NOUGH FOR
OU NOW?
YIELD, ODIN.
YIELD THIS FIGHT. YIELD YOUR THRONE.
AND TAKE YOUR PLACE IN THE DUST AND SHADOWS, LIKE THE RELIC YOU ARE.

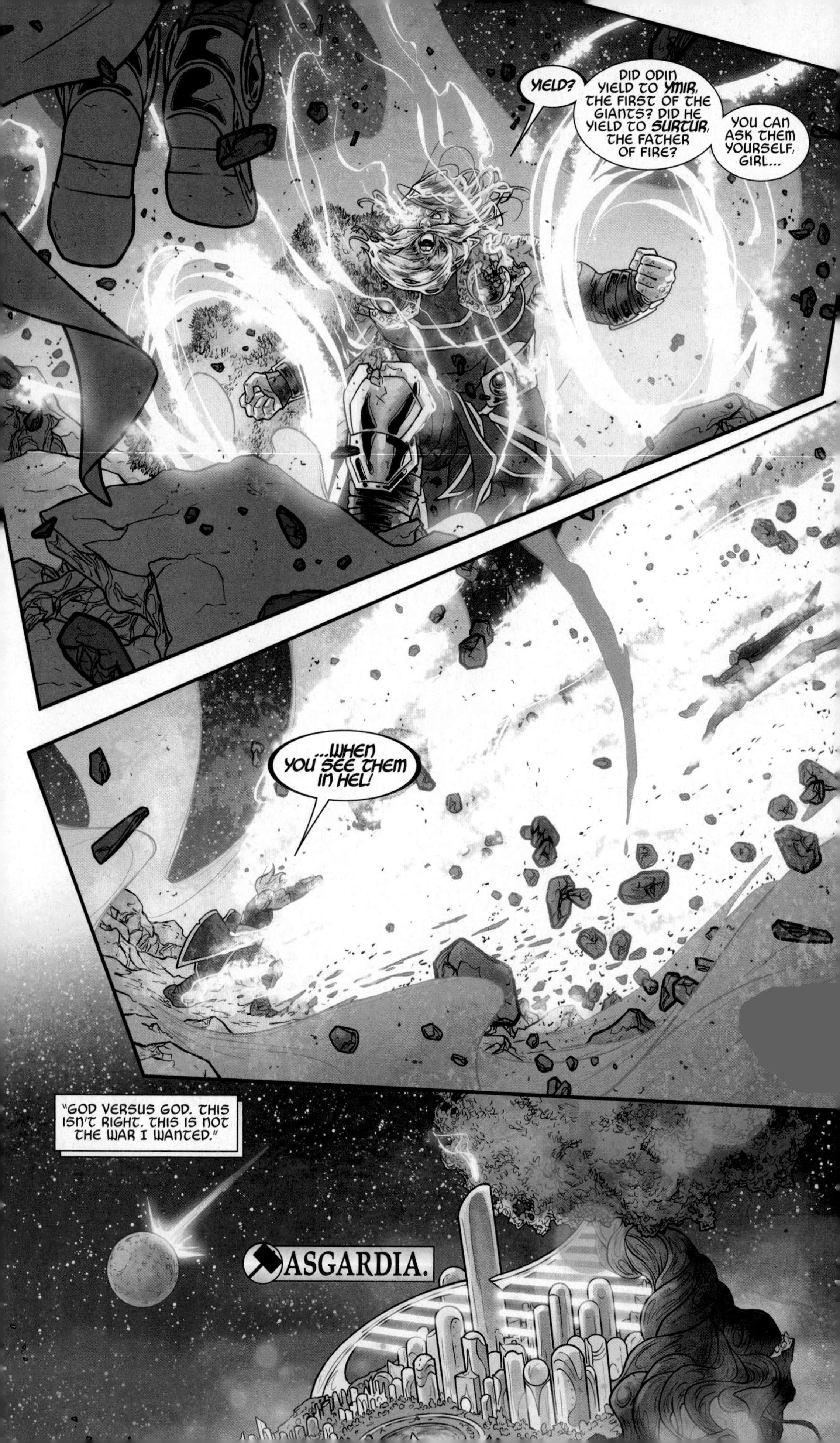
YIELD?
DID ODIN YIELD TO YMIR, THE FIRST OF THE GIANTS? DID HE YIELD TO SURTUR, THE FATHER OF FIRE?
YOU CAN ASK THEM YOURSELF, GIRL...
...WHEN YOU SEE THEM IN HEL!
"GOD VERSUS GOD. THIS ISN'T RIGHT. THIS IS NOT THE WAR I WANTED."
ASGARDIA.

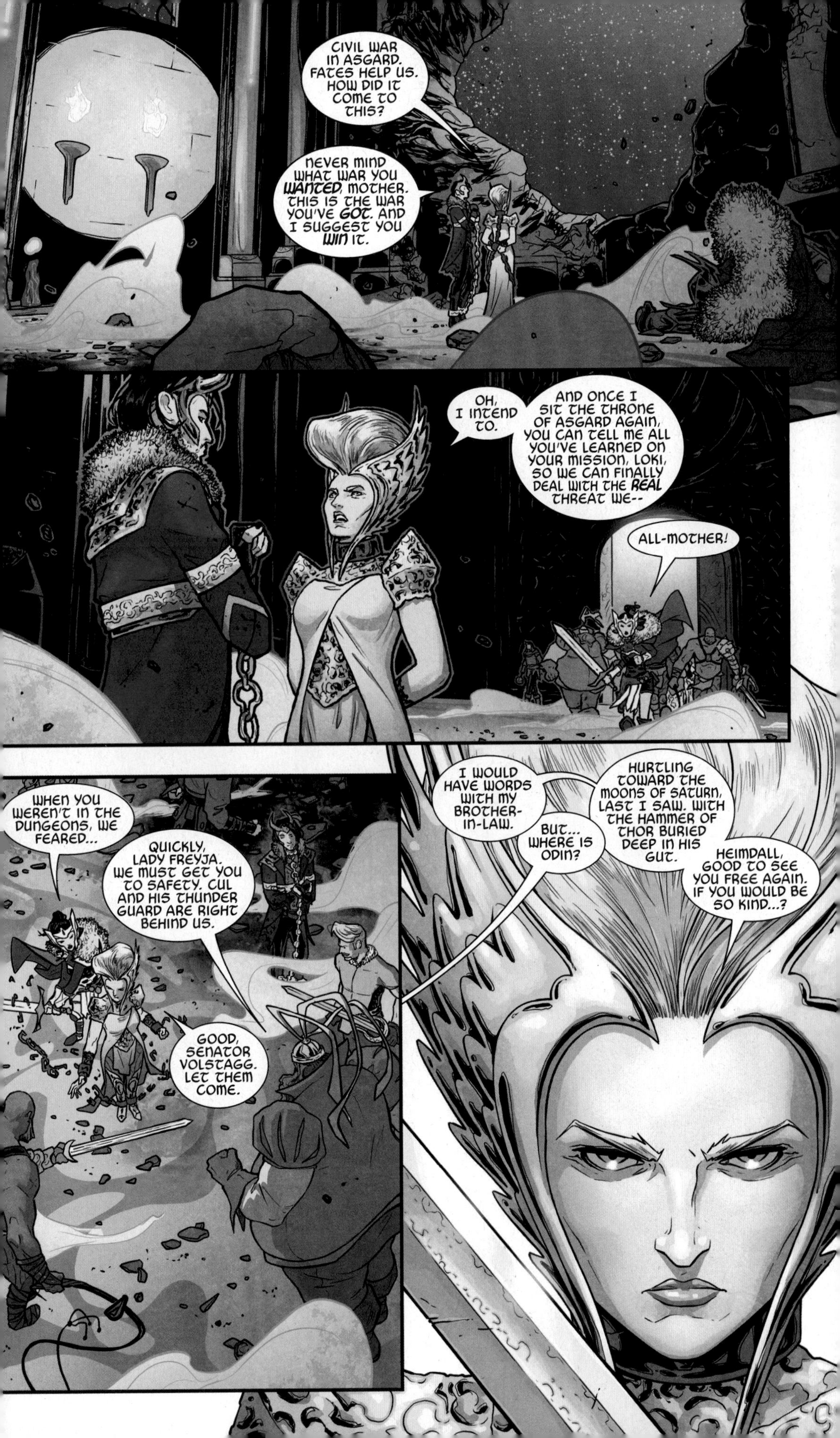

CIVIL WAR IN ASGARD. FATES HELP US. HOW DID IT COME TO THIS?
NEVER MIND WHAT WAR YOU WANTED, MOTHER. THIS IS THE WAR YOU'VE GOT. AND I SUGGEST YOU WIN IT.
OH, I INTEND TO.
AND ONCE I SIT THE THRONE OF ASGARD AGAIN, YOU CAN TELL ME ALL YOU'VE LEARNED ON YOUR MISSION, LOKI, SO WE CAN FINALLY DEAL WITH THE REAL THREAT WE--
ALL-MOTHER!
WHEN YOU WEREN'T IN THE DUNGEONS, WE FEARED...
QUICKLY, LADY FREYJA. WE MUST GET YOU TO SAFETY. CUL AND HIS THUNDER GUARD ARE RIGHT BEHIND US.
GOOD, SENATOR VOLSTAGG. LET THEM COME.
I WOULD HAVE WORDS WITH MY BROTHER-IN-LAW.
BUT... WHERE IS ODIN?
HURTLING TOWARD THE MOONS OF SATURN, LAST I SAW. WITH THE HAMMER OF THOR BURIED DEEP IN HIS GUT.
HEIMDALL, GOOD TO SEE YOU FREE AGAIN. IF YOU WOULD BE SO KIND...?

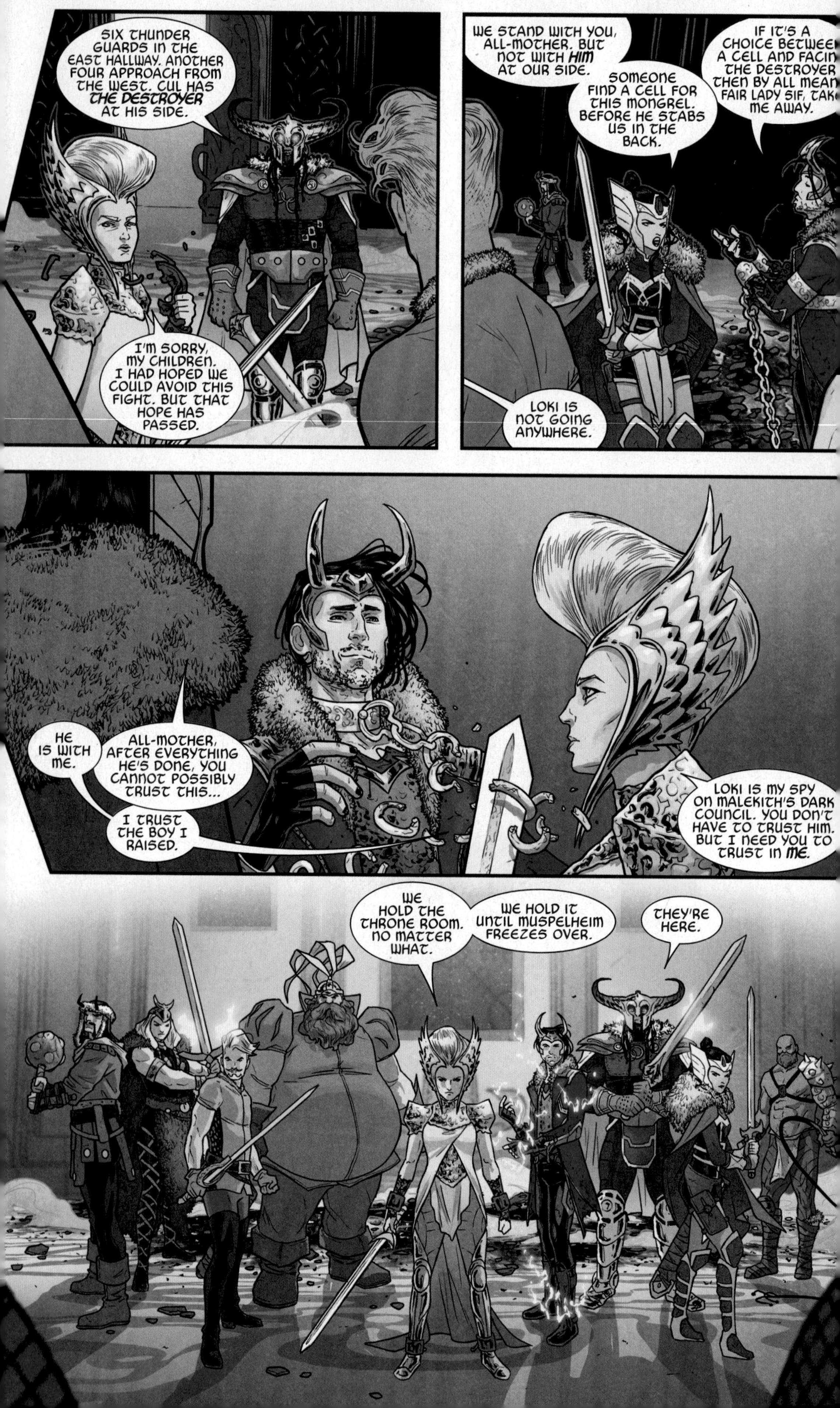
SIX THUNDER GUARDS IN THE EAST HALLWAY. ANOTHER FOUR APPROACH FROM THE WEST. CUL HAS **THE DESTROYER** AT HIS SIDE.
I'M SORRY, MY CHILDREN. I HAD HOPED WE COULD AVOID THIS FIGHT. BUT THAT HOPE HAS PASSED.
WE STAND WITH YOU, ALL-MOTHER. BUT NOT WITH **HIM** AT OUR SIDE.
SOMEONE FIND A CELL FOR THIS MONGREL. BEFORE HE STABS US IN THE BACK.
IF IT'S A CHOICE BETWEE A CELL AND FACIN THE DESTROYER THEN BY ALL MEAN FAIR LADY SIF, TAK ME AWAY.
LOKI IS NOT GOING ANYWHERE.
ALL-MOTHER, AFTER EVERYTHING HE'S DONE, YOU CANNOT POSSIBLY TRUST THIS...
HE IS WITH ME.
I TRUST THE BOY I RAISED.
LOKI IS MY SPY ON MALEKITH'S DARK COUNCIL. YOU DON'T HAVE TO TRUST HIM. BUT I NEED YOU TO TRUST IN **ME**.
WE HOLD THE THRONE ROOM. NO MATTER WHAT.
WE HOLD IT UNTIL MUSPELHEIM FREEZES OVER.
THEY'RE HERE.

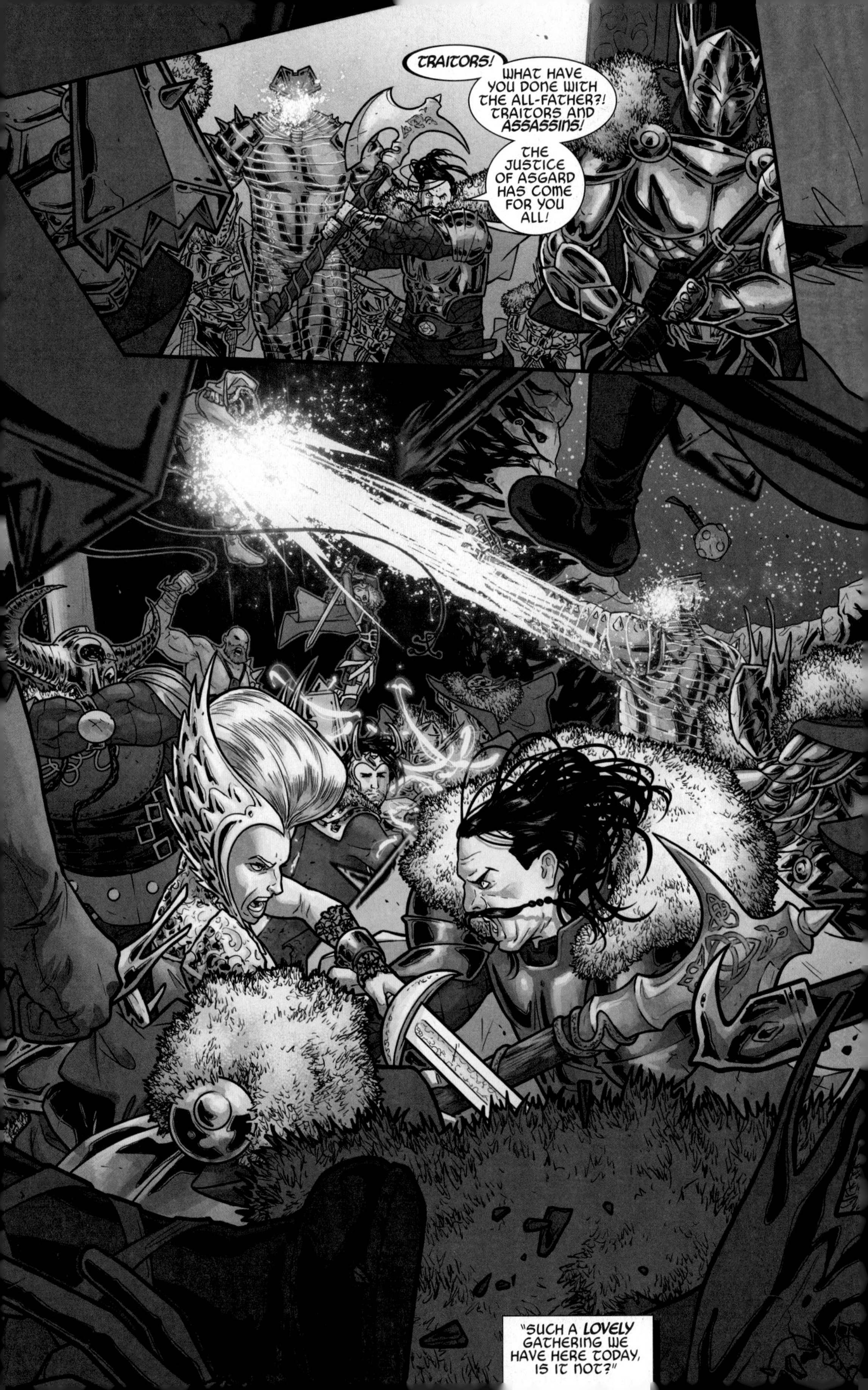
TRAITORS!
WHAT HAVE YOU DONE WITH THE ALL-FATHER?! TRAITORS AND ASSASSINS!
THE JUSTICE OF ASGARD HAS COME FOR YOU ALL!
"SUCH A LOVELY GATHERING WE HAVE HERE TODAY, IS IT NOT?"

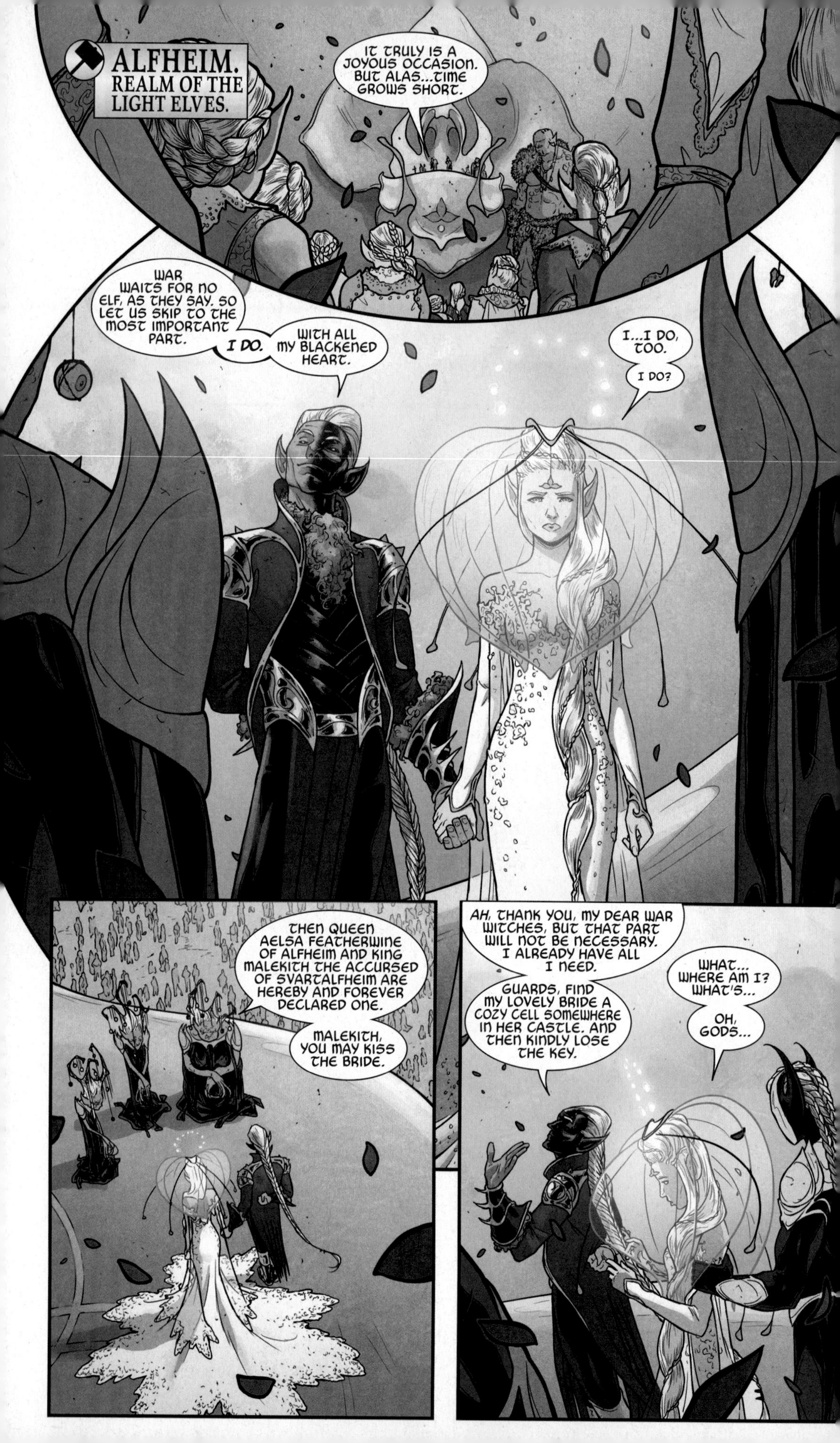
ALFHEIM. REALM OF THE LIGHT ELVES.
IT TRULY IS A JOYOUS OCCASION. BUT ALAS...TIME GROWS SHORT.
WAR WAITS FOR NO ELF, AS THEY SAY. SO LET US SKIP TO THE MOST IMPORTANT PART.
I DO.
WITH ALL MY BLACKENED HEART.
I...I DO, TOO.
I DO?
THEN QUEEN AELSA FEATHERWINE OF ALFHEIM AND KING MALEKITH THE ACCURSED OF SVARTALFHEIM ARE HEREBY AND FOREVER DECLARED ONE.
MALEKITH, YOU MAY KISS THE BRIDE.
AH, THANK YOU, MY DEAR WAR WITCHES, BUT THAT PART WILL NOT BE NECESSARY. I ALREADY HAVE ALL I NEED.
GUARDS, FIND MY LOVELY BRIDE A COZY CELL SOMEWHERE IN HER CASTLE. AND THEN KINDLY LOSE THE KEY.
WHAT... WHERE AM I? WHAT'S...
OH, GODS...

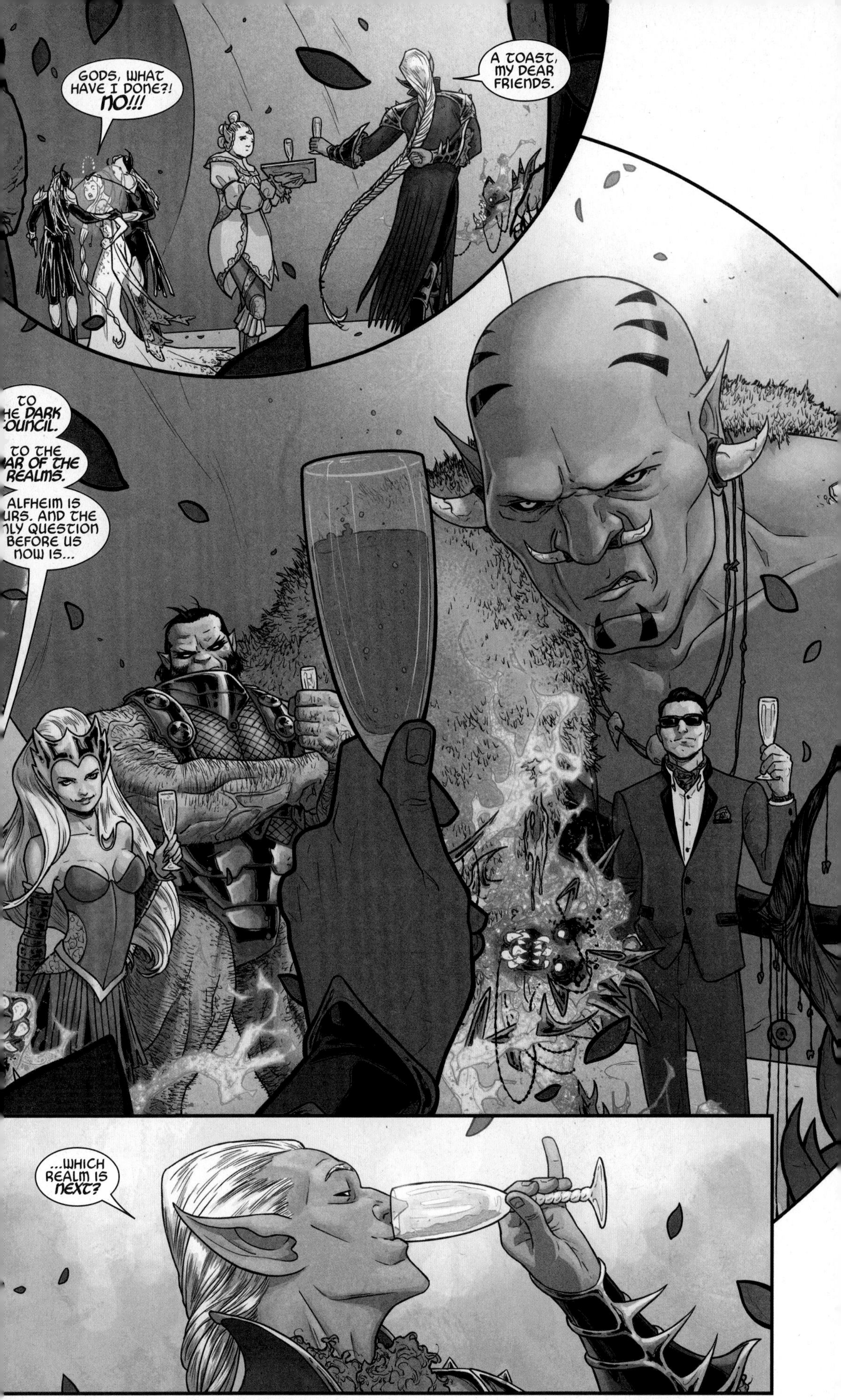
GODS, WHAT HAVE I DONE?! NO!!!
A TOAST, MY DEAR FRIENDS.
TO HE DARK OUNCIL.
TO THE AR OF THE REALMS.
ALFHEIM IS URS. AND THE NLY QUESTION BEFORE US NOW IS...
...WHICH REALM IS NEXT?

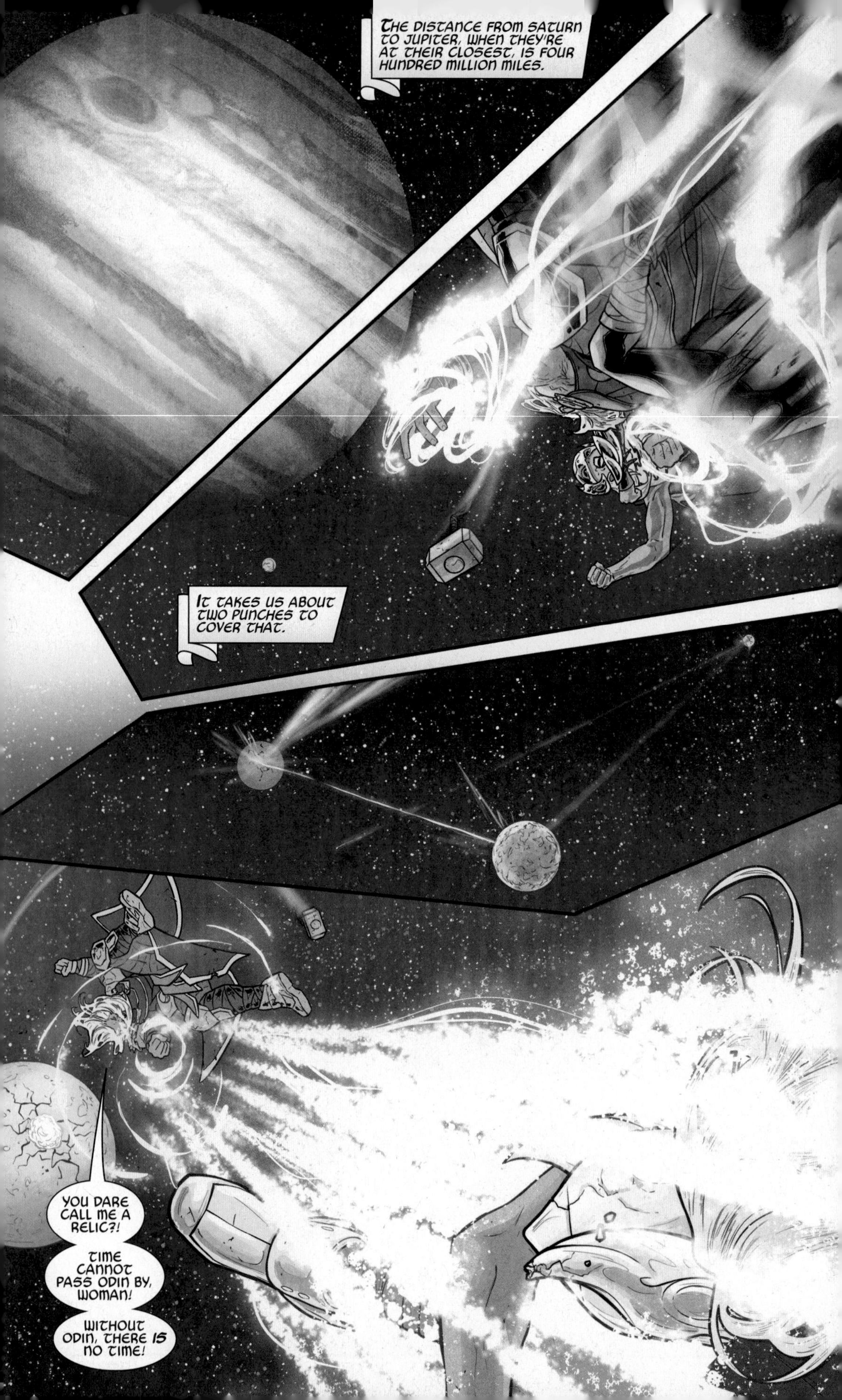
THE DISTANCE FROM SATURN TO JUPITER, WHEN THEY'RE AT THEIR CLOSEST, IS FOUR HUNDRED MILLION MILES.
IT TAKES US ABOUT TWO PUNCHES TO COVER THAT.
YOU DARE CALL ME A RELIC?!
TIME CANNOT PASS ODIN BY, WOMAN!
WITHOUT ODIN, THERE IS NO TIME!

NO SUN, NO MOON, NO STARS!
RIGHT. NO FOUR-HUNDRED-YEAR-OLD, PLANET-SIZED JOVIAN SUPER STORMS!
JUPITER'S GREAT RED SPOT ERUPTS AROUND ME. THE HAMMER CONVULSES VIOLENTLY IN MY HANDS.
IF I DIDN'T KNOW BETTER...I'D SWEAR I COULD HEAR MJOLNIR LAUGHING.

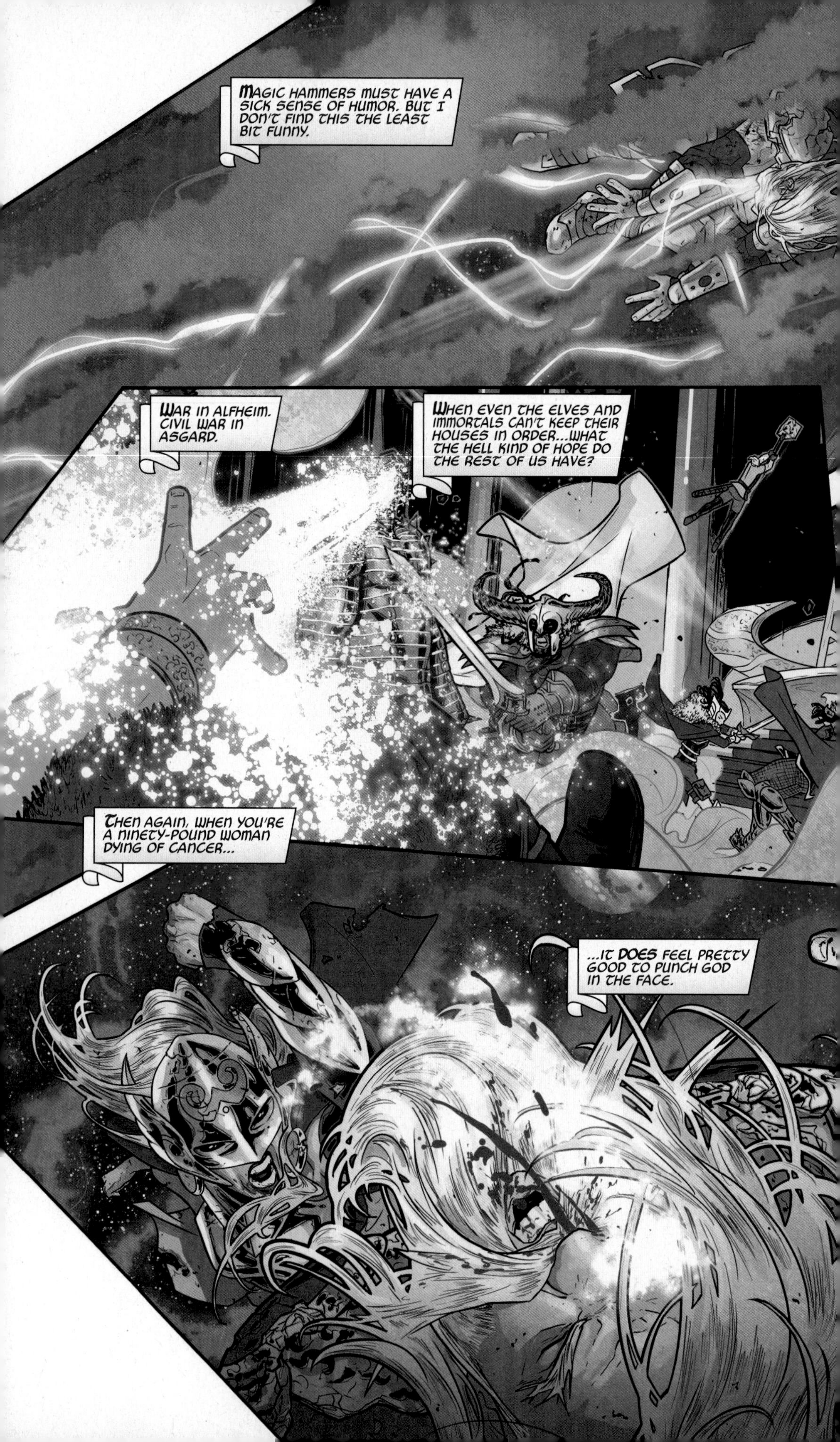
MAGIC HAMMERS MUST HAVE A SICK SENSE OF HUMOR. BUT I DON'T FIND THIS THE LEAST BIT FUNNY.
WAR IN ALFHEIM. CIVIL WAR IN ASGARD.
WHEN EVEN THE ELVES AND IMMORTALS CAN'T KEEP THEIR HOUSES IN ORDER...WHAT THE HELL KIND OF HOPE DO THE REST OF US HAVE?
THEN AGAIN, WHEN YOU'RE A NINETY-POUND WOMAN DYING OF CANCER...
...IT DOES FEEL PRETTY GOOD TO PUNCH GOD IN THE FACE.

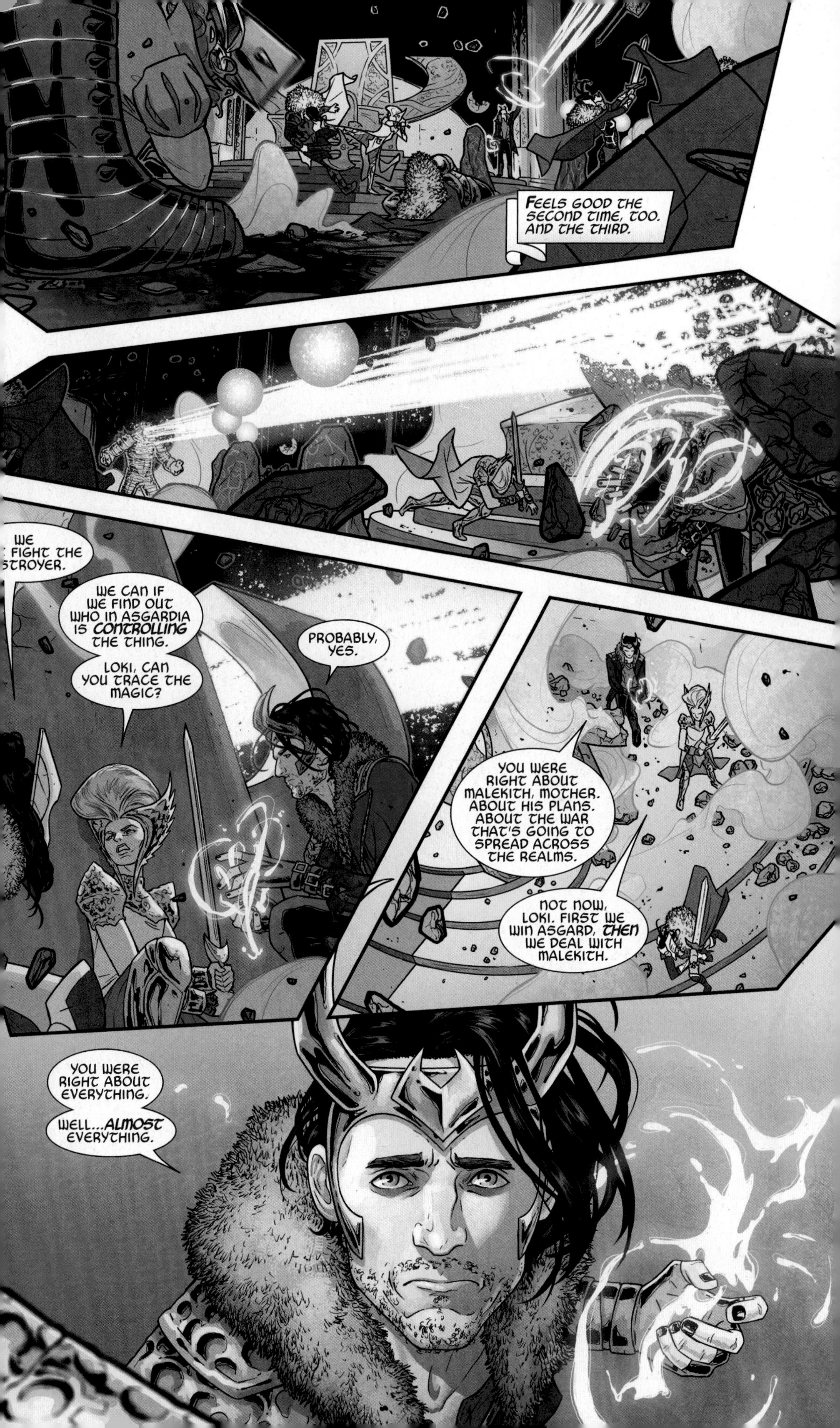

FEELS GOOD THE SECOND TIME, TOO. AND THE THIRD.
WE FIGHT THE STROYER.
WE CAN IF WE FIND OUT WHO IN ASGARDIA IS **CONTROLLING** THE THING.
LOKI, CAN YOU TRACE THE MAGIC?
PROBABLY, YES.
YOU WERE RIGHT ABOUT MALEKITH, MOTHER. ABOUT HIS PLANS. ABOUT THE WAR THAT'S GOING TO SPREAD ACROSS THE REALMS.
NOT NOW, LOKI. FIRST WE WIN ASGARD, **THEN** WE DEAL WITH MALEKITH.
YOU WERE RIGHT ABOUT EVERYTHING.
WELL...**ALMOST** EVERYTHING.

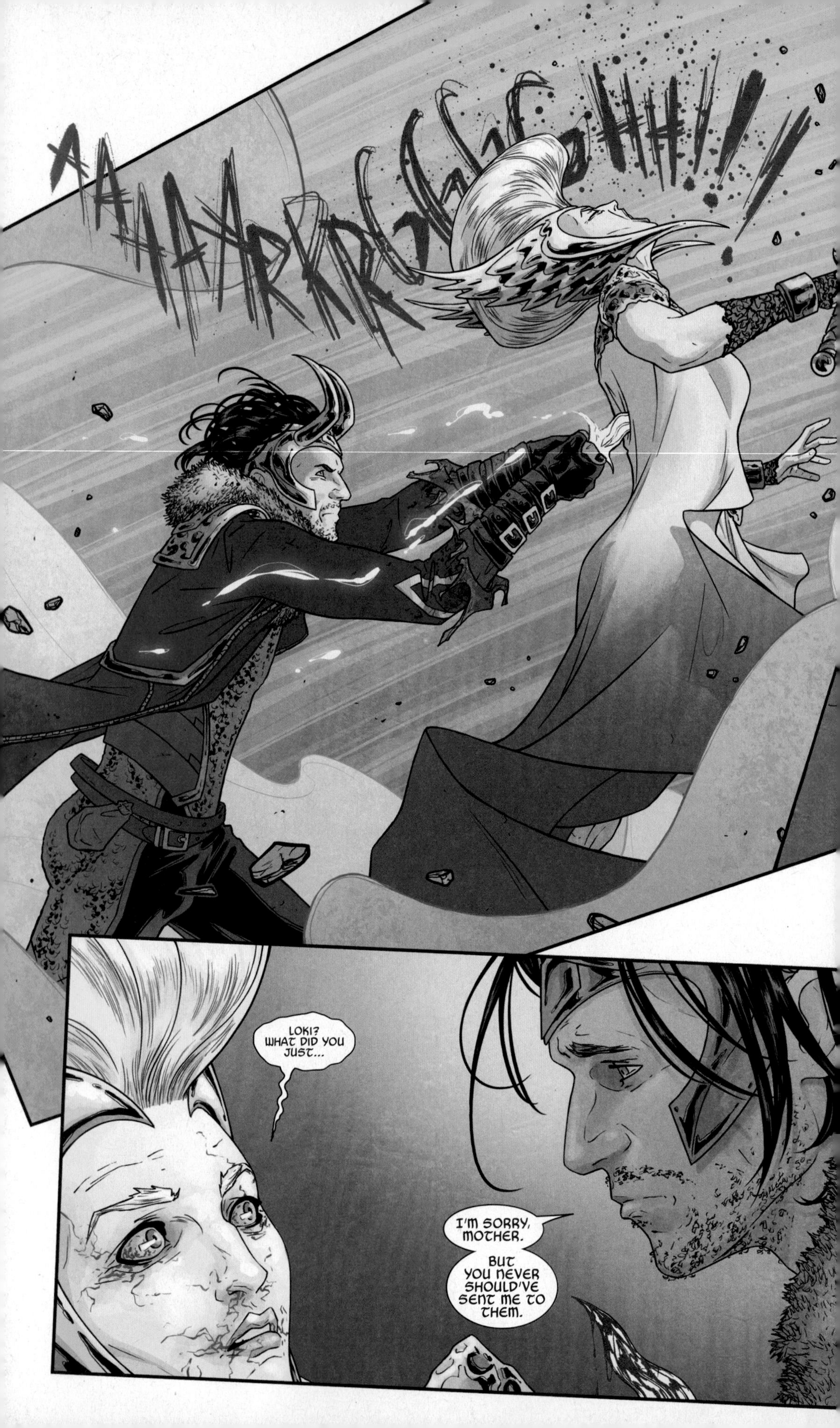
AAAARRRGHHH!!!
LOKI? WHAT DID YOU JUST...
I'M SORRY, MOTHER.
BUT YOU NEVER SHOULD'VE SENT ME TO THEM.

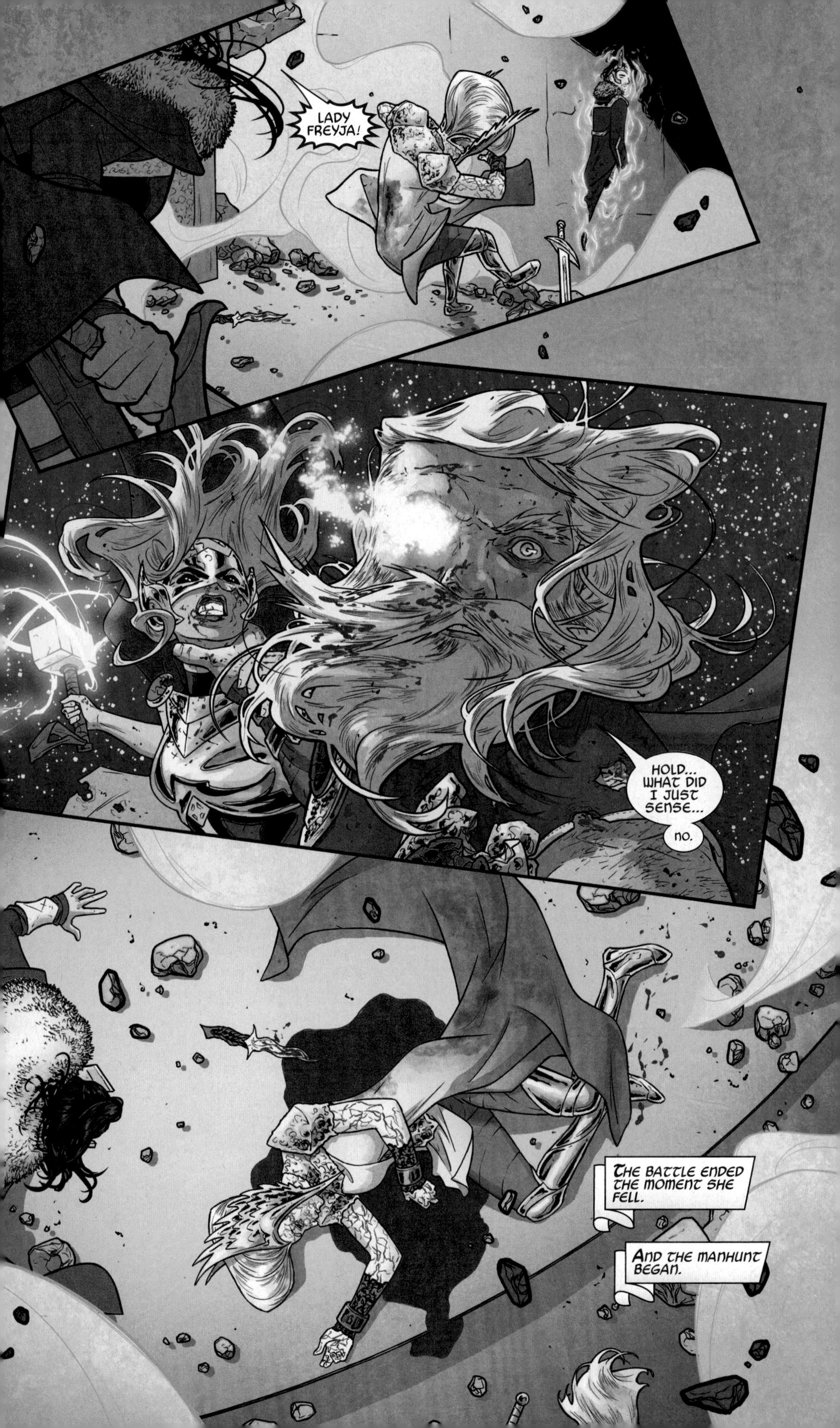
LADY FREYJA!
HOLD... WHAT DID I JUST SENSE...
no.
THE BATTLE ENDED THE MOMENT SHE FELL.
AND THE MANHUNT BEGAN.

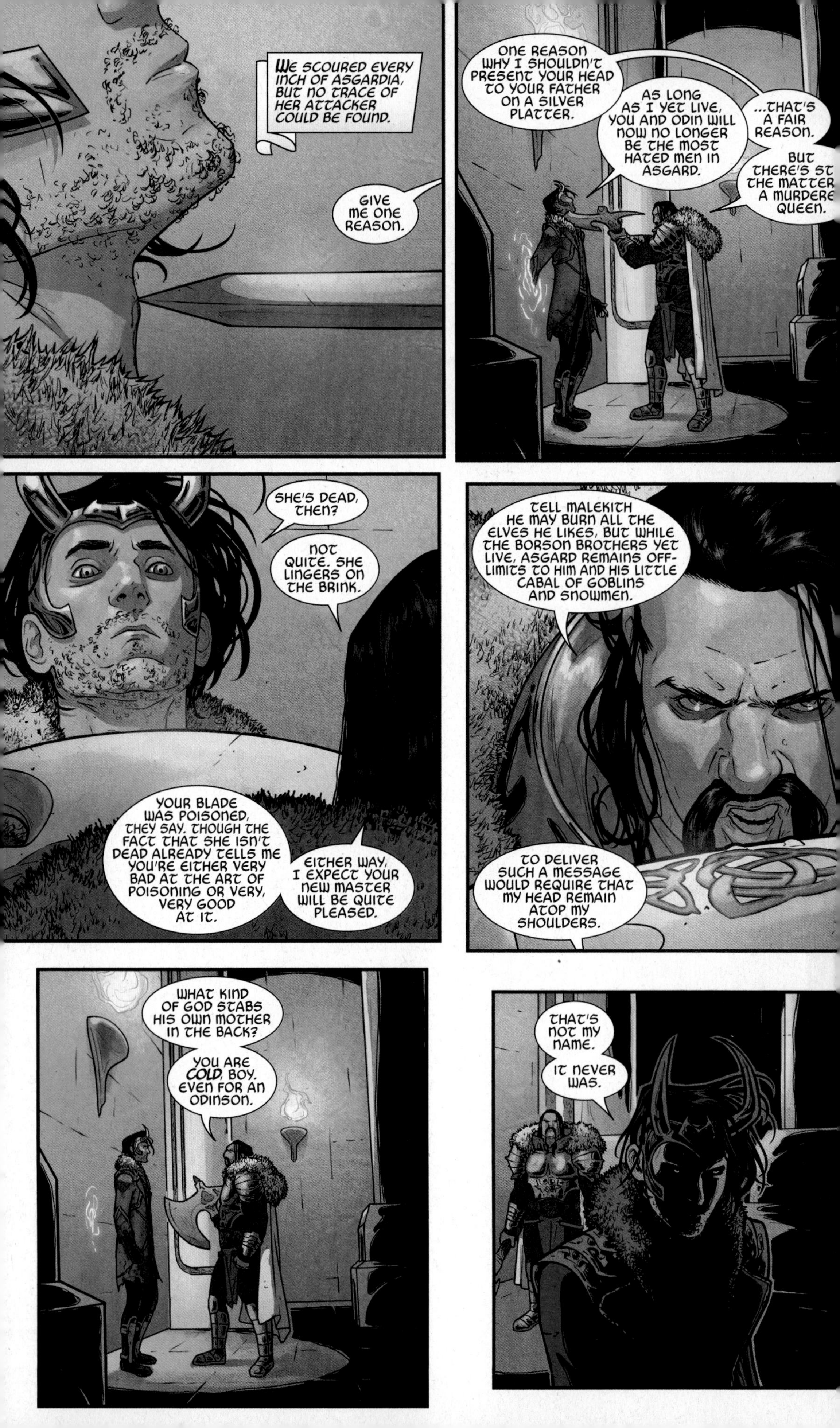
WE SCOURED EVERY INCH OF ASGARDIA, BUT NO TRACE OF HER ATTACKER COULD BE FOUND.
GIVE ME ONE REASON.
ONE REASON WHY I SHOULDN'T PRESENT YOUR HEAD TO YOUR FATHER ON A SILVER PLATTER.
AS LONG AS I YET LIVE, YOU AND ODIN WILL NOW NO LONGER BE THE MOST HATED MEN IN ASGARD.
...THAT'S A FAIR REASON.
BUT THERE'S ST THE MATTER A MURDERE QUEEN.
SHE'S DEAD, THEN?
NOT QUITE. SHE LINGERS ON THE BRINK.
YOUR BLADE WAS POISONED, THEY SAY. THOUGH THE FACT THAT SHE ISN'T DEAD ALREADY TELLS ME YOU'RE EITHER VERY BAD AT THE ART OF POISONING OR VERY, VERY GOOD AT IT.
EITHER WAY, I EXPECT YOUR NEW MASTER WILL BE QUITE PLEASED.
TELL MALEKITH HE MAY BURN ALL THE ELVES HE LIKES, BUT WHILE THE BORSON BROTHERS YET LIVE, ASGARD REMAINS OFF-LIMITS TO HIM AND HIS LITTLE CABAL OF GOBLINS AND SNOWMEN.
TO DELIVER SUCH A MESSAGE WOULD REQUIRE THAT MY HEAD REMAIN ATOP MY SHOULDERS.
WHAT KIND OF GOD STABS HIS OWN MOTHER IN THE BACK?
YOU ARE COLD, BOY. EVEN FOR AN ODINSON.
THAT'S NOT MY NAME.
IT NEVER WAS.

...IN WOULDN'T
T ANYONE
UCH HER.

HE CARRIED FREYJA INTO HIS INNERMOST SANCTUM, THE CHAMBER OF THE ODINSLEEP, WHERE THE DESTROYER GUARDS THE DOOR DAY AND NIGHT.

THEY SAY HIS HALL SMELLS OF PRIMAL MAGIC. AND THAT SOMETIMES YOU CAN HEAR HIS WEEPING THROUGH THE WALLS.

THE CONGRESS OF WORLDS WAS RESTORED, AND WITH IT, SOME SENSE OF ORDER.

ALL FIGHTING HAS ENDED. ALL ARMS HAVE BEEN LAID ASIDE.

FOR NOW.

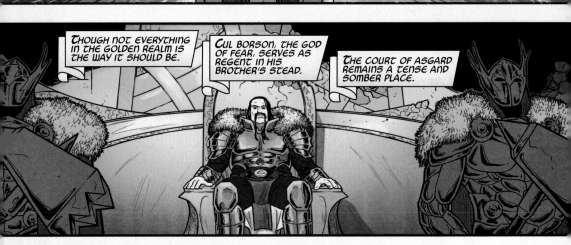

THOUGH NOT EVERYTHING IN THE GOLDEN REALM IS THE WAY IT SHOULD BE.

CUL BORSON, THE GOD OF FEAR, SERVES AS REGENT IN HIS BROTHER'S STEAD.

THE COURT OF ASGARD REMAINS A TENSE AND SOMBER PLACE.

AND CANCER REMAINS ONE HELL OF A DISEASE.

NO ONE IS QUITE SURE WHO WON THE CIVIL WAR IN ASGARD, ESPECIALLY THOSE OF US WHO FOUGHT IN IT. BUT OF ONE THING I AM DEFINITELY CERTAIN...

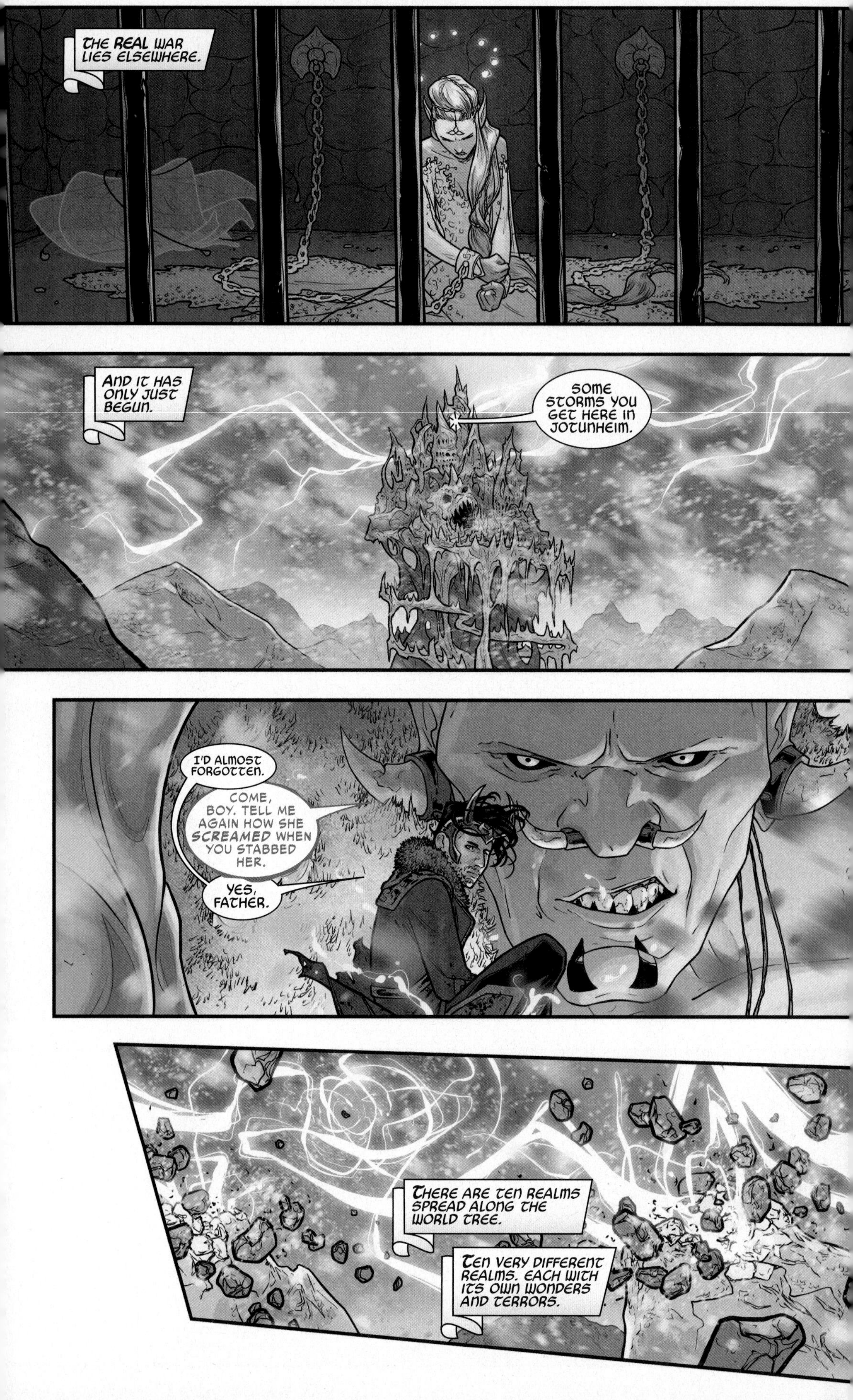
THE REAL WAR LIES ELSEWHERE.
AND IT HAS ONLY JUST BEGUN.
SOME STORMS YOU GET HERE IN JOTUNHEIM.
I'D ALMOST FORGOTTEN.
COME, BOY. TELL ME AGAIN HOW SHE SCREAMED WHEN YOU STABBED HER.
YES, FATHER.
THERE ARE TEN REALMS SPREAD ALONG THE WORLD TREE.
TEN VERY DIFFERENT REALMS. EACH WITH ITS OWN WONDERS AND TERRORS.

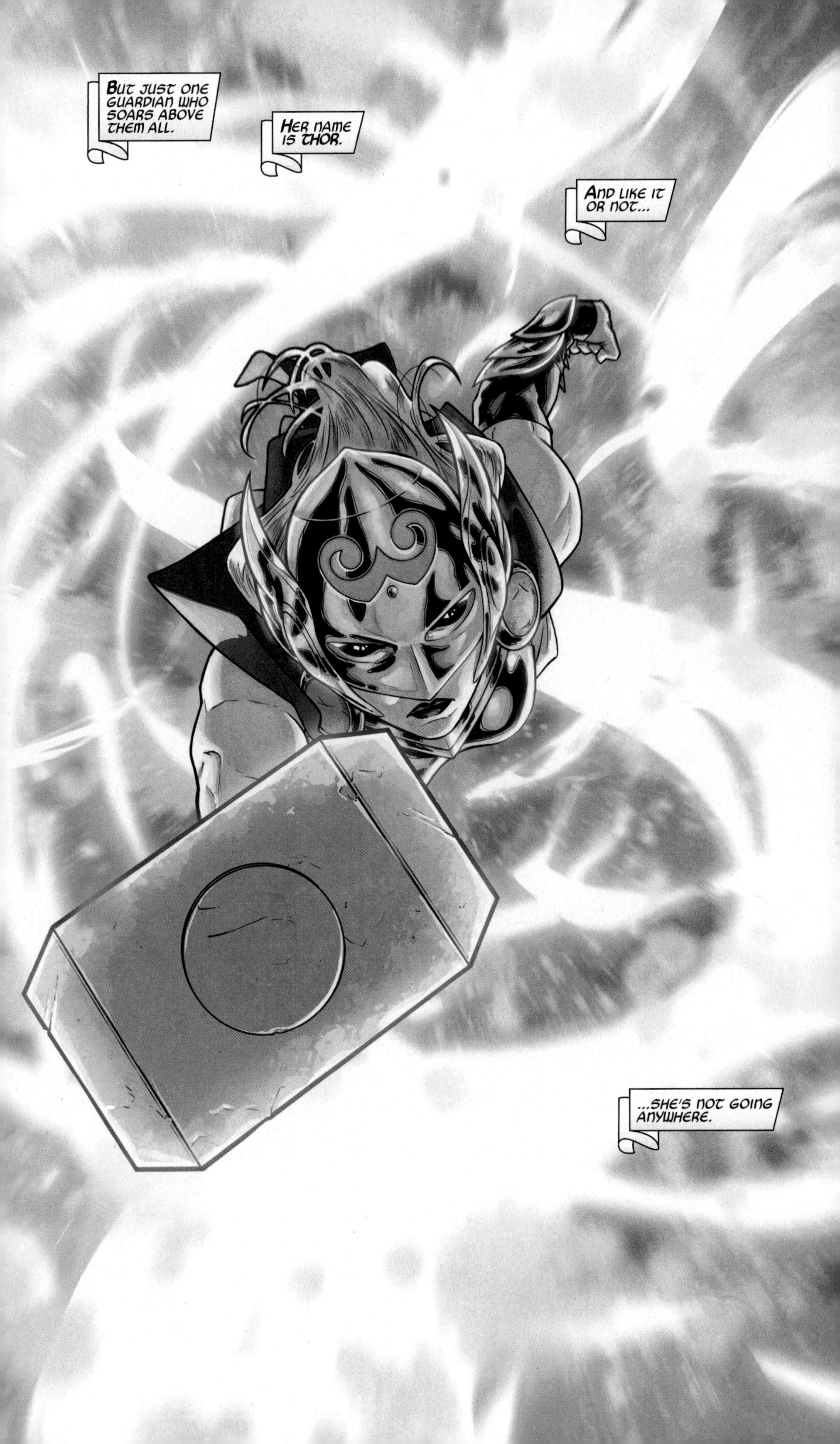
BUT JUST ONE GUARDIAN WHO SOARS ABOVE THEM ALL.
HER NAME IS THOR.
AND LIKE IT OR NOT...
...SHE'S NOT GOING ANYWHERE.

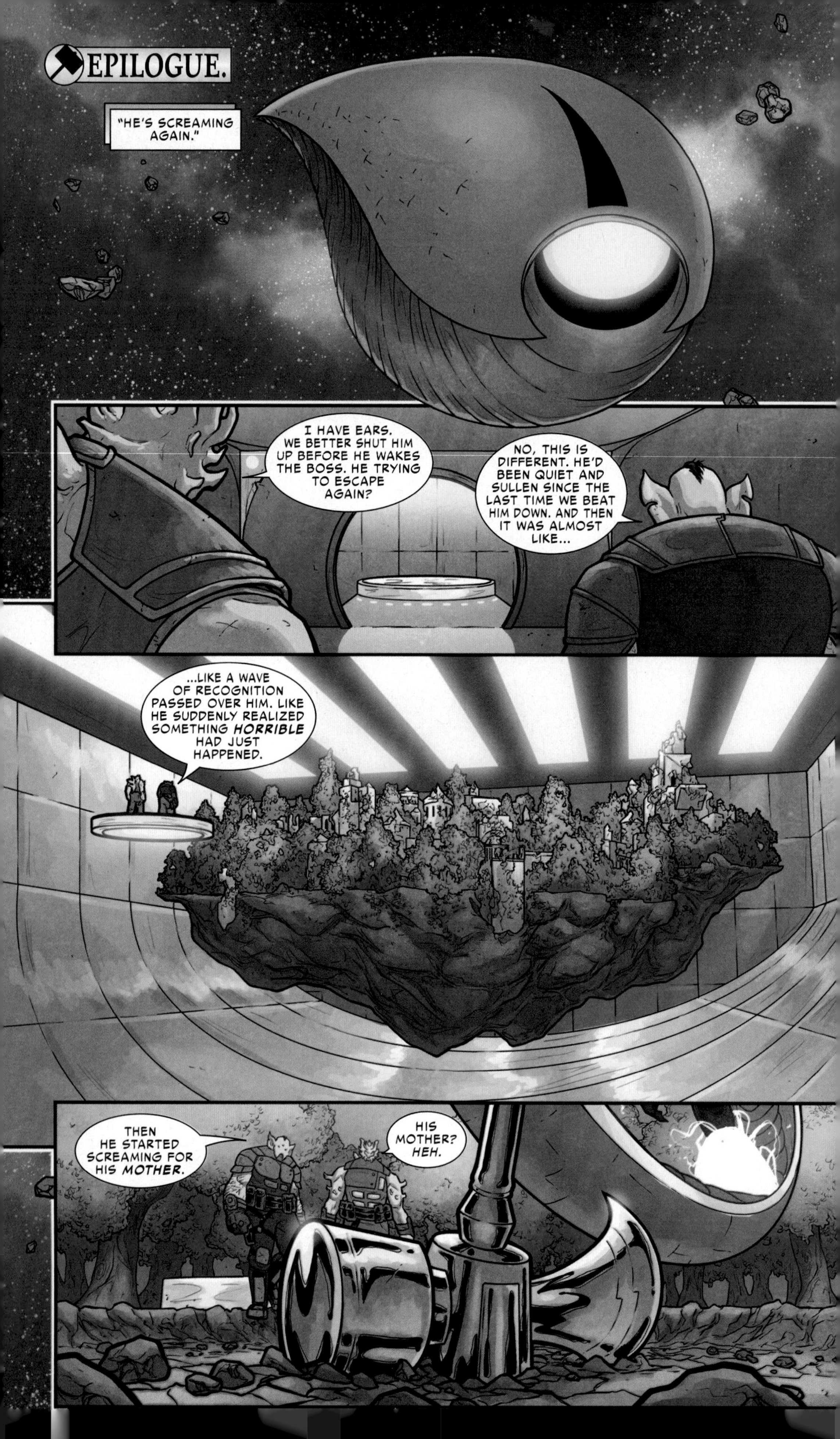
EPILOGUE.
"HE'S SCREAMING AGAIN."
I HAVE EARS. WE BETTER SHUT HIM UP BEFORE HE WAKES THE BOSS. HE TRYING TO ESCAPE AGAIN?
NO, THIS IS DIFFERENT. HE'D BEEN QUIET AND SULLEN SINCE THE LAST TIME WE BEAT HIM DOWN. AND THEN IT WAS ALMOST LIKE...
...LIKE A WAVE OF RECOGNITION PASSED OVER HIM. LIKE HE SUDDENLY REALIZED SOMETHING *HORRIBLE* HAD JUST HAPPENED.
THEN HE STARTED SCREAMING FOR HIS *MOTHER*.
HIS MOTHER? *HEH*.

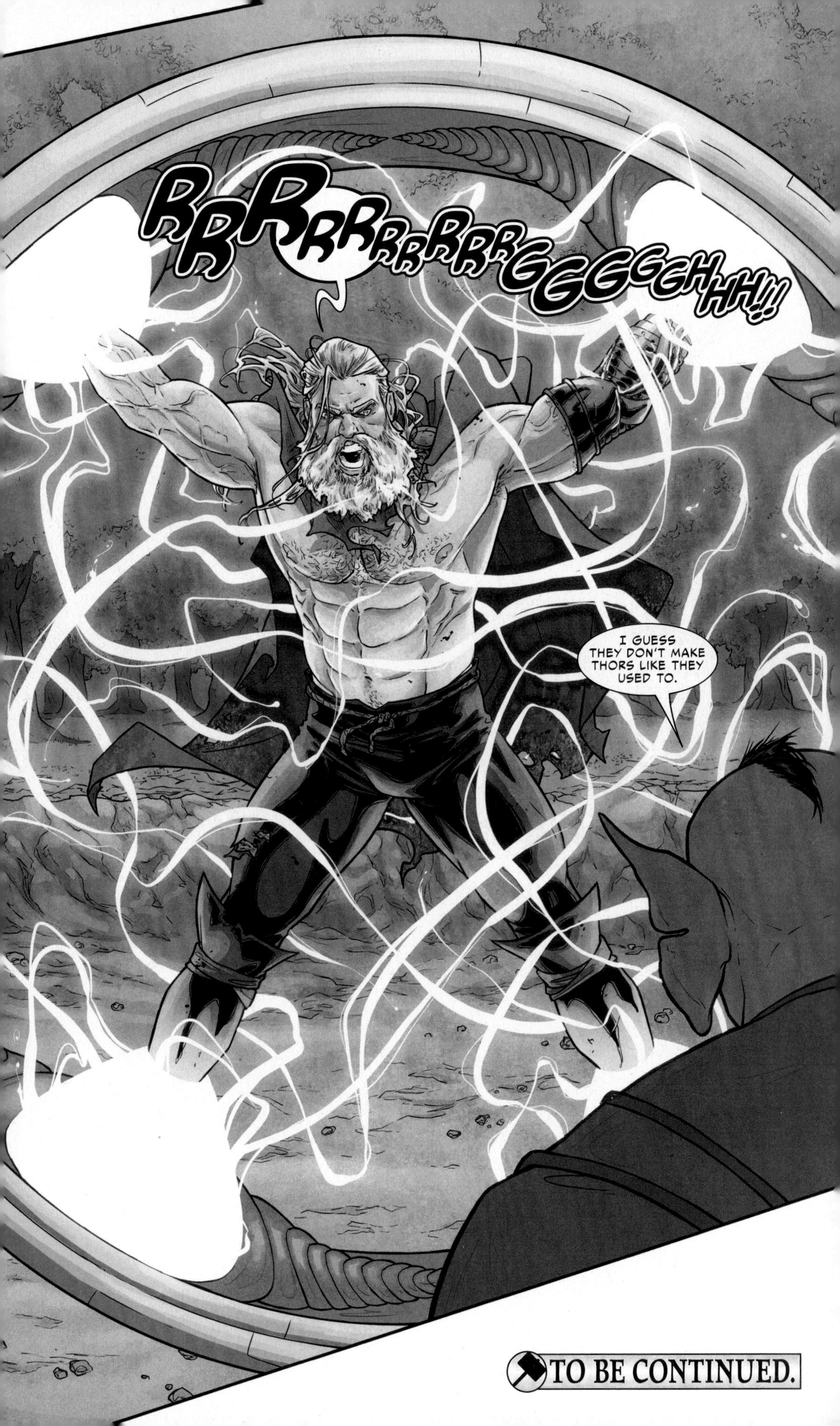
RRRRRRRRRRGGGGGHHH!!!
I GUESS THEY DON'T MAKE THORS LIKE THEY USED TO.
TO BE CONTINUED.

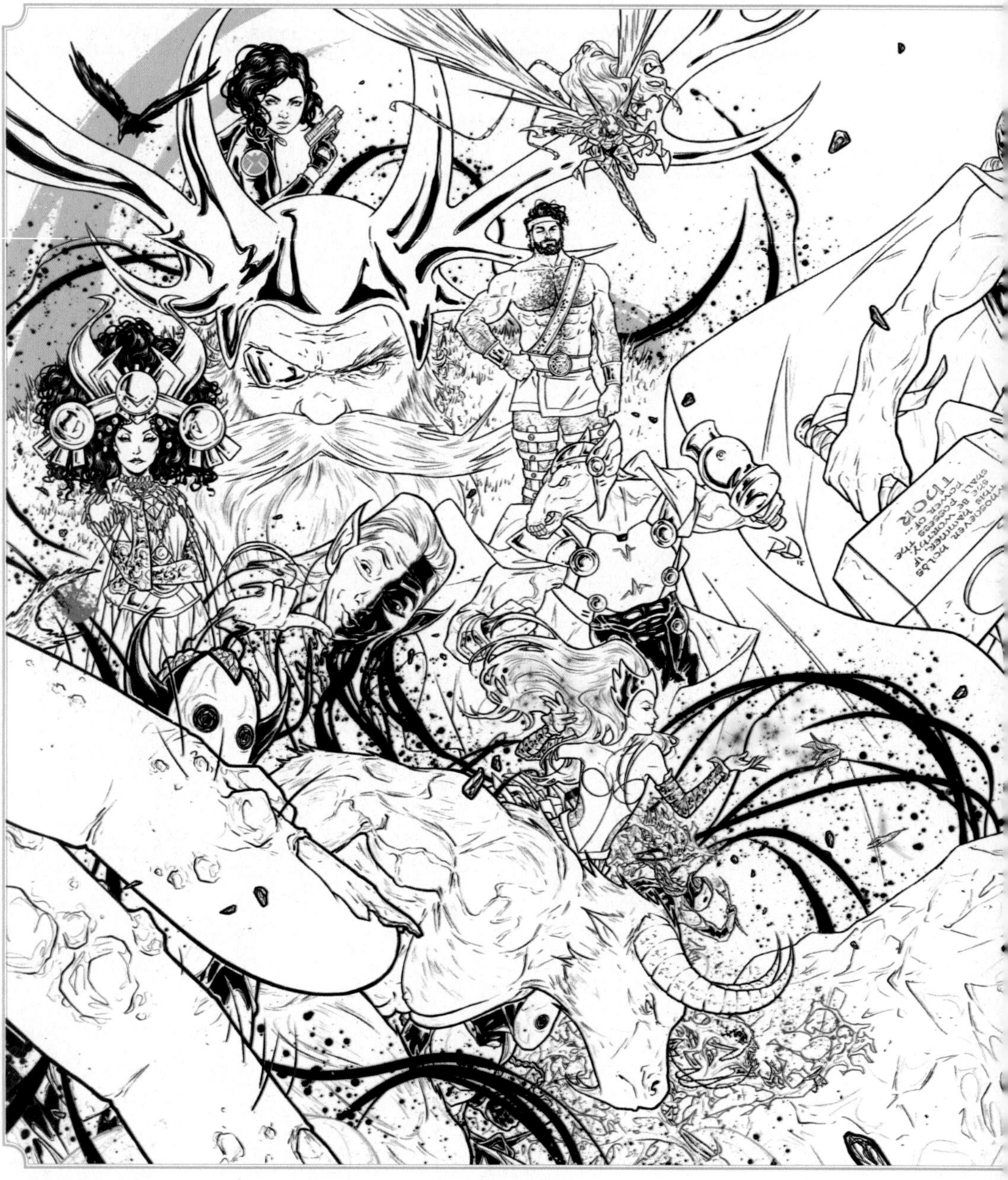
WHOSOEVER HOLDS
THIS HAMMER, IF
SHE BE WORTHY, THE
SHALL POSSESS
POWER OF...
THOR

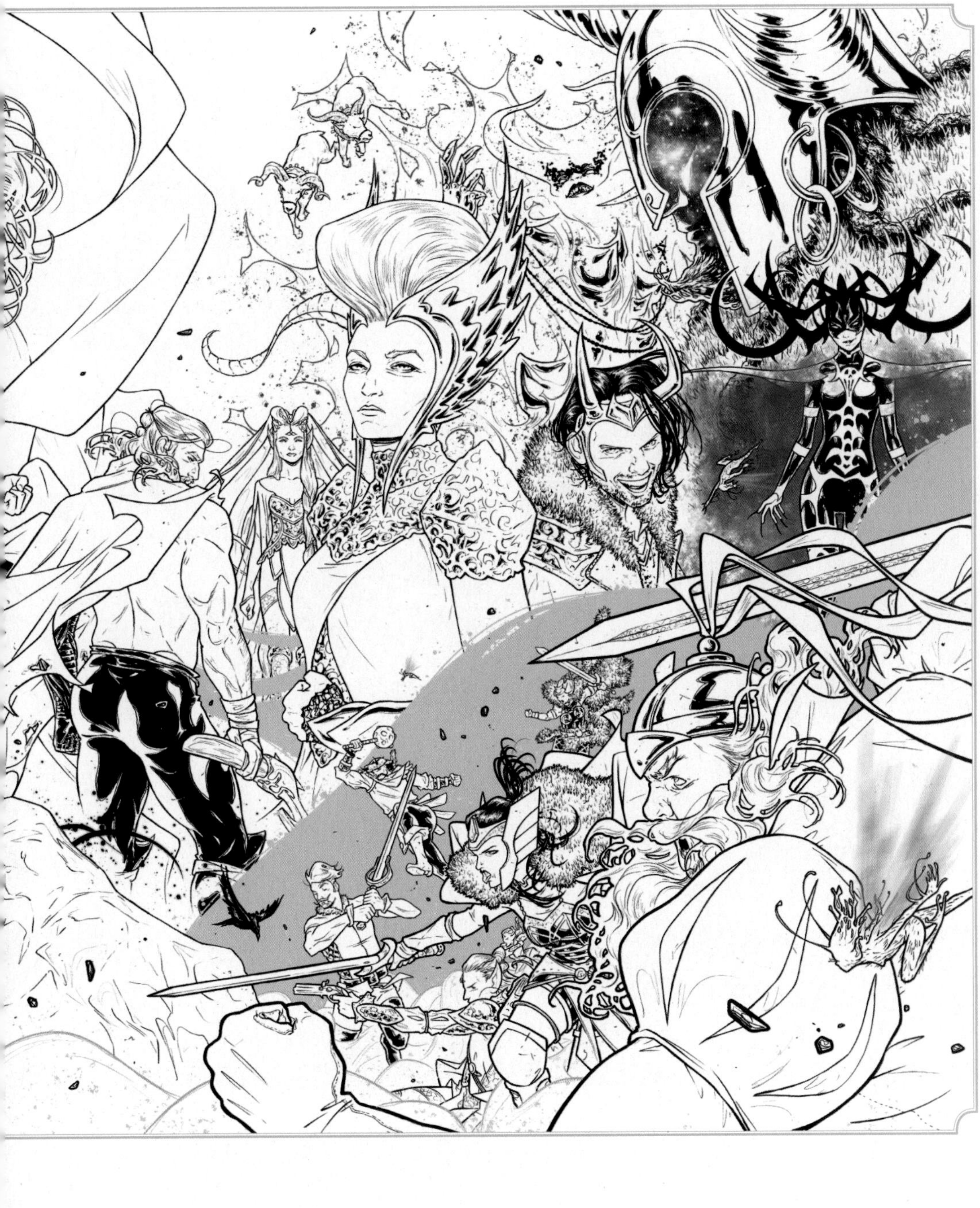

MIGHTY THOR # 1 COVER INKS
BY **RUSSELL DAUTERMAN**

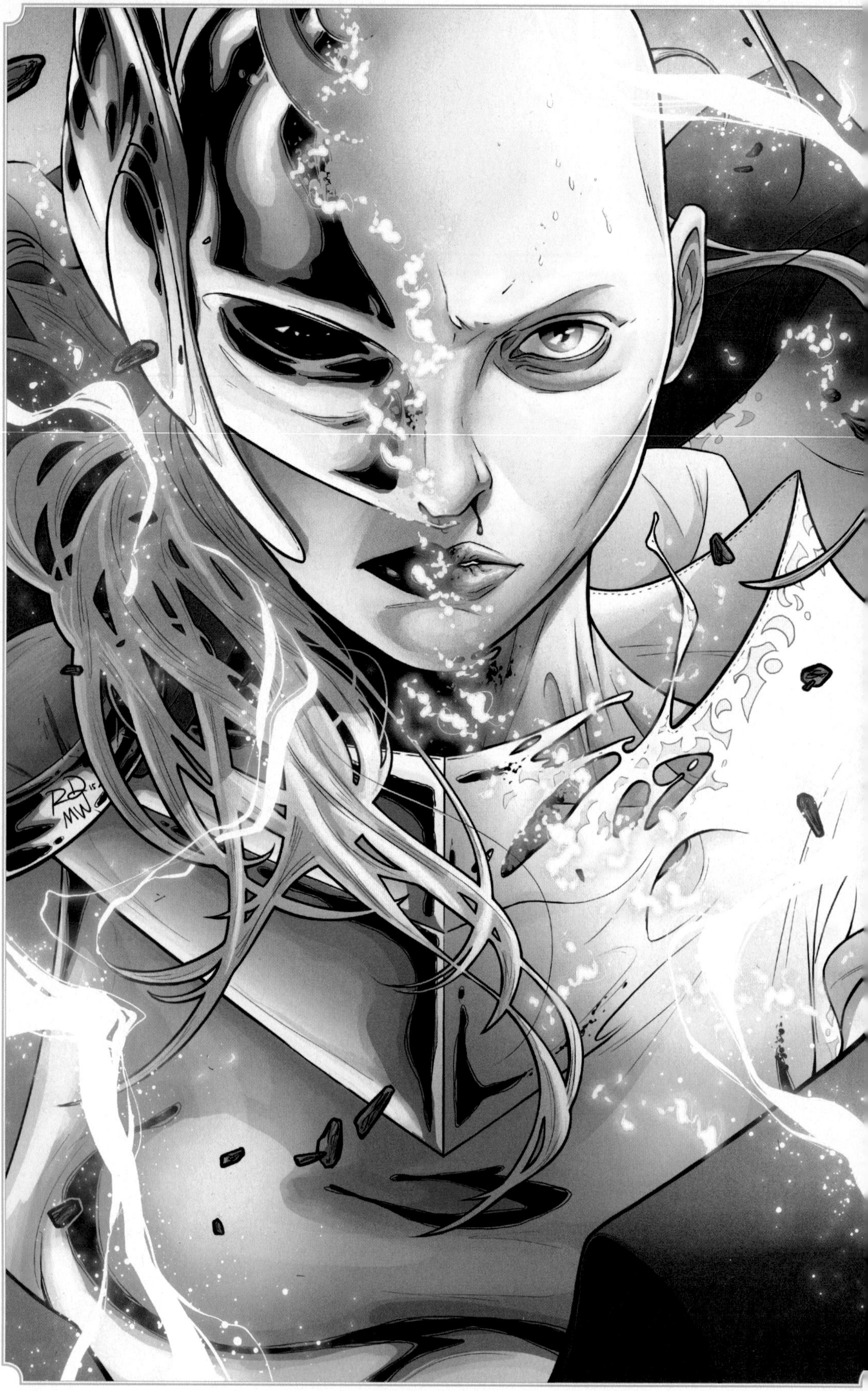

MIGHTY THOR # 1 VARIANT
BY **RUSSELL DAUTERMAN & MATTHEW WILSON**

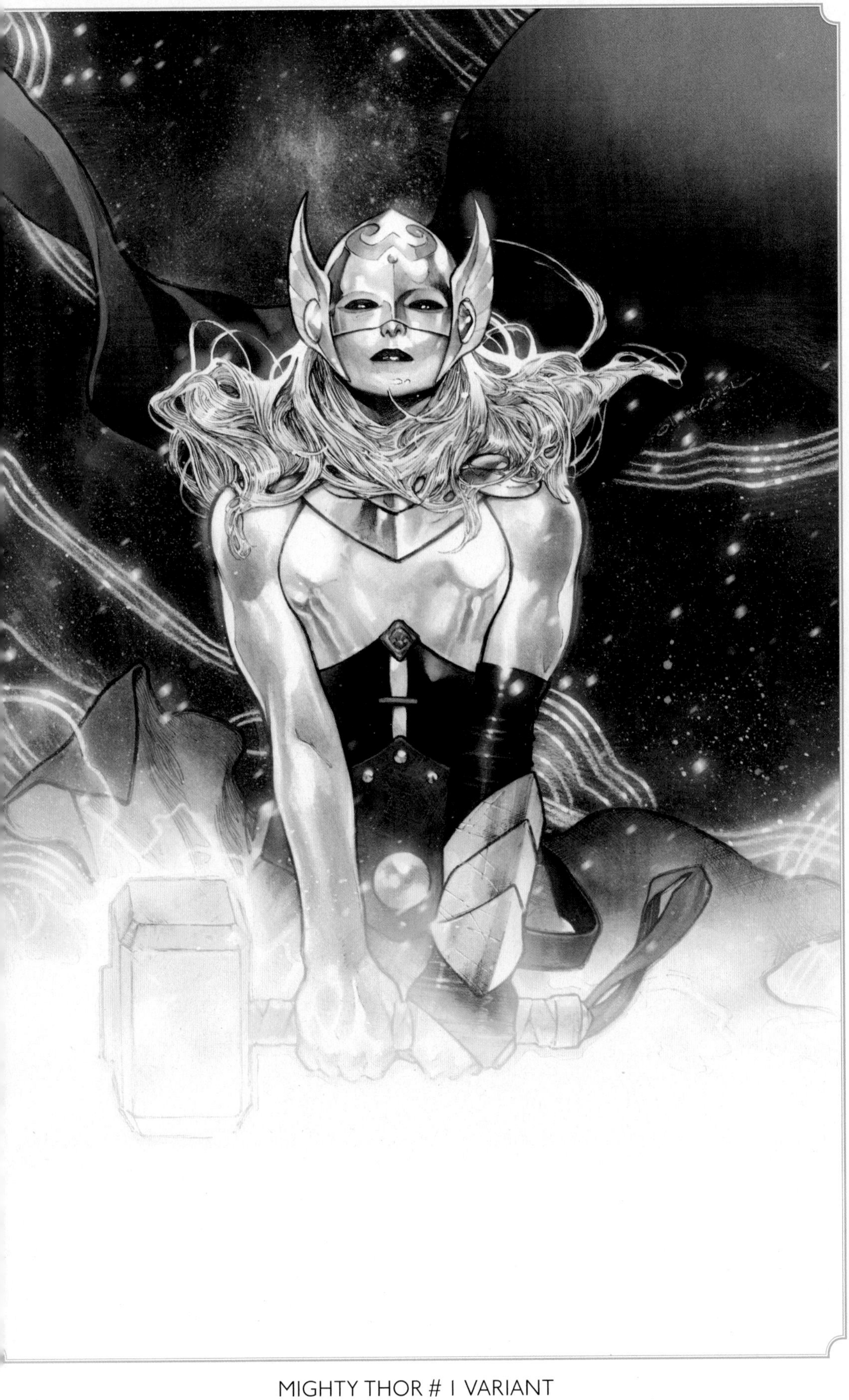

MIGHTY THOR # 1 VARIANT
BY **OLIVIER COIPEL**

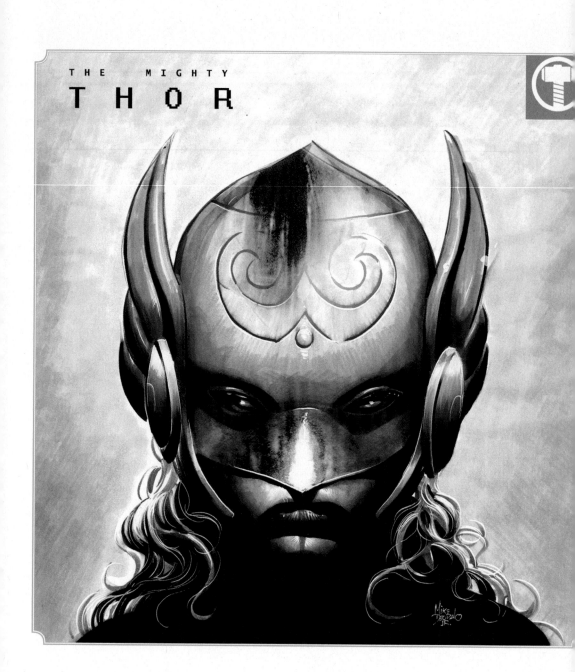

MIGHTY THOR # 1 HIP-HOP VARIANT
BY **MIKE DEODATO JR.**

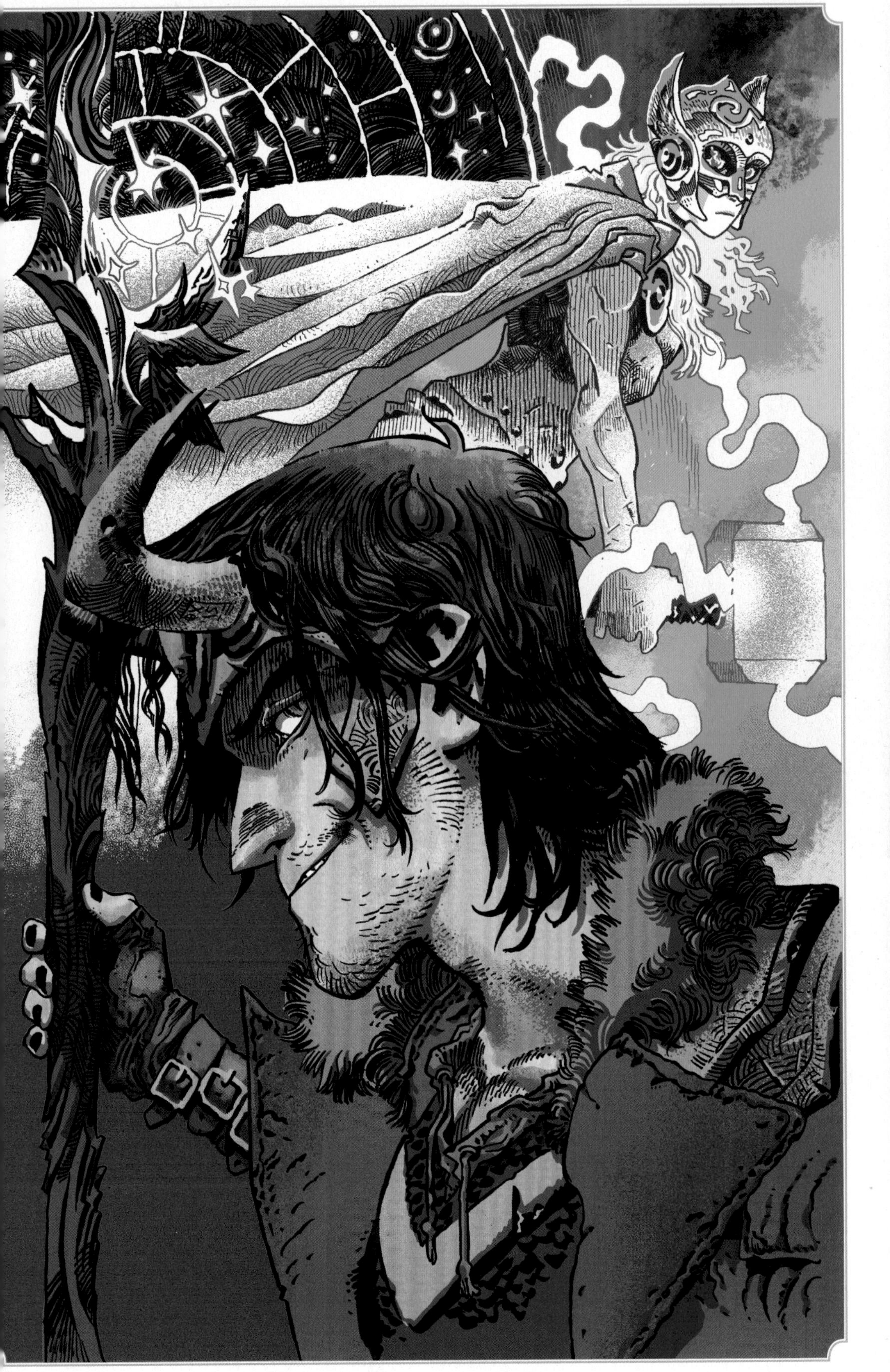

MIGHTY THOR # 2 VARIANT
BY **ARTYOM TRAKHANOV**

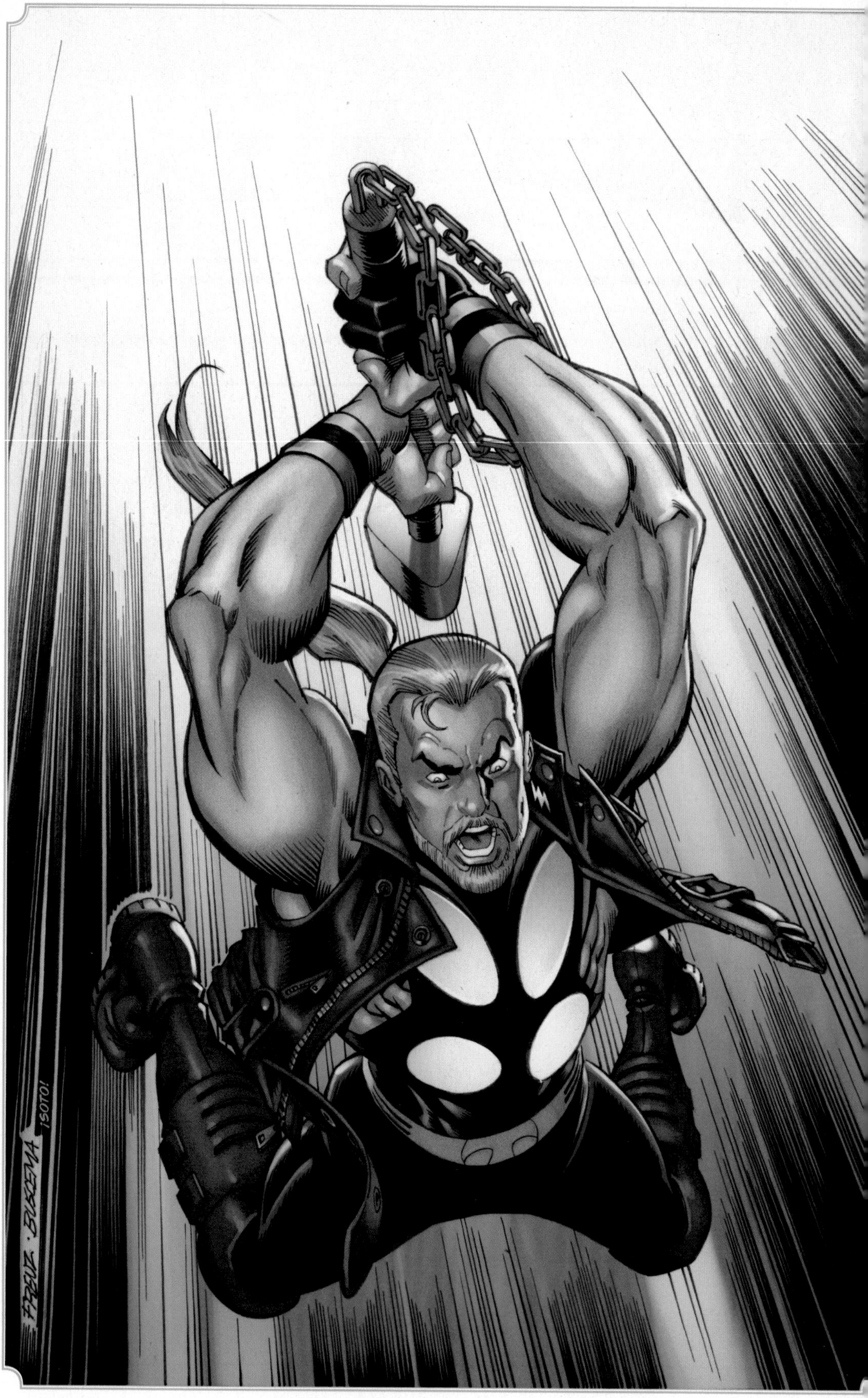
FRENZ · BUSCEMA
¡SOTO!

MIGHTY THOR # 2 MARVEL '92 VARIANT
BY **RON FRENZ**, **SAL BUSCEMA** & **CHRIS SOTOMAYOR**

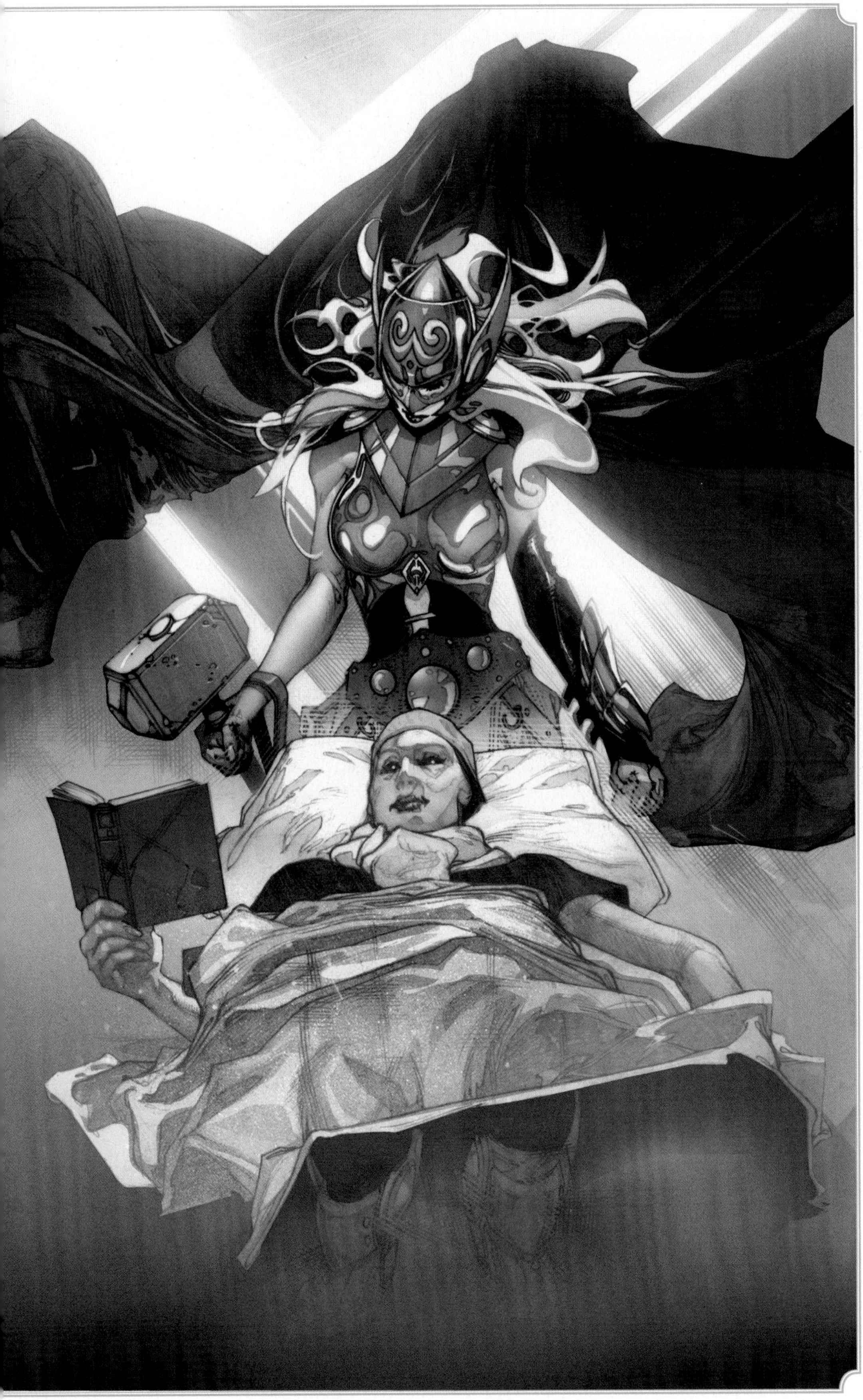

MIGHTY THOR # 3 VARIANT
BY **SIMONE BIANCHI** & **DAVID CURIEL**

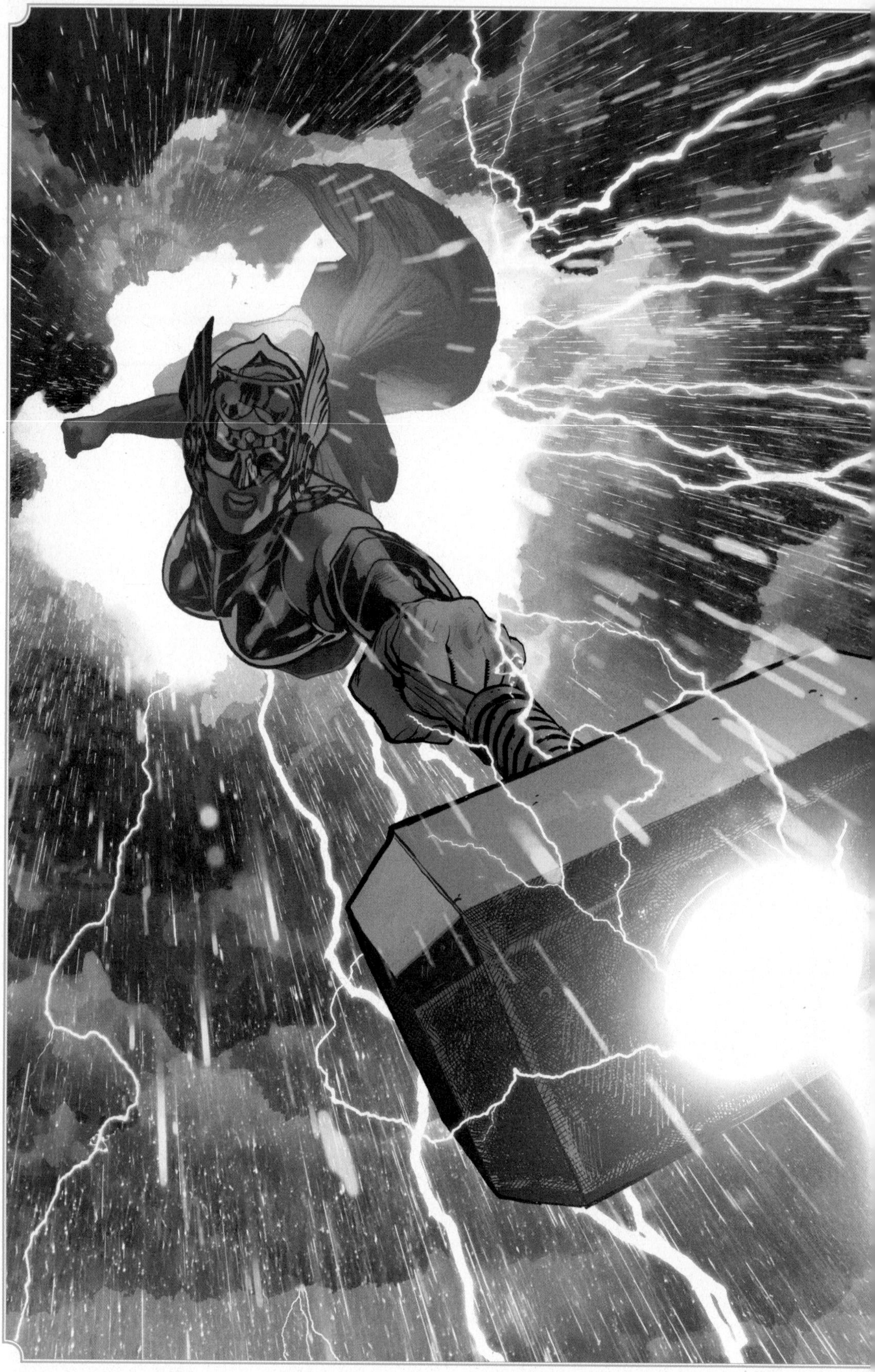

MIGHTY THOR # 4 VARIANT
BY **ADAM HUGHES**

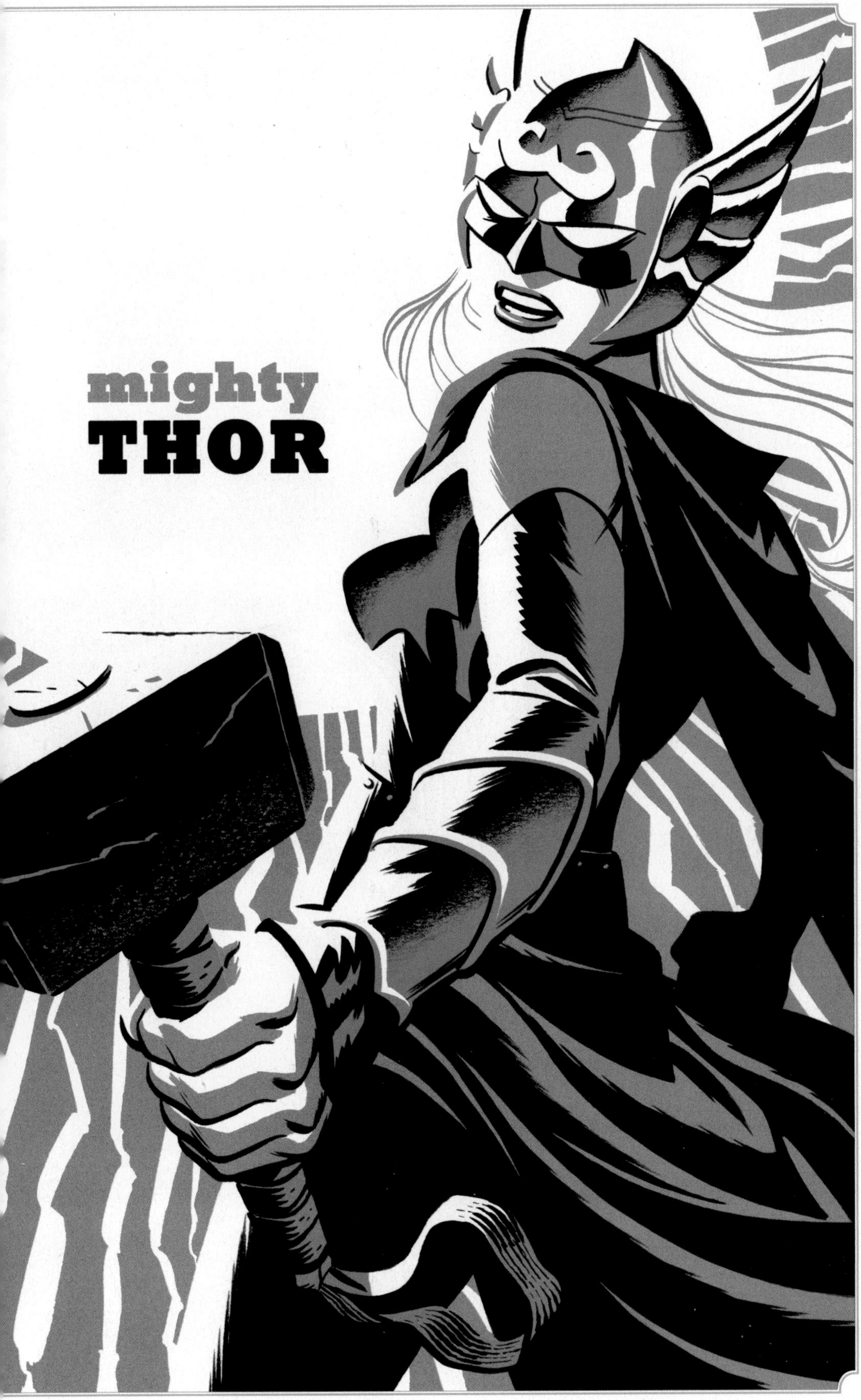
mighty
THOR

MIGHTY THOR # 4 VARIANT
BY **MICHAEL CHO**

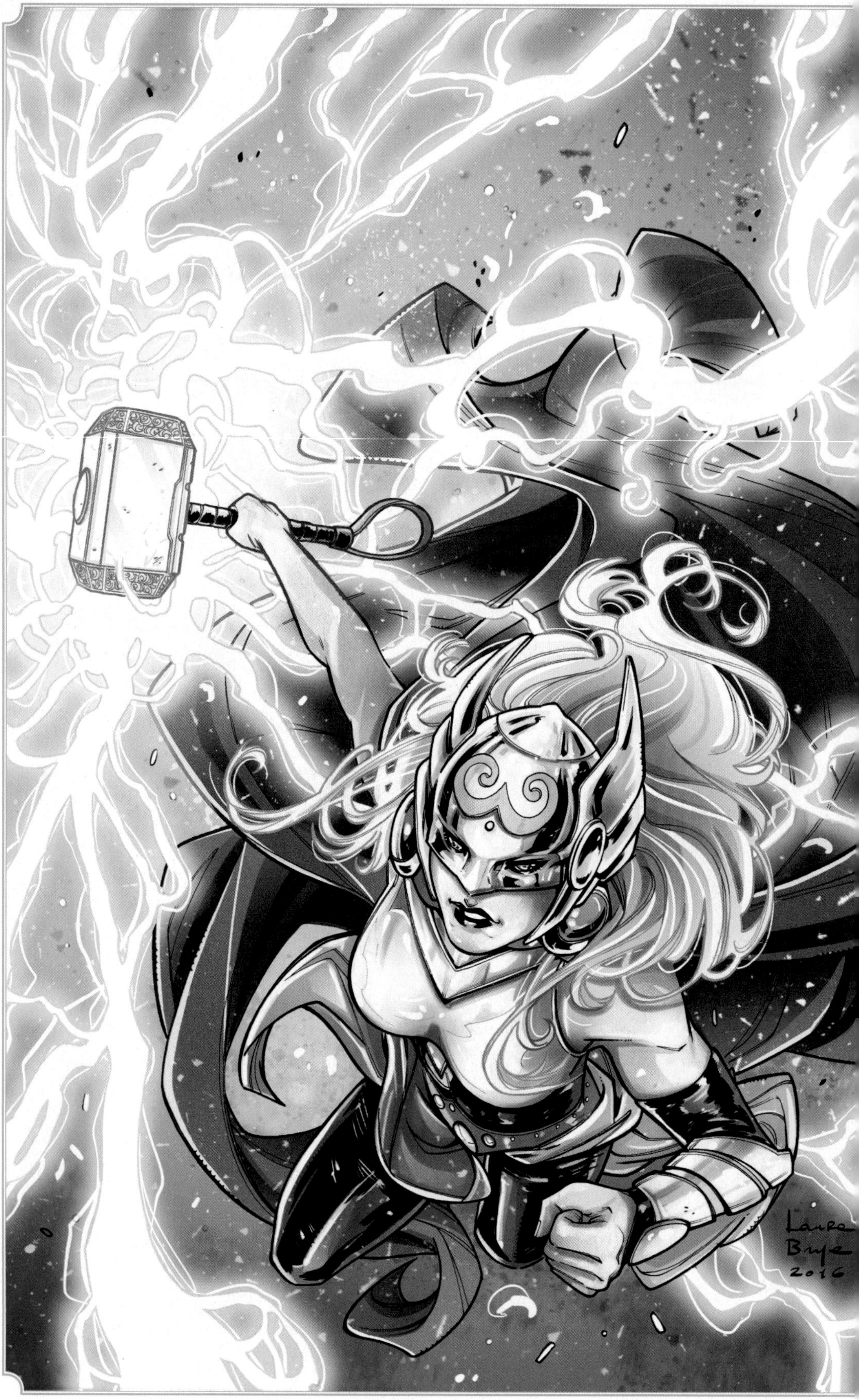

MIGHTY THOR # 5 WOMEN OF POWER VARIANT
BY **LAURA BRAGA**

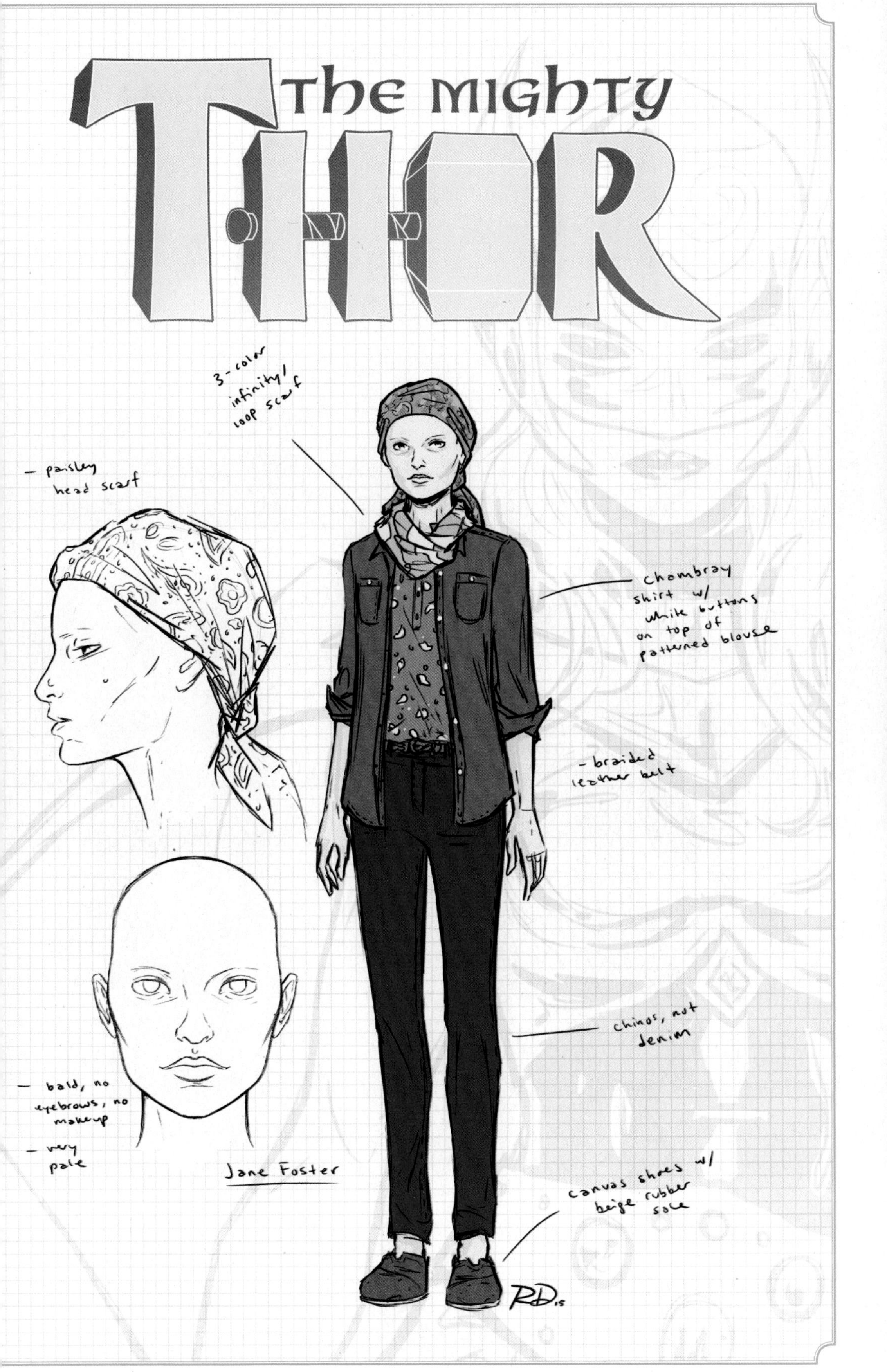
THE MIGHTY
THOR
3-color infinity/loop scarf
- paisley head scarf
chombray shirt w/ white buttons on top of patterned blouse
- braided leather belt
chinos, not denim
- bald, no eyebrows, no makeup
- very pale
Jane Foster
canvas shoes w/ beige rubber sole
RD 15

MIGHTY THOR # 1 DESIGN VARIANT
BY **RUSSELL DAUTERMAN**

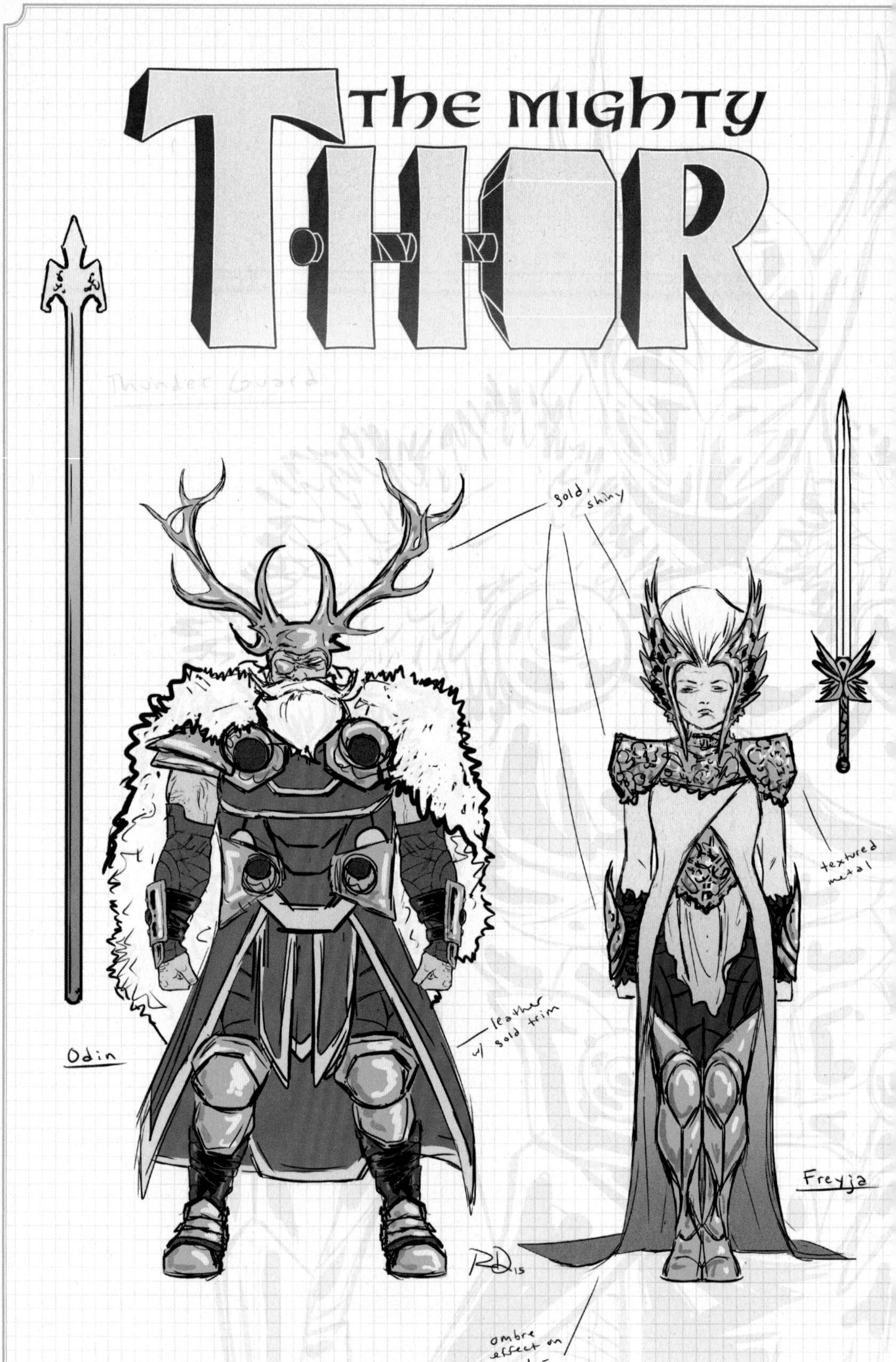
The Mighty
THOR
Thunder Guard
gold, shiny
textured metal
leather w/ gold trim
Odin
Freyja
ombre effect on skirt - rust to gold

MIGHT THOR # 2 DESIGN VARIANT
BY **RUSSELL DAUTERMAN**

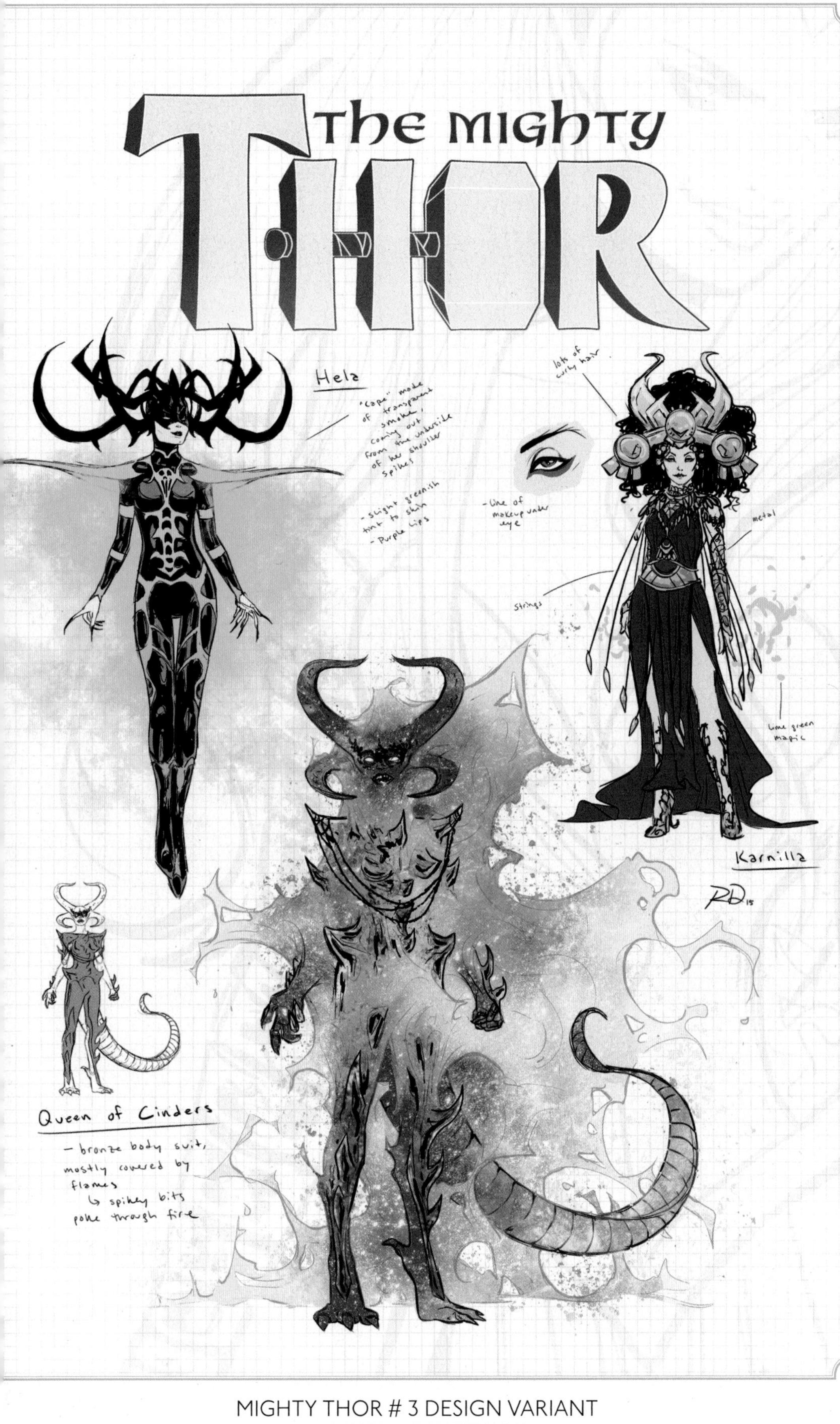
THE MIGHTY THOR
Hela
"cape" made of transparent smoke, coming out from the underside of her shoulder spikes
- slight greenish tint to skin
- purple lips
- line of makeup under eye
lots of curly hair
metal
strings
lime green magic
Karnilla
RD '15
Queen of Cinders
- bronze body suit, mostly covered by flames
↳ spikey bits poke through fire

MIGHTY THOR # 3 DESIGN VARIANT
BY **RUSSELL DAUTERMAN**